Reflexivity in L[anguage and]
Intercultural Educa[tion]

With the impact of accelerated globalization, digital technologies, mobility, and migration, the fields of applied linguistics, language, and intercultural education have been shifting. One shift in need of further exploration is that of systematic and coherent reflexivity in researching language and culture. This unique and timely book thus examines the significance of reflexivity as an integral process, particularly when researching the multifaceted notions of multilingualism and interculturality in education. It also contributes to current critical approaches to representations of languages and cultures in identity politics. As such, the authors offer innovative ways of engaging with reflexivity in teaching, learning, and research through multimodal and complex ways. The chapters span a diverse range of educational settings in Asia, Australia, Europe, and North America.

Julie S. Byrd Clark is Associate Professor of Applied Linguistics and French Language Pedagogy at the Faculty of Education at Western University, Canada.

Fred Dervin is Professor of Multicultural Education at the University of Helsinki, Finland.

Routledge Studies in Language and Intercultural Communication

Edited by Zhu Hua, Birkbeck College, University of London
Claire Kramsch, University of California, Berkeley

1 **Language and Intercultural Communication in the New Era**
   Edited by Farzad Sharifian and Maryam Jamarani

2 **Reflexivity in Language and Intercultural Education**
   Rethinking Multilingualism and Interculturality
   Edited by Julie S. Byrd Clark and Fred Dervin

Reflexivity in Language and Intercultural Education
Rethinking Multilingualism and Interculturality

Edited by Julie S. Byrd Clark
and Fred Dervin

Routledge
Taylor & Francis Group
LONDON AND NEW YORK

First published 2014 by Routledge

2 Park Square, Milton Park, Abingdon, Oxon OX14 4RN
711 Third Avenue, New York, NY 10017, USA

Routledge is an imprint of the Taylor & Francis Group, an informa business

First issued in paperback 2016

Copyright © 2014 Taylor & Francis

The right of the editors to be identified as the author of the editorial material, and of the authors for their individual chapters, has been asserted in accordance with sections 77 and 78 of the Copyright, Designs and Patents Act 1988.

All rights reserved. No part of this book may be reprinted or reproduced or utilised in any form or by any electronic, mechanical, or other means, now known or hereafter invented, including photocopying and recording, or in any information storage or retrieval system, without permission in writing from the publishers.

Notice:
Product or corporate names may be trademarks or registered trademarks, and are used only for identification and explanation without intent to infringe.

Library of Congress Cataloging-in-Publication Data

Reflexivity in language and intercultural education : rethinking
  multilingualism and interculturality / edited by Julie S. Byrd Clark and
  Fred Dervin.
    pages cm — (Routledge studies in language and intercultural
communication ; 2)
    Includes bibliographical references and index.
    1. Grammar, Comparative and general—Reflexives. 2. Multicultural
education. 3. Intercultural communication. 4. Language and
languages. I. Clark, Julie Byrd, editor of compilation. II. Dervin,
Fred, 1974– editor of compilation. III. Series: Routledge studies in
language and intercultural communication ; 2.
    P299.R44R46 2014
    306.44'6—dc23
    2013044726

ISBN: 978-0-415-71659-8 (hbk)
ISBN: 978-1-138-24532-7 (pbk)

Typeset in Sabon
by Apex CoVantage, LLC

Julie: To my sister, Jennifer, for her wisdom and courage; to Ryan, for healing; to sweet Trevor, who was taken far too young from us; and to the memory of my grandmother, Asunta Mazzoli Cernaro, who loved and took care of us all.

Fred: To my coeditor, who was a joy to work with and more than an equal partner in this adventure; and to all of the great memories made during my visit in June 2012.

Contents

Acknowledgments   ix

Introduction   1
JULIE S. BYRD CLARK AND FRED DERVIN

1 The Process of Becoming Reflexive and Intercultural: Navigating Study Abroad and Reentry Experience   43
JANE JACKSON

2 'Or, Just It's My Fault, Right?': Language Socialization through Reflexive Language Writing Feedback   64
JÉRÉMIE SÉROR

3 Reflexivity and Self-Presentation in Multicultural Encounters: Making Sense of Self and Other   81
ALEX FRAME

4 Researching Chinese Students' Intercultural Communication Experiences in Higher Education: Researcher and Participant Reflexivity   100
PRUE HOLMES

5 Critical Reflexive Ethnography and the Multilingual Space of a Canadian University: Challenges and Opportunities   119
SYLVIE A. LAMOUREUX

6 Reflexivity in Motion in Language and Literacy Learning   138
DAVID MALINOWSKI AND MARK EVAN NELSON

7 Uses of Digital Text in Reflexive Anthropology: The Example of Educational Workshops for Out-of-School/Educationally Excluded Adolescents   158
ERIC CHAUVIER

8 Reflexivity and Critical Language Education at Occupy LA   172
   CHRISTIAN W. CHUN

9 Weaving a Method: Mobility, Multilocality, and the Senses
   as Foci of Research on Intercultural Language Learning   193
   ULRIKE NAJAR

10 Everyday Practices, Everyday Pedagogies: A Dialogue
   on Critical Transformations in a Multilingual
   Hong Kong School   213
   MIGUEL PÉREZ-MILANS AND CARLOS SOTO

   Conclusion: Reflexivity in Research and
   Practice: Moving On?   234
   FRED DERVIN AND JULIE S. BYRD CLARK

   Commentary   240
   CLAIRE KRAMSCH

   Contributors   245
   Index   249

Acknowledgments

We would like to thank, first and foremost, Claire Kramsch and Zhú Huà for their encouragement, enthusiasm, and unwavering support for this project. We would also like to express our sincere thanks to Felisa Salvago-Keyes, Andrew Weckenmann, and Margo C. Irvin of Routledge for offering us their excellent editorial expertise throughout this process. We also thank them for their willingness in allowing us the space to engage with and represent some unconventional ideas and approaches to research as well as to writing. In addition, we wish to thank the anonymous reviewers of our original proposal, who gave us valuable criticism and suggestions. Particular thanks go out to all of the authors who contributed to this volume. Finally, we want to thank our families and loved ones for all of their love, support, and stability, which give us the luxury of imagining new ways of doing research, of trying to change the world . . . and that, in the end, is what reflexivity is all about.

Introduction

Julie S. Byrd Clark[1] *and Fred Dervin*[2]

The purpose of this book is to draw attention to the importance of reflexivity in language and in intercultural education research, especially in relation to the notions of multilingualism and interculturality. With the impact of accelerated globalization, digital technologies, mobility and migration, the fields attached to these notions (among others, applied linguistics, language and intercultural education,[3] and intercultural communication) have been experiencing a shift in adapting social and postmodern approaches to the studies of multilingualism and intercultural communication. The chapters of this volume represent a coherent and serious attempt to take these changes into account and to make the case that reflexivity is intricately woven throughout all facets of the research and/or educational process and practice. This attempt permits us as authors to approach some of these unstable aspects from a more complex viewpoint. Thus, what we endeavor in this volume is to explore what people (including researchers, language teachers, students) do in the process of being and becoming reflexive, or rather how they (co-)construct, perceive, and represent what they do because reflexivity is a process as well as an act of discoursing.[4] In other words, what does reflexivity mean for them and for those who research *multilingualism* and *interculturality* in education? How, when, and where do different social actors take into account the impact of their varied positioning(s) in regard to learning, teaching, and research and, beyond as these contexts, also have an impact on other social and interactive contexts outside academia?

The aim of our book is to illuminate the need for a *reflexive turn* in applied linguistics, language, and intercultural education, and intercultural communication. However, it is not our intention to define or constrain reflexivity to a singular, static phenomenon but rather to shed light on the intricate and multimodal ways in which we come to understand and practice reflexivity as an ongoing, multifaceted, and dialogical process. At the same time, we understand reflexivity to be a social construct, one that is continually evolving, open to interpretation and reconstruction. In this sense, we hope that reflexivity can play an important part in informing both approach and practice.

Our goals in this book are to:

1. Situate our understandings of reflexivity in relation to multilingualism and interculturality by examining some ways in which reflexivity has been conceptualized (as critical reflection, awareness, and hyper-reflexivity in what follows) and at the same time to shed some light on how our understandings of these constructs have been shaped through different historical, social, philosophical, and political approaches across time and space.
2. Discuss some of the potential blind spots and challenges when attempting to engage conceptually and methodologically with these notions.

We conclude the book by underscoring some ways of developing and promoting reflexivity as an integral, multimodal process that may lead to a deeper engagement of what constitutes the multilingual and intercultural in education, as well as offer ways to advance research in the field(s). Though our context of study is education, scholars and practitioners working in other fields—such as communication, business, health, and cultural studies, to name just a few—will find this volume of interest.

We turn now to our own situated positions and ways of understanding reflexivity.

WHAT DO *WE* MEAN BY 'REFLEXIVE'?

> If men define situations as real, they are real in their consequences.
> (W. I. Thomas & D. S. Thomas, 1928)

> [M]an is both knowing subject and the object of his own study.
> (Foucault, *The Order of Things*, 1966/1970)

It is important to situate our work in relation to reflexivity because, as we look at positions taken up by different social actors (namely, practitioners and researchers), we can see that the notion can also come to mean different things to different people: For example, some people associate the word 'critical' with being congruous to reflexive, while others distinguish between reflexivity and self-reflexivity (i.e. one's own reflexivity), and as such, there are varied degrees of reflexivity (e.g., ways of engaging with complexities, the social construction of difference, etc.)

First and foremost, the authors of this volume understand reflexivity as a multifaceted, complex, and ongoing dialogical process that is continually evolving. Our understanding of reflexivity or the process of becoming reflexive is greatly influenced by social, sociopsychological, and poststructuralist theories in that reflexivity is socially situated but at the same time always in motion. In other words, reflexivity is neither a given nor a static element and, in this regard, involves not only a willingness to recognize and engage with complexities but also necessitates as well as exudes multimodal ways of engaging with representations of social life, particularly those that are unexpected. The multimodality of everyday communication and interaction in contemporary social life is significant, particularly as it relates to reflexivity, because we need to take into account not only all of the ways in which we[5] make and index meaning (e.g., through gestures, voice, movement, music, online discussions, signing, texts, styles, recordings, drawings, etc.)—that is, the complex, overlapping, and multiple modes of representations that allow us to configure (and reconfigure) the social world—but also the ways in which we invest in certain social meanings and representations, as well as in our performances of them. In other words, multimodality offers us great insights into the opportunities, challenges, and complexities involved when investigating what it means to be and become reflexive. Multimodality plays an instrumental part in reflexivity because it permits us to make visible the multidimensionality of meanings, interpretations, strategies, positionings, representations (experiences), and voices that we encounter and engage in research and teaching. Drawing upon reflexivity through multimodality helps to make us aware that neither our representations (e.g., identities) nor our social and linguistic practices (as well as others') are transparent, unidimensional entities sitting in isolation—that we are connected by more than simple words on a page. At the same time, multimodality combined with reflexivity enables us to see that there are multiple (and contradictory) ways of seeing, doing, experiencing, and representing life in the social world, and that we (whoever 'we' are) are always becoming—although we (or others) may have written and represented ourselves in certain ways through our pasts in different time-spaces, this doesn't mean that *this is the way we are* and that *this is the way it is*, permanently, so to speak[6]. For example, in an interview with a newspaper journalist, we may identify ourselves differently than we would during a recorded video of a teaching demonstration with an educational researcher in a language-learning context. Several of the upcoming chapters in this volume (see Séror, Malinowski and Nelson, Chun, Chauvier, and Najar) indicate that reflexivity combined with multimodality helps us to uncover the instabilities, uncertainties, overlappings, and complexities that challenge unhelpful conventional conceptions of writing as a stable representation of the world. But as we will see, reflexivity represents much more than revealing these instabilities and complexities. Reflexivity through intersecting and multimodal processes can help to move researchers and teachers away from dogmatic, essentialized truths about themselves and others, and possibly get at the deeper, underlying ideological conditions and attachments, which may have led to such 'truths' in the first place. When we just look at or accept one truth about someone, we really do miss out and cut ourselves short because there's so much more to all of us than some of the categories, labels, and stories we've received, become invested or attached to, and in many cases, had to endure. Furthermore, drawing upon multimodal processes as they relate to reflexivity, whereby we appropriate, negotiate, and expropriate meanings through different mediums such as video, audio, digital texts/texting, and the like, could also serve to lessen the disconnect between the academic and creative uses of language (e.g., writing).

Second, as authors, we understand the difficulty and contradiction in trying to articulate reflexivity as a process in relation to representations and varied degrees of reflexivity (e.g., be it critical reflection, awareness, or hyper-reflexivity, as we shall see in the next section). Though reflexivity can appear dynamic, this process cannot be understood outside of our own interactional, social, and historical experiences. This challenges us not only to be cognizant of and strategic in the ways in which we question realities in different contexts but also to be aware of the conditions that make it possible for us to question such realities. Of course, this is not easy because, as already stated, reflexivity can shift and make visible the potential for creative human agency; yet being and becoming reflexive also demand an understanding of how, when, why, and with whom to operationalize more fixed and concrete notions of languages, identities, and cultures for strategic purposes (this is perhaps what is implied by having a *"feel for the game"*; see Bourdieu, 1990: 66). The chapters of this book will address some of the challenges when attempting to situate representations of reflexivity in different contexts and to do research on them.

Third, in an attempt to engage with conceptualizations of reflexivity, we try to take into account the multidimensional facets, such as the intense self–other interactions; issues of power; the self-criticism; the ego musings and narcissistic, self-promoting confessionals; the skepticism and constant questioning of representations; the narratives and issues of bias; the vulnerabilities, contradictions, instabilities; and the imaginative resourcefulness and positive engagements with variation; certainly not least, we discuss some of the blind spots and challenges related to reflexivity when researching the multilingual and intercultural. To understand this multimodal and multifaceted process, we must consider briefly how reflexivity has been conceptualized and the ways in which we ourselves have tried to understand and represent different facets of reflexivity here.

Thus, in the upcoming sections, we examine the ways in which reflexivity has been conceptualized and talked about in different fields. As such, we have identified three notions/representations that continually recurred when reading or researching the notion of reflexivity: (1) critical reflection, (2) awareness, and (3) hyper-reflexivity. Although we locate certain social, political, and historical dimensions in relation to each notion, we also want to clarify that these notions are not completely separate from one another; that is to say, researchers can use these terms interchangeably because the meanings appear similar and interrelated. Researchers can navigate among these different notions *nolens volens* because they are not always in control of their academic discourses, which are also co-constructed with different entities: the (multilingual and intercultural) research community, the publishing platform, research participants, decision makers who fund their research, the media, and so on. In many cases, implicit or explicit censorship may lead researchers to showing less reflexivity—whereas they would, in fact, want to be represented as more reflexive. In recent reviews of an article that one of us submitted in Canada, the reviewers accused the author of being too reflexive and of using the pronoun 'I' too much. When the author complained about this to the journal editors, the latter used the culture-as-an-excuse argument. According to them, Canadian/North American journals have very precise scientific criteria (the rest of the world does not!) and fear the utterance of personal ideologies. They continue: The use of 'I' can ruin the credibility of the work ...

On that note, before proceeding into our more in-depth discussion of reflexivity, the reader might be wondering at this point who or what the 'we' represents in this introductory chapter.

OUR OWN COMPLEX POSITIONINGS, REPRESENTATIONS, AND ENGAGEMENTS WITH REFLEXIVITY

As we (Julie and Fred) worked on this collection and reread, rereviewed, and reengaged with the continually evolving contributions about reflexivity, we felt compelled to include our own complex positionings and representations here as well as our engagements with language learning, intercultural communication, and applied linguistics. First, we certainly don't want you (the readers) to feel that you are reading some disembodied or disengaged text with some abstract all-knowing voice that produces (yet another) hegemonic discourse. Second, we hope that having an understanding of our own positionings (or the ways we have represented ourselves in this chapter), as well as our commonalities, will shed light on how and why we have gone about engaging with the notion of reflexivity in the ways that we have and, more importantly, clarify why it was significant for us and the authors of this book to have our voices heard. Finally, in sharing our own ways of engaging with reflexivity and adding some self-disclosure as researchers, we wish not only to inspire the act of doing reflexivity but also to invite reflexive engagement on the part of you, the readers.

Let us start by stating that we (Julie and Fred) share chameleonic ways of self-identifying; that is, sometimes being able to cross both traditional linguistic and cultural boundaries, yet at varied degrees with varying levels of success and difficulty. For example, when asked the question 'Where are you from?' we both have difficulty giving a simple, straightforward response because we've each lived and spent considerable time in several different geographical places (e.g., the United States, Ireland, France, Canada, the UK, Hong Kong, and Finland). Similarly, we both grew up in places that have been represented to the world as nationalist and mono-ideological (the United States and France), even though our family households were quite heterogeneous (linguistically and socially[7]). To add to this complexity, though our family names are Anglophone (Byrd Clark and Dervin), in certain spaces and in different interactions, we are recognized as Francophones even though neither of us is representative of a Francophone in the traditional sense (despite one of us having been born in France). Nevertheless, we use French for the majority of our communication, and when we are together speaking in public places, very often people assume or want to know whether we're French. Some will ask for affirmation ('So, you guys are from France?') and others out of curiosity ('Are you from France?'). Whether amused or annoyed (depending on the way the questions are asked), we strangely find ourselves trying to give a quick, simple (static) response by stating, 'No, we're not. I'm Canadian, and he's Finnish.' Ironically, when one of us (Julie) has traveled to France, she is often identified as a Québécoise, a French Canadian from Québec, and gets some surprised, astonished looks when saying that she's from Toronto, Ontario. 'Il y a des Francophones à Toronto?' ('Are there Francophones in Toronto?') is a question that is frequently asked. On other occasions, when responding 'I'm Canadian' to the question 'Where are you from?' in France, she often hears, 'Oui, on s'entend,' meaning, 'Yes, it's [the sound is] evident.' Interestingly, when in Canada, Julie has often been told that she speaks more 'Euro-French' and has often been identified as Swiss (because of her intonation?!), even though she's yet to reside in Switzerland. Fred also experiences similar phenomena: In Finland, when he speaks Finnish, people ask him if he is German or Russian; in Sweden, when he uses Swedish, people identify him as a Finn; in the United States, his interlocutors often refer to him as 'the Brit'; while in France, he is often mistaken for a Swiss, Canadian, or Belgian.

Nevertheless, our ways of speaking and identifying can dismantle traditional frames, leaving a lot of people looking baffled or downright confused. On the other hand, this is not to say that our identities don't get called into question or that we constantly experience ease when trying to claim membership or legitimacy with particular groups (e.g., ethnolinguistic, social, academic, etc.). For instance, we recently published an article with a special issue of a journal in France, and when we received the initial feedback from one of the reviewers, it stated, 'L'auteur n'est pas francophone, mais le style est à revoir.' ('The author is not Francophone, so the style has to be re-examined'). On a more serious note, we have each endured different struggles over trying to claim (or reclaim) such social and linguistic identities, particularly after what seems like a lifetime's investment in what Bourdieu calls "a reflexive mastery of language" (1977: 659), or rather a symbolic investment in a dominant usage of language. Paradoxically, our Canadianness and Finishness are frequently being challenged, regardless of our many years of living in these contexts. There appears to be something about the ways in which we sound or pronounce certain words that unmasks our difference and that has people trying to figure us out (not always willing to accept us as a 'real' Canadian or a 'real' Finn). Yet in other international contexts, people think we sound 'so Canadian' or 'have a Finnish accent when speaking English'). As such, there are moments when our apparent fluidity gets stuck in ideological debates and attachments over who or what constitutes *a certain identity (someone as something)*. Furthermore, as mentioned, there are moments when our positionings are mistaken, when people have made incorrect assumptions about us that have led us to experience some interesting and disturbing consequences as well (e.g., different dimensions of discrimination). This is related not just to how we sound but also to how we might look to others in a given situation.

It is also important to note that at different moments, we can appear to be and have been represented/labeled in the traditional sense as *multilinguals* because we have both formally studied languages in a variety of settings (e.g., school, university, exchange programs, etc.), where our linguistic practices have been measured, labeled, and enumerated (L1, L2, L3, etc.). So we can state that Julie's linguistic repertoire consists of English, French, Italian (San Fratedani variety and Florentine variety), with some German and Spanish and that Fred's linguistic repertoire comprises French, English, Swedish, Finnish, and German, with some Italian and Chinese. However, we must signify that how we came to be and become multilinguals is quite different because each of us has his/her own complex life trajectory and experiences as well as social class background.[8] Having said this, we also identify as *multilinguals* in the nontraditional sense (see Weber & Horner, 2012; Canagarajah, 2013, as well as the upcoming sections on the intercultural and multilingual) because our practices and identities shift and flow at times in different interactions with particular people in different contexts. As such, and like many, we have the capacity to do a lot of creative, imaginative play with our language uses/practices (and/or multiple codes) and can access a great range of varied linguistic varieties, genres, registers, accents, and styles. For example, we are very good at imitating different ways of speaking (we like to think so anyway!), and do a lot of code meshing, or translanguaging, when we talk or write e-mails to one another. Sometimes this works out great to our advantage,[9] where we have similar experiences to those of David Block, who in his narrative regarding language and culture, details the ability of getting by in Italy while speaking 'Romance-esque' (see Block, 2010) and sometimes our creative play and multiple identities cause 'road blocks', confusion, misconceptions, disaffiliation, and, to a larger extent, exclusion—feelings of shame, and (at times) that we don't *really* belong anywhere (e.g., not being recognized as legitimate and/or authentic for certain social group affiliation and membership, ethnolinguistic or national belonging, etc.).

In lieu of wanting to represent candidness, we feel it significant to disclose that we have also endured difficult childhoods and have had to overcome different yet similar kinds of adversity (e.g., emotional and verbal abuse; loss of a parent at a young age; discrimination based on social class, gender, language, ethnicity, and race, to name a few). One of us, who grew up in North America, did not come from a privileged social class background, even though many people (including scholars) tend to make assumptions about people from North America as having a so-called privileged voice. Unfortunately, it's much more complicated than this. To quickly counter this, we suggest that you begin by listening to a song by the rock band U2 from the late 1980s, entitled, 'In God's country,' particularly the lyrics 'sad eyes, crooked crosses, in God's country,' for another point of view. Then follow this up with the song 'Fast Car' by Tracy Chapman. Let's be clear: Speaking English and growing up in North America do not automatically render one a privileged voice. Ironically, the people who often make such generalized statements, such as 'It's the privileged voice from North America' happen to be in positions of privilege themselves.

Finally, with our own investigations, engagements, and work with the notions of multilingualism and interculturality (which we address more fully in the next section), we have found a significant need for researchers, in particular, to (re)examine what it means to be and become reflexive, especially with the problematic use of (and attachment to) social categories and our own underlying ideological positionings (Byrd Clark, 2012). Before turning to our understandings of what reflexivity has come to mean and how reflexivity has been represented (including some of the significant dimensions that have contributed to our understandings of reflexivity in contemporary times), we now highlight our own positionings in relation to multilingualism and interculturality.

From a reflexive and critical point of view, we have placed these two terms or notions, the intercultural and the multilingual, front and center in this volume because of their current political relevance as well as our personal investments in them as researchers and social beings (as will be conveyed in the upcoming section). In the chapters throughout this book, these notions are often implicit.

POSITIONING THE INTERCULTURAL AND THE MULTILINGUAL

> The very process of identification through which we project ourselves into our cultural identities, has become more open-ended, variable, and problematic. Within us, we have, contradictory identities pulling in different directions, so that our identifications are continuously being shifted about. (Hall, 2006: 251)

> I argue that in all cultures people can be observed to project multiple, inconsistent self-representations that are context-dependent and may shift rapidly. At any particular moment a person usually experiences his or her articulated self as a symbolic, timeless whole, but this self may quickly be displaced by another, quite different 'self,' which is based on a different definition of the situation. The person will often be unaware of these shifts and inconsistencies and may experience wholeness and continuity despite their presence'. (Ewing, 1990: 251)

The two notions of multilingual and intercultural have played and are still playing an important part in applied linguistics and education, under the guise of political forces, such as the Council of Europe, whose voice is spreading across the world rapidly (alas!). As the political, educational, and scientific tend to overlap in the use of these notions, a lot of confusion and polysemy ensue. This is why we feel the need to say what we mean by these notions and how they will thus be used in this volume.

First of all, we do not see these two notions as completely separate from one another, and in many instances each notion implies (or often assumes) the other. However, we want to acknowledge and highlight some of the current work that has been done regarding each notion in order to demonstrate the complex overlapping between the two.

We start with the intercultural. The notion is being increasingly described as polysemous and thus problematic in both research and practice (Dervin et al., 2011; Aikman, 2012). The approach to the intercultural in this volume critically reviews 'ahistorical, depoliticized and uncritical ethnocentric benevolence' (Andreotti, 2011: 144), which is often found in the treatment of the notion. We also attempt to move away from an overemphasis on the problematic concept of culture, which is often an 'ersatz of demonstration' (Bayart, 1996) when analyzing interactions between persons (from the Latin *persona*, mask) whose multifaceted identities [language, gender, social class, generation, etc. but also (inter-)subjectivity] should be taken into account. For V. Andreotti, an overemphasis on culture 'tends to confirm racist assumptions of the superiority of the self as seen through the eyes of the others, disguised in a politically correct discourse of mutual learning' and casts aside questions of inequality and privilege (2011: 156). In a similar vein, A. Sen argues that 'invoking the magical power of some allegedly predominant identity . . . drowns other affiliations' (2006: xv). Thus to the authors of the chapters, it is the 'inter-' of the intercultural that is important, not so much the '-cultural' because the concept tends to be too limiting, see essentializing in Holliday (2010). We argue that the 'self and other' are not separate but always in relation (or in dialogue) and situated (see Hall, 1992; Byrd Clark, 2009). This is in line with, for example, the recent upsurge in research on dialogism (Gillespie, 2006). For Gallagher, 'We are immersed in interactive relations with others before we know it' (2011: 48). This leads, he adds, to the ideas of 'self-in-the-other' and 'other-in-the-self' (2011: 492). The 'inter-' thus corresponds to the idea, which will be developed in the next section, that there is no self without other and vice versa. In other words, people co-construct their identities in intercultural encounters, and no culture can predetermine these negotiations—only discourses of culture and othering do! As such, it is only in terms of representing certain images of the people who interact that culture intervenes. This does not mean, of course, that people are free to identify as they wish. The intercultural—like any other context of social interaction—requires 'pulling and pushing' identity markers and objects determined by power relations and imaginaries. These processes are not always predetermined, and therefore the powerless might suddenly be/become empowered in a situation where their othering had led to negative identification.

But just as we argue that the self is not completely separate from the other, the intercultural is not separate from the multilingual because it is through language (or linguistic practices) that people co-construct, negotiate, impose, and represent their identities in such intercultural encounters in everyday life. Similar to culture, the notion of multilingual is also becoming blurred and at times, controversial because a monolingual view of languages has been perpetuated and dominant throughout many branches of applied linguistics and intercultural education—but also in politics. For example, within fields such as *second* and *foreign* language education, languages are still viewed as autonomous, separate systems (similar to the view of cultures as separate, homogeneous groups). This is problematic for a host of reasons, but mainly the constructed and (continued) use denies the multidimensional, heterogeneous nature of language(s) and identities as well as the complexity of contexts. Many situations, such as in lingua franca use, code mixing, and code switching (which are increasingly common in our *globalized* world), are thus often considered as 'second-class interactions' and not *real* multilingualism. The enumerating of languages (L1, L2, L3) reduces (essentializes) knowledge of languages and the spaces in which such knowledge is acquired as fixed, sedentary traits. This monolingual view of languages—that is, 'the mystic need for separate, perfect, well-balanced mastery of languages' (Moore & Gajo, 2009: 8)—and the ultimate goal of becoming, speaking, and feeling like an idealized native speaker are still being reproduced and promoted in language learning classrooms worldwide—though in certain contexts, such as in India or Malaysia, this is not always the case because access to the so-called native speaker is scarce (see Davies, 2003; Mahboob, 2005; Castellotti, 2008; Dervin & Badrinathan, 2011). As regards multilingualism, languages are still viewed as separate systems, not as a hybrid, overlapping system or as complex practices and social activities, even though scholars, such as Cook (2002), have demonstrated a unified linguistic competence in which knowledge of two or more languages exist (a multicompetence). Coste (2002) has equally challenged this bias by putting forth the notion of a *plurilingual and pluricultural competence* (see also Beacco & Byram, 2003), taking into account the situated mobilization of the linguistic and cultural components of the repertoire and its potential evolution and reconfiguration over time: 'a wholistic rather than segmented vision of language skills' (Moore & Gajo, 2009: 7). Perpetuating the use of monolithic categorizations [e.g., ESL (English as a second language); FSL (French as a second language); L1–L2)] does not appear to take into account any type of reflexivity on the hierarchical and problematic nature of the imposition of social categories or the recognition of transnational, diverse, plural identities (Byrd Clark, 2012). In other words, it does not reflect the researcher's awareness of his/her own investments in the employment of such categories (see Byrd Clark, 2008, 2009, 2010; Byrd Clark & Labrie, 2010) and still reflects a national, monolingual ideology (Risager, 2007) rather than the reality of multilingualism demanded by globalization (see Cenoz, 2013). We would argue that although recent forms of globalization have continued to spread capitalism in industrial and post-industrial countries, they have also, in particular, made such multimodal forms of communication more visible (as Canagarajah reminds us, 'there is a long history of texts and talk that have *meshed* languages' (2013: 2)).

With regard to globalization, there has been a shift in the field of applied linguistics within the last 15 years in viewing multilingualism from a critical perspective, that is, conceiving multilingualism as a social practice or as a set of resources (e.g., Pennycook, 2001, 2010; Budach, Roy, & Heller, 2003; Hornberger, 2005; Kramsch, 2006; Blackledge & Creese, 2010). Similar to the focus of the 'inter-' of the intercultural, the 'multi-' in multilingualism has been a more recent preoccupation among scholars (e.g., *societal multilingualism* proposed by Fishman, 2002; *flexible multilingualism*, as recently put forth by Weber & Horner, 2012; and the newest construct, *translingual practice* offered by Canagarajah, 2013). Through a critical perspective,[10] which underscores some types of emancipation (see Habermas, 1962, 1974; Marcuse, 1964*)*, it has become problematic to define or continue to use the term '*multi*lingualism' because it implies an ideal objective, a mastery of three separate or parallel monolingual systems. Yet, as argued by Heller (2008: 252), a critical perspective enables us to interrogate the notions of multilingualism and bilingualism themselves. For example, through such a perspective, one questions who or what constitutes a multilingual person? Is there an advantage to being/becoming multilingual? In other words, does being seen as a certain kind of multilingual enable privilege? If so, where, when, why, and according to whom? However, if we're looking more at performance, strategies, representations and uses of language(s), and culture(s), we might ask why do we still use the terms 'multilingual' and 'intercultural'?

The authors of this volume will also critically interrogate the notions of multilingualism and interculturality, but they will likewise critically interrogate the *critical*, meaning that multilingualism and interculturality through a critical perspective often entails a binary oppressor/oppressed relationship (dominant/marginalized) or a dichotomous relation between structure and agency (e.g., see Giddens, 1984, for a discussion of structure and agency). We see this also being played out with the celebration of linguistic diversity whereby monolingualism is seen as the problem and multilingualism as the solution. But the ways in which people use languages and position themselves are much more complex and complicated than an oppressor/oppressed relationship in everyday life, particularly when we look at how people perform varied identities through their language use in everyday spaces. In this book, the authors argue for a *reflexivity of reflexivity* (see Bourdieu, 1991) when looking at peoples' everyday life activities and performances through linguistic and communicative practices (including their own!).

REFLEXIVITY AS MULTIDIMENSIONAL: CRITICALITY, AWARENESS, AND HYPER-REFLEXIVITY

As mentioned in the previous section, when researching reflexivity and trying to make sense of reflexivity for ourselves, we began to see complex positionings that involved discourses and processes of othering, of constructing self/selves, and of ongoing engagement with self and other. In conjunction with these complex positionings, three notions/representations continually recurred in our readings: (1) criticality, or critical reflection, (2) awareness, and (3) hyper-reflexivity. These three overlapping notions reflect some of the complicities involved in the process of reflexivity. However, as discussed here, there are particularities that we (the authors) have chosen to address with each notion. That said, we have not exhausted, by any means, the different interpretations of each notion and its relevance to understanding reflexivity.

Nonetheless, we want to signal two significant issues that help shed light on our positionings and understandings of reflexivity in relation to multilingualism and interculturality. The first is that reflexivity has been looked upon predominantly as a dimension of the researcher/researched relationship and has been most closely connected conceptually to (or with) ethnography (see Aull Davies, 1999; Rampton et al., 2004; Hammersely, 2007). This framing of reflexivity in a binary relationship (researcher/researched) has provided advancement but also significant limitations and some blind spots because most of the challenges with conceptualizing reflexivity in research and practice (have been and) are encountered at the methodological realm (as we shall see in the upcoming sections).

The second issue has to do with the ways in which we have represented the three notions in this introduction. Though we intended to look at the different ways that reflexivity has been conceptualized, we realize at the same time the contradictions within our own articulations and positioning(s) of these notions. For instance, after many discussions with one another, we see that these notions could be potentially interpreted as static categories that progressively lead to a more reflexive stance (from critical reflection to hyper-reflexivity). Therefore, we caution that these representations should not be viewed as diachronic, hierarchical, separate categories but rather as particular yet overlapping facets (or dimensions) of reflexivity that intersect and help us to understand the complexity of this process and its continual evolution and to tackle the issue of reflexivity in a different light in research. It is likewise important to recognize that each of these notions signifies ideological representations, representations that become symbolic, particularly for researchers who invest in and embody them (ourselves included). Although we feel that reflexivity should reflect a multidimensional process incorporating all three notions here, we cannot deny our own interests in hyper-reflexivity, which we will expound upon further in our conclusion chapter. We should also note that these elements are selective and do not mention, for example, phenomenology (Gadamer, 1976, 1997) and other such approaches to being and becoming reflexive.

CRITICALITY OR CRITICAL REFLECTION: GETTING AT THE COMPLEXITIES

Reflexivity is not a new phenomenon for the social sciences. Notions of reflexivity have been greatly influenced by the fields of anthropology (Clifford & Marcus, 1986; Aull Davies, 1999; Wikan, 2002; Chauvier, 2011), psychology (e.g., Garfinkel, 1967; Moscovici, 1984; Potter 1996; Edwards, 1997; Gillespie, 2006), and sociology (Bourdieu, 1990; Giddens, 1991; Lahire, 2008), and they even date back to the early 1900s (in philosophy, for example, see the work of Henri Bergson (1906), a clear precursor of postmodern thinking). In sociology, researchers, such as Thomas & Thomas (1928) encountered the significance of interpretation—that the interpretation of a situation causes the action and, more importantly, that this interpretation is not objective. Such investigations led to the notion of the 'self-fulfilling prophecy' (see Merton, 1948, whereby 'subjective impressions can be projected on to life and thereby become real to projectors' (Volkart & Thomas, 1951: 14). This idea of impressions becoming *real*, or primordial in a sense, links with the sociopsychological notion of representation (see Moscovici, 1984); in other words, how and why we come to represent our impressions and ideas in the ways that we do, as well as how and why these representations become meaningful (symbolic) to us and in many ways become positioned as 'common sense.' But how do we come to understand such representations, and how do we (even we researchers) represent them? When? And how do we work on/with/against them?

Representations are significant to understanding reflexivity because it is through representations that people come to understand the world and organize their constructions of reality and of one another. For Jovchelovitch: 'the reality of the human world is in its entirety made of representation: in fact there is no sense of reality for our human world without the work of representation' (2007: 11). However, in the traditional scientific method, representations were deemed illusions, taking people away from 'real things,' as if reality were an objective, ideal, and constant nature.

Nevertheless, these early discoveries led researchers to develop a sense of critical inquiry to question scientific objectivity and so-called absolute truths about reality. This questioning of reality fostered a moving away from objective, neutral, and positivist ways of understanding the world and led to the epistemological development of critical theory (see Horkheimer, 1937). Drawing from some of Karl Marx's ideas about capitalism and the exploitation of the working classes by the wealthy, a group of theorists from what is known as the Frankfurt School[11] (1930), set to distinguish social sciences from natural sciences, arguing that generalizations cannot be made from so-called experiences because the understanding of a 'social' experience itself is always fashioned by ideas that reside within the researchers themselves. Thus, for the theorists of the Frankfurt School, critical theory represented a social critique aimed at enlightenment and change by illuminating the need to break out of the ideological constraints that restricted them.

This seemed to mark an important beginning of what has been referred to as critical reflection because 'critical theory must at all times be self-critical' (Bohman, 1996: 190). For Horkheimer, one of the Frankfurt School theorists, a theory is critical only if it is explanatory. He adds that critical theory must combine practical and normative thinking in order to 'explain what is wrong with current social reality, identify actors to change it, and provide clear norms for criticism and practical goals for the future' (Horkheimer, 1972: 219). In short, socialist philosophical thought must be given the ability to criticize itself and 'overcome' its own errors. Although theory must inform praxis,[12] praxis must *also* have a chance to inform theory. As we can see, the main focus of critical theory has been centered on recognizing the need for some type of emancipation or improvement (from being oppressed or dominated) and that this is highly dependent upon society becoming self-critical of (questioning or grasping) the outside world or events that happen in the outside, or 'real,' world. Ironically, it offers a 'rationalist model of emancipation that does not do enough to question the righteousness of its own assumptions' (Pennycook, 2001: 41).

One can see the influence of critical theory in relation to more contemporary research. For example, critical discourse analysis (CDA) theorists' general understanding of critique is in line with and links back to social transformative and emancipatory aims offered by the Frankfurt School (e.g., see Discourse Historical Analysis, DHA in Titscher, Wodak, Meyer, & Vetter, 2000). Critical interventions aim to reveal and demystify power structures from the 'perspective of those who suffer' (Fairclough & Wodak, 1997: 258; Wodak, 2001a: 10). Enabling informed choices through a self-reflective stance (Reisigl & Wodak, 2001: 265; Wodak, 2001b: 65) and a rejection of a 'know-that-all or know-it-better attitude' (Reisigl & Wodak, 2001: 265) also remain shared goals.

Critical theory has had a great impact on researchers in different fields of applied linguistics and intercultural education to consider the importance of interpretation and how this has related to the construction of social norms, including how such norms have become appropriated and performed, how certain inequalities and inequities have come about, and, certainly not least, the significance of communication and use of power in different contexts. For instance, under the guise of critical theory, many researchers who work in applied linguistics, linguistic minority education, the sociology of language, language policy, and critical language pedagogy have produced some highly influential work (e.g., see Norton Pierce, 1995; Cummins, 1996; Heller, 1999; Norton & Toohey, 2004; Hornberger, 2005; Hawkins & Norton, 2009), as well as intercultural communication and education (Shi-xu, 2001; Abdallah-Pretceille, 2003; Holliday, 2013 Andreotti, 2011) on unequal relations of power between dominant and marginalized groups (in other words, the haves and the have-nots).

Nonetheless, it is important to highlight that this focus of the reflection has tended to be on the critical of the reflection, and the critical, in this sense, has tended to focus on the recognizing and questioning of the other, or outside world, rather than reflecting upon and/or including one's own positionings/subjectivities. In other words, the emphasis has been on trying to understand how and why who does what to whom, when, where, how often, and what the consequences are of these actions (influenced by anthropology, as we shall see in the next section). In general, most work has been critical of the social order; the macro structures of the larger social and political order, hegemony or hegemonic processes (where a small group of elites have control of valuable resources and run things that appear to be democratic but that actually serve only their interests); the distribution of resources (material, linguistic, social, symbolic); the construction of difference; language politics; the organization and operationalization of social institutions, nationalism, capitalism, and/or processes of socialization (e.g., indoctrination, linguistic regimentation). Although important, the critical in this case appears to reflect only one facet of reflexivity (e.g., see Gramsci, 1971; Heller, 1994, 1999, 2006; Duchêne & Heller, 2007, 2012; Jaffe, 2009; Fairclough, 2006) in the 'telling of such stories' (Sole & Wilson, 2002; Duranti, 2009). These works exude criticality, with particular emphasis on the materiality of social processes, but they appear unreflexive in their own ideological and social positionings (positions of power) and in the material conditions that enabled them to produce such critical work.

Having said this, many scholars in applied linguistics and intercultural communication and education have written about the importance of developing critical reflection and advocating for a critical approach (Heller, 1999, 2011; Pennycook, 1999; Block, 2003; Hawkins & Norton, 2009; Dervin, 2011). Yet blind spots and challenges remain when it comes to self-representation as researchers and the ways in which we represent data. For us, we see that reflexivity as a process and a construct requires us to be aware at every stage of the research [from engaging with theoretical concepts and their relationship with methodological and analytical practice to the researcher's (researchers') identities, contexts, and linguistic choices when representing data—from generation to communication].

Pennycook posits that 'self-criticism is a crucial element for critical work' (1999: 345). He adds that critical approaches should incorporate 'constant questioning and constant skepticism for the types of knowledge they operate with'; at the same time, he cautions that we need to employ candor as well as humility about the limits of what can be known through critical research and practice. According to Norton Pierce, the researcher's critical reflection plays a constitutive role in 'determining the progress of the research project' (1995: 570). However, how does being critical relate to being reflexive? Are the two notions one in the same? And, again, when we are being/becoming critical, have we included our *selves* in this criticality? For instance, in critiques of Norton Pierce's work, *Social Identity, Investment and Language Learning*, Canagarajah (1996) and Kramsch (1999) point out that Norton Pierce did not appear aware of her own representations as a researcher or of the complex representations of the immigrant women in Canada in her study, particularly positioning their use of diary writing entries as transparent reflections of their lives (and identities). Whereas Norton Pierce made the case for a theory of identity 'as multiple and a site of struggle', Canagarajah argued that Norton Pierce's own identity[13] was largely absent from the written research report. He states:

> For all practical purposes, the researcher is absent from the report, looming behind the text as an omniscient, transcendental, all knowing figure. This convention hides the manner in which the subjectivity of the researchers—with their complex values, ideologies, and experiences—shapes the research activity and findings. In turn, how the research activity shapes the researchers' subjectivity is not explored—even though research activity can sometimes profoundly affect the researchers' sense of the world and themselves. (1996: 324)

But this kind of critical reflection presents a dilemma and leads into another important dimension of reflexivity: awareness. Awareness, in this sense, is not only a question of representing our own subjectivities but also the ways in which we go about representing linguistic and cultural representations of the people with whom we do research, particularly those who are conceived of as marginalized. We need to ask ourselves are we critically defending their interests, or are we objectifying their diversity to serve our own? Certainly, this is not a *black-and-white* question that renders a neat, *black-and-white*, *either-or* answer (especially since the answer could be yes to both!). But this question signifies a start at getting at the complexities.

To recapitulate, most critical work has exemplified the significance of how difference is constructed and the importance of recognition in bringing about social transformation and change (be it through linguistic rights, modernity, identities, relations of power, and some kind of liberation from the unequal distribution of symbolic resources). One begins by trying to understand 'the problem(s) of the social world,' yet we are left wondering how can one be and become critical without necessarily being/becoming aware of one's own performances, life chances, experiences, and values, as well as, more importantly, his/her investments in such representations? And what do we mean by awareness anyhow?

AWARENESS: ON BECOMING OTHER

> You must be the *change* that you want to see in the world. (Mahatma Gandhi)

> "When you've made your secret journey, you will be a holy man" (The Police, 1982)

According to Aull Davies (2010: 4), reflexivity represents 'a turning back on to oneself; a process of self-reference.' When we think of awareness in relation to reflexivity, it seems to add a slightly different dimension or facet than 'critical' because awareness has been most associated with a type of betterment for the individual and at the same time may appear reminiscent of both Jürgen Habermas's notion of enlightenment as well as the Buddhist notion of enlightenment (awareness; spiritual awakening).[14] As far as mainstream representations of enlightenment go, one of us who grew up in the 1970s and 1980s (in North America) couldn't help but think back and remember the *Star Wars* series, particularly the films the *Empire Strikes Back* and *Return of the Jedi*, which depict young Luke Skywalker in the process of training to become a Jedi knight (and his transformation in becoming a Jedi) by the Jedi master, Yoda. This process, while illuminating, was often met with frustration and appeared to take time to master. Luke had to overcome his fear as well as transcend his ego in order to become a Jedi. Awareness as a means of enlightenment, in this sense, was not exclusively centered on being critical of what was happening on the outside or taking action, but, more importantly, it focused on getting in touch with and understanding feelings, emotions, and experiences from within; in a way, mastering our fears in order to become other. Related to research, this facet of awareness fosters a process that has preoccupied researchers, to be and become (in ethnographic terms) both 'insider' and 'outsider' (to which we will further attend toward the end of this chapter). Consequently, awareness in research (e.g., such as counseling) has additionally been treated as a heuristic phenomenon (Braud & Anderson, 1998; Moustakas, 1990, 2001), mainly focusing on the researcher's lived experiences (the transformative effect of the inquiry on the researcher's own experience or self-discovery). It has been described as a psychological and emotional state and as particularly linked with becoming other or something more (be it better, more effective, etc.) than you were or happened to be before—a transformation, an altered or heightened sense achievable through a particular experience(s).

Researchers of multilingual and intercultural education have discussed, at different moments, although not at lengths, this notion of awareness. At the end of her 1994 book, *Crosswords*, Monica Heller discusses her ethnographic study on Francophone Canada and talks about the research that made her both a researcher and a human being, signifying the importance of research for one's own humanity—that emancipation/transformation is not solely reserved for the participants in a study but likewise for the researcher. Although Heller mentions this at the end of her book, we are left wondering how do we know that we have become better or more aware? Often what appears missing is a discussion or details of the moments of how, when, and why a researcher experiences becoming enlightened or more aware.

Lorenza Mondada (1998) illuminates the power of the researcher and the ways in which researchers interpret or *'fabriquer le terrain'* ('construct the field') the moment they enter it. She has likewise underscored the importance of having awareness of this *fabrication du terrain* throughout the research process, from the researcher's epistemological and ontological stance to the selection, analysis, and presentation of the data. Having such an awareness of self can contribute to a more deeply engaged study because the researcher is not trying to hide, conceal, or cover up any bias or preconceived notions but actively engages with his/her own ideological attachments.

Along similar lines of awareness as betterment, Michael Byram has discussed the significance of awareness in relation to language education and *cosmopolitan* citizenship by elucidating the need for effective human capital, that is, well developed, critically thinking citizens of the world in this new knowledge economy (Byram, 2010). Canagarajah reminds us that cosmopolitanism doesn't have to involve travel because we can experience it in our own neighborhoods 'in forms of super-diversity constructed by people of different language and cultural backgrounds' (2013: 193). Although different in their conceptions of cosmopolitanism, both Byram and Canagarajah seem to stress that awareness entails an openness to diversity that will lead to some introspection or ways of becoming self-critical.

However, we must ask, does such awareness lead one to inspect one's own ideologies and life chances in relation to the kinds of research one does, or might it serve to reinforce class prejudice and continue to separate people from one another? In qualitative research, the representation of the historical 'neutral observer' or scientific method continues to dominate,[15] and this representation harkens back to anthropologists' work from the early 1900s (see Boas, 1928, 1940; Malinowski, 1927, 1944).

If we return to the criticisms made by Canagarajah of Norton Pierce in the former section, it is not completely surprising to witness the absence of the researcher's identity and apparent lack of self-awareness because a couple of issues are at hand. The first details late 19th-century anthropologists (e.g., the famous armchair anthropologists) who claimed that a major preoccupation of theirs was how to avoid imposing their own biases and preconceptions on the people they were studying. They sought objectivity through detached observations (see Mead, 1928). The irony occurs when researchers are taking a critical (nonobjective) stance without questioning the validity of their representations of others, thus remaining uncritical of their own interpretations and experiences. We, like many, have certainly been guilty of doing this in our earlier research, whereby we provide our critical and candid interpretations (based on our own social and lived trajectories) but do not go far enough in analyzing our own analyses or representations of data. Of course, without collaborative engagement or interaction with others, this makes it very difficult to become aware of one's own investments and use of representations (more on this in the final section).

For Boas and Malinowski, two early 19th-century anthropologists, the only way one could hope to understand the *native* point of view, uncontaminated by one's own preconceptions, was to immerse oneself in the native world, rather than to set oneself as apart as possible (i.e., in one's armchair).

Therefore, reflexivity, for these anthropologists (as well as for many applied linguists and interculturalists), was something to be overcome. As time went on, particularly as participant observation became the norm, anthropologists slowly began to consider how far it was really possible to be objective (especially when one considers the fact that many anthropologists in the 19th century were working for governments and for colonization!); immersing oneself in native life may remove one from one's own world but not from one's own mind, itself formed in the context of one's own world (e.g., see Wikan, 2002) or worlds. For Eric Chauvier (2011), this consisted in 'desinterlocuting' the observed, negating her as an interlocutor but also negating the power of language.

On the social side, French sociologist Pierre Bourdieu also conceived of reflexivity as something to overcome (as a static state) in relation to objectivity (as seen previously with anthropologists) but one that equally inclines us to look at our own illusions of the social world. Bourdieu (1991) called for reflexivity when he argued for a *sociology of sociology* insofar as social scientists are inherently laden with biases as well as illusions, and as such they must at all times conduct their research with conscious attention to the effects of their own position, their own set of internalized structures (*habitus*), and how these are likely to distort or prejudice their objectivity. He argued that social scientists ought to conduct their research with one eye continually reflecting back upon their own habitus, in other words, their dispositions (which he argued were learned through long social and institutional training). Bourdieu emphasized that it is only by maintaining such a continual vigilance that the sociologists can spot themselves in the act of importing their own biases into their work. He chastised academics (including himself) for judging their students' work against a rigidly scholastic linguistic register, favoring students whose writing appeared 'polished,' marking down those guilty of using 'colloquial language.' In this vein, we concur that many academics appear to be blinded by class prejudice whereby there is some ideal or objective, 'normalized' way of writing (teaching, and research included).

Without a reflexive analysis of the ways in which the academics judge students' work, Bourdieu argued that academics will unconsciously reproduce a degree of class prejudice. And we argue, so too will researchers! Lakoff (1990: 17), who takes a similar position to Pierre Bourdieu (1982, 1991), reminds us that 'our every interaction is political, whether we intend it to be or not; everything we do in the course of a day communicates our relative power, our desire for a particular sort of connection, our identification of the other as one who needs something from us, or vice versa.' If aware of this, one might purport that the researcher should be able to be critical of the injustices that research can contribute to and potentially try to have an impact on them. Anthropologists have been quite pioneering in this sense as, increasingly, it is expected of them to have a positive impact on their field (political promotion). This, of course, contributes to confuse the boundaries between research and politics. Yet one could argue that research cannot be anything but political, especially when it is done reflexively.

In regard to becoming aware and critical of these elements, anthropologists distinguished between self-reflexivity and reflexivity. According to Kelly and Grenfell:

> Self-reflexivity of anthropologists is distinct from the reflexivity of the people whom anthropologists study, the ways that people perform socially, that they 'tell stories about themselves', but the two are related; both acknowledge that people (both those being studied and those doing the studying) are 'contextualised persons', and that what they say about themselves and others emerges from that context, and does not because such represent an objective reality. (2004: 4)

Moving from the stance of detaching oneself in order to avoid imposing one's bias to including one's own voice or positionings as a researcher in the research process has led to some controversy, which brings us to a second issue. The second issue of awareness deals with issues of navigating the different degrees and performances of including one's self-reflexivity or what Pillow has referred to as an 'uncomfortable reflexivity—a reflexivity that seeks to know while at the same time situates this knowing as tenuous' (2003: 188). This 'reflexivity of discomfort' pushes toward the unfamiliar and the uncomfortable.

Nevertheless, some anthropologists had become self-reflexive to the point of self-obsession (see Kelly & Grenfell, 2004), bringing themselves so much to the center of the text that the story was much more about themselves than about the people being studied (e.g., see Behar, 1993; Lawless, 1992). For example, they wrote detailed personal accounts of their own experiences: 'they begin to believe that they *are* the world they study, or that the world revolves around them' (Burawoy, 2003: 673). But how do we include or make space for self-disclosure without being construed as overbearing or self-indulgent? In conventional writing, "to write the 'self' into the text is seen as problematic and always presents a dilemma to the author who does not fit the authoritative model of a white male self" (Minh-ha, 1989 as cited in Day, 2012: 69). Of course, we must remember the category 'white male self' represents a complex social construction (heterogeneous as well). However, "Minh-ha's work reminds us that not all authors are powerfully positioned, and the conventions of writing authoritative accounts are such that the heterogeneity of authors is erased" (Day, 2012: 69).

Many researchers (including the authors in this volume) have written from voices of authority without being aware of how we present our data and subjectivities as transparent rather than as symbolic representations from particular moments and times. At the same time, many researchers are afraid to include what they understand to be their own positionings and engagements for fear of losing face among their colleagues, of being told that what they're doing isn't *real* research and that there is far too much *navel gazing* going on in their texts. In her autobiography, Pavlenko (2003) recounts what she deems as failure in that one of her research participants happened to "see through her" and her attempt to hide behind others' life stories in order to whisper her points "objectively". Although Pavlenko signals that this was an important moment for her to include her subjectivity "as an interested and invested scholar rather than a hidden puppet-master," she goes on to state: "I still work with language learning autobiographies; I no longer use them to tell my story . . ." (p. 188). But one must question, is such an experience really a *failure* or is it perhaps an invitation for reflexivity? For example, how does one select and use others' stories without revealing a bit of one's own biases/positionings (as Trinh T. Minh-ha argues: "questions are always loaded with the questioner's prejudices" (1989:69); and who is this "I"? Building upon Goffman's (1967) notion of saving face and Butler's (1990) work on performativity, Pennycook, in his 2005 article, 'Performing the Personal,' draws our attention to the use of 'I' in both writing and research as a performance and, in doing so, highlights an important dimension of awareness and positionality that many reflexive moves in qualitative research do not take into account. He states, 'the point here is that the textual I, the invitation to these reflexive accounts, is not so much a transparent representation of an author, but a textual production of one' (2005: 301): The 'I' of research writing is a performed form of identification. One of Pennycook's aims is to make a case for the centrality of writing as research that is distinct from the call for endless confessional writing activities, which can all too quickly appear self-indulgent (2005: 302) or as 'navel gazing' (Heller, 2011, forum discussion). Aside from this, it is important to note that there are also consequences by including one's vulnerabilities (or identity negotiations) in writing to a general public; as Lin recounts, 'Exposing one's own mistakes, conflicts, confusions, and dilemmas to the public through writing this critical reflexive account is not only an intellectual task, but also a political action, full of psychological and social risks . . .' (2004: 287, as cited in Pennycook, 2010: 302). Yet to do justice to our fields, to participants, and to others, this ('leaning into the discomfort') should be a compulsory component of research. This also contributes to signaling that research cannot but be a process during which certain things succeed, while others do not work. The current obsession with success in research should make way for more modest accounts of 'failure' through reflexivity. It takes courage to show one's imperfections, but sometimes through what we construe as failure and imperfection may actually lead us to a deeper engagement and connection with one another. Reflexivity in this vein does not mean dismissing the importance of examining issues of power, but rather that reflexivity is inextricably linked to power and privilege that cannot be easily or 'comfortably' erased (as will be discussed further in the upcoming section on Hyper-reflexivity).

Similar to criticality, the chapters in this volume attend to some of these issues of awareness in relation to reflexivity but will also focus on some of the potential blind spots, one being a question of opportunities to develop a deeper understanding around self–other relations, including navel gazing, which is something we all do at different moments in different spaces. However, rather than quickly judging or singularly categorizing people, we could perhaps look at how and why we do such navel gazing. We need to have some kind of awareness of the experiences, life chances, representations, power issues, and identities that we bring with us throughout the research process as well as those of our research participants. Contrarily, these narcissistic, self-confessional ego musings may potentially lead to some kind of awareness if provided the conditions where we are willing to critically revisit our own writings, engage with one another, particularly about the discomfort, drawing from a diversity of disciplines, and reflect on our understandings, strategies, and employment of representations at particular moments in time. Again, awareness represents an important facet of reflexivity, but, at the same time, awareness of self alone may not be enough.

Very often absent from multilingual and intercultural research is awareness of the relations of power taking place between the different actors as well as the ways in which dogma is established, embodied, and performed, how a black-and-white or an us-and-them is constructed (Gumperz, 1982). This would additionally include how invested we become in certain approaches and groups that can also blind us. For example, in a recent ethnographic forum, Jan Blommaert (2012) interacted with a group of students and researchers in response to a question about dogmatism in relation to ethnography, stating:

> It is good to distinguish between 'dogmatism' and 'methodological firmness'. The latter is a commitment towards a perpetual improvement of theory and methodology, casting robust foundations and working from that basis up to specific techniques and methods of analysis. The first is the refusal, so to speak, to change and adjust, replacing the dynamics of scientific dialogue by a 'catechismic' attitude in which everything should fit the theory. If it doesn't fit, the data are dropped, simplified or disqualified as unreliable. I guess all of us are familiar with that phenomenon. The spirit of ethnography is precisely its openness. . . . The key thing about ethnography is what I have called elsewhere 'the ethnographic invitation': the constant openness to critically check what we believe against the available evidence; to keep exploring things even when—or especially when—they appear to be well-known. It's, as we can see, a fundamentally anti-dogmatic stance in science. I hope that distinction, between dogmatism and firmness, is clear now. (Forum discussion retrieved September 15, 2012, from www.jiscmail.ac.uk/cgi-bin/webadmin?A0=LING-ETHNOG)

Although we appreciate and understand Blommaert's positioning here, we must ask whether the distinction is so clear-cut? Certainly there are moments when and where we can all appear dogmatic and other times when we appear 'firm.' What one might question here would be is ethnography (alone) enough to foster openness and keep us from being dogmatic? To echo

Bourdieu, are ethnographers under some kind of illusion or illusions about certain approaches (ethnography)? Do all ethnographers practice reflexivity in their own writing and everyday lives? Often, scholars will talk about the tough questions that they had to ask themselves during the research process and issues of power, but do not fully address their own stance, life trajectories, struggles (including the unfamiliar), negotiation of positionalities (e.g., questioning transparency of self-representations), or engagements throughout the research (e.g., Block, 2005, 2010; Heller, 2011; Duchêne & Heller, 2012; Jaffe, 2009; Pavlenko, 2003; Piller, 2012). Other times, researchers' written accounts appear eloquent, well poised, down-to-earth, and inspiring, yet when coming into contact through face-to-face interaction, some researchers don't often seem to put into practice those wonderfully written accounts and sadly appear the very opposite of the representations they so skillfully craft (perform) in their writings. But again this reflects back to the political nature of writing, and Pennycook's (2005) argument of performing the personal.

For many ethnographers and qualitative researchers alike, the interaction centers on the researcher and the researched but, again, does not account for the complexity, intersectionality[16], and polyvocality of representations, subjectivities, and performances taking place between the interlocutors. The interactions are presented in an interpretivist manner, but usually we hear only the interpretations of the researcher of/on/about the research participants (as traditional objects of study) and seldom any engagement of these interpretations with/between the participants in the research and the researcher(s). We also seldom hear any recounts of the questioning of our methods (see Bensa, 2010). Lastly, are we as researchers practicing what we preach in our work? Are we aware of the hegemonies (e.g., class prejudice) to which we (re)produce and ascribe, how we form research groups and allow some to be included and recognized (in our groups and publications) while others are not? Are we aware of the 'hierarchies of credibility' (see Becker, 1967) that we ourselves construct? Again, we return to the question, how do we know we are reflexive or doing reflexivity?

Awareness, in this section, appears to carry with it at least three issues/aspects: (1) a betterment of the human being/citizen/person through research and/or lived experiences and learning about one's self via others, (2) something to overcome, and (3) a need to become aware of the illusions of the social world as well as our own representations and engagements with them.

In the spirit of awareness, we now move to discussion of the third dimension of reflexivity, hyper-reflexivity.

HYPER-REFLEXIVITY: THE COMPLEX MESHING OF SELF AND OTHER

The use of the word 'hyper' is currently being used as a prefix with terms such as 'diversity' (e.g., Moyer et al., 2012), 'mobility' (e.g., Dervin, 2008), and in this case, 'reflexivity' (e.g., Kapoor, 2004; Byrd Clark, 2012). The prefix signifies going beyond, exceeding what is conceived of as 'normal,' mega, extreme, and existing in more than three spatial dimensions. The notion of hyper-reflexivity, in this sense, demonstrates a moving away from and going beyond some of the traditional ways that reflexivity has been conceived or at least how one engages with reflexivity as a complex, multifaceted process. With regard to our understandings of the notion hyper-reflexivity, there is a demand for a heightened awareness of our use (and misuse) of representations, methodological dilemmas, and our own positionings and engagements throughout the research process. Collaboration serves an important piece of doing hyper-reflexivity, whether it be ongoing between the researcher and the people willing to participate in a study, the collaborative efforts of a research partnership or team, the revisiting of strategies, discussions of previous writings with fellow colleagues or friends, or all of the above.

This notion of hyper-reflexivity puts forth a call for a so-called reflexive turn in applied linguistics but owes some of its credit to what has been coined the 'social turn' in applied linguistics and intercultural education (in the early to mid-1990s) whereby researchers started to look more closely at the identities of their participants, including themselves and their investments in research—not just in a specific section of one's work but throughout, especially when analyzing data and confronting data with theory. For example, Ben Rampton reminds us of the importance of recognizing one's own engagements throughout the research process:

> Researchers cannot help being socially located persons. We inevitably bring our biographies and our subjectivities to every stage of the research process and this influences the questions we ask and the ways in which we try to find answers. (1992: 5)

But a reflexive turn incorporates not only a constant inspection of one's positionalities throughout the research process at every stage but also the openness to variation, to failure, and to imagination in each of our self–other engagements. The itinerary toward representing the other 'over there,' requires scrutiny of the 'here' (Visweswaran, 1994: 112), or it necessitates reversing the gaze, reimagining what we mean by the 'field' or the 'there.'

Coming from critical literacy and postcolonial studies, Gayatri Spivak has argued that because we are all 'subject-effects' (1988: 204, as cited in Kapoor, 2004: 641)—that is, inescapably positioned in a variety of discourses—our personal and institutional desires and interests are unavoidably written into our representations. We need, then, to be unscrupulously vigilant (e.g., hyper-self-reflexive) about our complicities as researchers and human beings. This means that we need to be cognizant and critical of our own constructions, strategies, investments, and social backgrounds throughout our engagements. Drawing upon Spivak's (1988) work on the subaltern[17] and the politics involved in othering processes, we are presented with the problematic nature of both colonial and native representations of the Third World and the implications of such representations. Spivak invites a heightened sense of criticality and awareness of representations. This dimension of hyper-reflexivity requires that we examine how our discursive constructions are intimately linked to our life experiences, positionings (socioeconomic, gendered, cultural, linguistic, geographic, historical, institutional) and (often) our failure to recognize heterogeneity. Invoking Foucault, Spivak underscores the implication of *pouvoir-savoir* (being able to do something only because you are able to make sense of it, 1993: 34) and argues that we produce the other, or Third World in this case (Said, 1978: 3; Beverly, 1999: 2), and, to a rather large extent, we produce them to suit our own images and desires. Although Spivak acknowledges her own involvements, she does not distinguish that there are varying degrees of complicity. For example, as argued in our positionings and understandings in relation to multilingualism and interculturality, we are constructing otherness, but at the same time we are continuously constructing a sense of self or selves (e.g., see also Hall, 1992, 2006; Gallagher, 2011).

Perhaps of most interest to us here regarding reflexivity is Spivak's insistence on a vigilant self-implication and painstaking, ethical engagement that permits space for becoming aware of or at least engaging with the vulnerabilities and blind spots of one's power and representational systems. It is accepting of failure or, put positively, 'seeing failure as success' (Kapoor, 2004: 644).

Going a little further, hyper-reflexivity, as a third component of reflexivity, demands resourcefulness and openness on the part of the person involved, a willingness to go and sit with the uncomfortableness and messiness of one's own ideological attachments, ways of representing and investing, and a willingness, at the same time, to flexibly engage and negotiate meanings with one another. But hyper-reflexivity also means that one is aware that this does not happen in every situation, and varies considerably in different contexts. Reflexivity is a process that is collaborative, interactive and inherently social: a collective effort (Bourdieu 2004 as cited in Day, 2012: 81).

In his recent book, Canagarajah has introduced Khubchandani's work on the strategies of *synergy* (putting forth one's own efforts) and *serendipity* (accepting the other on his/her own terms) as a means to discuss linguistic pluralism and everyday practices. He explains that subjects living in linguistically pluralistic local contexts have to be radically other centered, open to unexpectedness, and 'imaginative and alert to make on the spot decisions in relation to the forms and conventions employed by the other' (2013: 41). This could also aptly apply to researchers in regard to fostering a more candid, multidimensional understanding and deeper engagement with reflexivity—one that allows us space to perform the personal, embrace our vulnerabilities, and bring methodological dilemmas to the forefront.

Reflexivity in this vein demands a constant reinspection of and engagement with our shifting and complex self-othering involvements, as relates to representations of power, our linguistic and social practices, our emotions (reactions and discernments), our biases, and constructions of difference throughout the research process. However, there is some caution about practicing hyper-reflexivity. One can become hyper-reflexive to the extent of over-analyzing (a potentially "endless process", see Lynch, 2000:45) whereby one is no longer able to make decisions and in turn becomes blind to hegemonic relations of power. One of us had a family member who was in a spiritual community for nine years as an active devotee of a guru—a guru who claimed to be enlightened. This guru alleged to be leading the spiritual community members toward awakening by having them transcend their egos—as if the ego represents a 'bad' thing. One of the greatest outcomes of this involvement was that this family member helped many to feel their heart's desires and vulnerabilities, and become more attuned to their own patterns, karma, and embodiments of energy. Although this family member became very adept at discerning peoples' intentions (energy/energies), constantly and continuously analyzing hers as well as others' actions, and seeing how attached we all become to the material world, she was unable to see the ways in which she separated herself from others, nor the hegemonic gatekeeping power behind the guru's persuasive, indoctrinating discourse. Being part of the guru's community, this family member was afforded an upper-middle class lifestyle and introduced to what she construed as unique practices/activities (not privy to everyone). Interestingly, no one in this spiritual community ever reached the enlightened state that the guru claimed to promote and possess. This experience, though particular, bears similarities to how doctoral students position and give recognition to their thesis supervisors (as guru or god-like) and to academia. Because of such positionings, both students and thesis supervisors can become blinded or have blind spots when it comes to their own attachments, investments, and representations of power (particularly 'conventional' knowledge). Hyper-reflexivity then demands not only an openness to the invitation of continuous introspection but also the capacity as well as the conditions to be able to take time to 'go outside' (removing oneself, whether mentally, geographically, physically, socially, etc.) and then revisit one's own immersed ways of thinking, doing, and being from particular moments of time (as Holmes and Malinkowski and Nelson have shown, in their upcoming chapters). For instance, to be able to have the insight of your own positionings as well as how you are positioned and conceived by others, including how you might become positioned differently at different times is not easy to figure out or predict. Finally, hyper-reflexivity cannot be assumed, is not a universal 'cure-all' and similar to different dimensions of awareness, necessitates intersectionality, time and opportunities (or conditions) for inspecting, engaging, experiencing and weaving through complex meshings of self-other relations in everyday life to inform both research and practice.

In this section, we have highlighted three intricately overlapping dimensions of reflexivity in relation to historical, philosophical, social, and political approaches vis-à-vis the continual evolution of reflexivity specifically in relation to multilingualism and interculturality. Table 0.1 indicates some

Table 0.1 Dimensions and Representations of Reflexivity

Representation of reflexivity	References	Characteristics
Critical reflection	Frankfurt School CDA Heller, Norton, Pennycook	Questions scientific objectivity and so-called absolute truths about reality
		Reveals and demystifies power structures
Awareness	Byram, Bourdieu, Mondada, Pennycook, Rampton	The power of the researcher and the ways in which researchers interpret or 'construct the field'
		A betterment of the human being/citizen/person through research and/or lived experiences and learning about one's self via others
		Becoming aware of the illusions of the social world as well as our own representations and performances of them
Hyperreflexivity	Rampton, Spivak Gallagher, Hall, Kapoor, Canagarajah	Ways of going beyond some of the traditional ways that reflexivity has been conceived, or at least to present reflexivity as a complex, multifaceted process
		Heightened awareness of our use (or misuse) of representations, strategies, and our own positionings
		Personal and institutional desires and interests are unavoidably written into our representations

of the main points of each representation. It is important to note, however, that the three representations are mutually informative and are not separate from one another (in that they intersect and can inform one another, at times multidirectionally). Some of the authors' works/references may appear to be more representative of one of these notions in particular, whereas some of the references are reflective of all of these facets, demonstrating that the dimensions we have employed here are not static, yet at the same time they do offer and represent our particular understandings of what constitutes or should constitute reflexivity.

In light of our positionings of the multifaceted and polysemous notions of intercultural and multilingual as related to our understandings of reflexivity, including how reflexivity has been conceptualized, we now turn to our final section, which looks at some of the work that has been done on reflexivity in relation to multilingualism and interculturality.

PREVIOUS RESEARCH ON REFLEXIVITY IN RELATION TO MULTILINGUALISM AND INTERCULTURALITY

Reflexivity has been given some consideration, theoretically speaking, for example, in applied linguistics and discourse analysis. For example, conceptions of reflexivity in terms of looking at the role of context, intersubjectivity, and the socially and culturally embedded nature of language (Fairclough, 1995; Kramsch, 2005; Byrd Clark, 2008; Pennycook, 2010; Dervin & Risager, 2014), particularly through the use of critical ethnographic methods (Rampton et al., 2004; Creese, 2008) and linguistic discourse analyses (Shi-xu, 2001; Fairclough, 1995) have contributed to transforming the ways in which multilingualism and interculturality have been traditionally conceived (Byrd Clark, 2009; Blackledge & Creese, 2010; Pennycook, 2010; Dervin, 2011). As already mentioned, several scholars have written about reflexivity in relation to critical awareness, particularly for TESOL (Teachers of English for Speakers of Other Languages) and language teacher education (e.g., Sarangi, 2003, Pennycook, 1999, 2005; Hawkins & Norton, 2009; Canagarajah, 2004, 2005). Upon its inception, Alastair Pennycook's work (2001) in particular, has shaken the traditional field of applied linguistics and has broken much needed new ground with his seminal work, entitled *Critical Applied Linguistics*, or linguistics with an attitude, as he likes to put it.

With the impact of globalization, digital technologies, mobility, and migration, we see that research on these topics is also increasingly moving away from the appeal of structure to the examination of normal daily phenomena such as exceptions, contradictions, instabilities, and processes. Most importantly, these epistemological and global shifts have rendered psycholinguistic, objectivist, and essentialist views of language, culture, and identity no longer tenable because they are not reflective of people developing transnational, *mélanged* identities and complex linguistic repertoires (Byrd Clark, 2009, 2012; Dervin, 2011).

In a reflexive turn, this focus on the local use of language(s) has led to some fascinating work, challenging nationalist conceptions of multilingualism, identities, and cultures.[18] Pennycook has recently proposed the locality of language, whereby language is not a pregiven structure but rather a product of practice, a repeated social action (something that we do) in what he refers to as a 'relocalized difference', inasmuch as 'language creativity is about sameness that is also difference' (2010: 51). This creativity for research vis-à-vis multilingualism and interculturality has been emerging in the ways that youth, in particular, draw upon multiple, hybrid, and mixed linguistic resources or features, capturing the dynamic and evolving relationship between open semiotic (meaning) systems and languages and, as Pennycook (2010) would concur, the negotiation of identities through languages in urban, modern spaces. Pennycook opens discussions about considering how we might look at language (in this case, performing the multilingual) as a practice. However, does this mean that we completely throw away language as a fixed system? Is it possible to move from A to Z in our approaches, or is there some achievable in-between among language as systems and as social practices? What about the ways in which people become attached to what counts as language, grammatically or meaningfully? And how do we engage with one another and co-construct meanings in relation to our ideological attachments and existing norms in everyday interactions? Being able to engage in such discussions with colleagues and students is one important facet of what reflexivity represents for us.

In addition to language as local practice, Pennycook (drawing upon Michel de Certeau's work), argues for the ordinariness of language, that is, the inclusion of everyday practices that people perform, particularly in social structures like school. We both agree and very much support this position. But this begs the question of how many of us, as academics, use everyday language or practices, especially when it comes to writing? If we do use everyday language, we're scrutinized by our peers and told that our use of language is far too colloquial or trite or tangential—in other words, not academic enough sounding. We have no problem demonstrating how participants in our research studies 'do language,' be it through hip hop, translingual practice, metrolingualism, translanguaging, etc. (see Creese & Blackledge, 2010; Alim, Ibrahim & Pennycook, 2009; Otsuji & Pennycook, 2010; Canagarajah, 2013;), but we almost never demonstrate or include our own ordinary uses of language. And if we do, we often have those sections rejected or not included in our publications. So conditions must be given consideration when discussing reflexivity.

Building upon Pierre Bourdieu's work (*Outline of a Theory of Practice*, 1977), Kramsch (2005) has likewise argued for a theory of practice that takes into account how real-world problems (e.g., see Davies, 1999) become problems by 'not only exploring the conditions that make the real world possible, but the conditions that make possible the very exploration of the *real* world' (Kramsch, 2005: 560). Although it is not explicitly expressed, Kramsch draws attention to the need for a (practical) reflexive approach ('a symbolic component to Communicative Language Teaching,' see Kramsch, 2011). The authors of this book thus take into account these more recent arguments via their engagements with reflexivity and build further upon these in relation to the notions of the intercultural and multilingual.

Although there have been great advances made in linguistic anthropology (e.g., Meyerhoff, 1978; Duranti, 1997; Aull Davies, 1999), anthropology (e.g., Wikan, 2002; Bensa, 2010; Chauvier, 2011), and sociology (e.g., Bourdieu, 1990; Erikson, 1994) whereby reflexivity is not a new concept, very few studies in applied linguistics, language and intercultural education, and/or intercultural communication have deeply and systematically engaged with reflexivity, especially in data analysis. Describing one's positions in relation to a field in one paragraph in a methodological section of, say, an article is not enough anymore. Such acts of reflexivity should be throughout! It is the hope of the authors that this book will serve as an important point of departure.

CONCLUSION

What does it mean to be and become reflexive as a learner, teacher, and researcher? The chapters in this volume put forth multimodal ways of thinking about languages, methods, 'cultures,' and identities by investigating what it means to be and become reflexive in relation to the notions of multilingualism and interculturality. As such, we can begin to better understand how and why we, as teachers, learners, and researchers, become invested in the ways that we do and perhaps, at the same time, find ways to embrace our own vulnerabilities and varied performances. Our objectives for this book are guided by following key questions:

1. (How) do teachers represent their practice of reflexivity in their teaching?
2. (How) do learners represent the development of reflexivity in their learning?
3. How does the researcher practice reflexivity in his/her research? How is reflexivity represented? According to whom?
4. (How) do all of these actors' positions regarding reflexivity intersect simultaneously? More importantly, how does this get represented?

The book is comprised of 12 sections, and each author addresses these very questions in compelling and intriguing ways. We have organized the chapters in and around some of the components of reflexivity discussed in this introduction. When reading through the chapters, it may be possible to locate some of the different dimensions of reflexivity that we have highlighted in this introduction. For example, some of the authors deal with and reflect on the reflectivity of others (students, research participants), whereas others reflect on innovative methods as well as on their own reflexivity as researchers and practitioners, and some do a bit of both. Some of the authors also incorporate multimodality explicitly in their chapters and discuss what this offers reflexivity in particular. On a closing note, we would like to highlight that this book is comprised of both prominent and emerging scholars from a range of international contexts, representative of the fields of applied linguistics, language and intercultural communication, and intercultural education.

We now turn to the organization of this volume.

REFLEXIVITY OF THE OTHER

In the first three chapters of this volume, by Jackson, Séror, and Frame, we can see the importance of developing reflexivity for learners, whether it be through their intercultural sojourns, their writing feedback, or their engagements of self and other. These chapters focus on the reflexivity of the other (research participants/language users, in this case) and on helping them to develop reflexivity or become aware of its components.

The first chapter, by Jane Jackson, 'The Process of Becoming Reflexive and Intercultural: Navigating Study Abroad and Reentry Experience,' offers evidence of the benefits of multimodality and reflexivity in L2/intercultural education within the context of education abroad. At the Chinese University of Hong Kong, the author explains how she developed a credit-bearing elective course, Intercultural Transitions: Making Sense of International Experience, in order to promote reflexivity and interculturality in students with recent or current international experience. To illustrate the process of being and becoming reflexive, Jackson focuses on one participant—a multilingual Hong Kong Chinese woman (English major) who joined the course after taking part in a year-long exchange program in Canada and an intensive summer language program in Germany. Through an intense period of guided, critical reflection, Endora (a pseudonym) unpacked the emotions of her 'lived experience' (sojourn/reentry) in oral and written narratives and class discussions. A thematic analysis of a selection of the triangulated data reveals that a complex mix of sociocultural factors (e.g., host–sojourner power relations), degree of reflexivity/openness, and agency (choice to invest in language/(inter-)cultural growth) impacted on Endora's developmental trajectory and evolving, hybrid sense of self.

Chapter 2, '"Or, Just It's My Fault, Right?": Language Socialization Through Reflexive Language Writing Feedback' by Jérémie Séror, examines the socialization impact of a common but to date still controversial form of interaction between university second language learners and their instructors: L2 writing feedback at the University of Ottawa. Arguing for an expanded sense of reflexive feedback as a pedagogic tool designed to achieve linguistic goals (i.e., improving students' mastery of grammatical and rhetorical structures) and navigating the author's own experiences of teaching and doing research on writing, this chapter stresses the importance of paying attention to the affective and identity work embedded within these literacy events.

The third chapter, "Reflexivity and Self-Presentation in Multicultural Encounters: Making Sense of Self and Other" by Alex Frame, seeks to highlight the ways in which reflexivity, as a process involved in multimodal communication, shapes intercultural encounters. The chapter discusses the way participants may develop self-presentation strategies, including identity strategies, or adopt strategic 'orientations' to their relationships with others, along with the underlying questions of agency and intentionality and the types and limits of reflexivity as it occurs in interpersonal communication.

REFLEXIVITY OF THE SELF

In the next set of chapters, by Holmes, Lamoureux, and Malinowski and Nelson, the focus of reflexivity shifts to the importance of discussing and problematizing one's own reflexivity, the reflexivity of self (in this case, the researcher/practitioner). This particular grouping of chapters details the willingness of the researcher to go back and revisit past experiences as well as former publications and writings in order to reflect upon the power relations, opportunities, and challenges of conducting research in university contexts, drawing upon multimodality when addressing not only the experiences, emotions, and feelings but also the instabilities and challenges of representation that one encounters when writing.

Chapter 4, 'Researching Chinese Students' Intercultural Communication Experiences in Higher Education: Researcher and Participant Reflexivity' by Prue Holmes, examines the process of researcher/practitioner reflexivity in relation to ethics. Holmes explains how researchers prepare ethics forms and receive approval from 'legitimated' university ethics committees to conduct research with so-called at risk people who volunteer to participate in their research. However, what issues emerge when researchers 'do' research 'on' these individuals who share neither the language nor the culture of the researcher? And how does the researcher's performance of doing the research impact his/her participants' experiences vis-à-vis the research itself? This chapter draws on reflexive insights from research participants themselves to uncover their sense making of an ethnographic study of their intercultural communication experiences

The fifth chapter, by Sylvie A. Lamoureux, 'Critical Reflexive Ethnography and the Multilingual Space of a Canadian University: Challenges and Opportunities,' draws upon the fieldwork experiences of two mixed-methods research projects exploring language policy issues related to French as an object of study and language of instruction in a minority context in Ottawa, Canada. She explores the important question of power relations in relation to reflexivity, for example, complications arising when conducting research in one's place of employment, particularly when research explores language ideology, language representations, and notions of linguistic identity.

In the Chapter 6, 'Reflexivity in Motion in Language and Literacy Learning,' David Malinowski and Mark Evan Nelson present a reflexive analysis of their own previous research into multimodal meaning making: dismantling, connecting, and textually reconstructing the research itself, their written representations of it, and, significantly, their own positions as *textualizing subjects*. Not unlike the learners with whom they have worked, their own ideological commitments were challenged and reformulated in creating this chapter, through confronting the words and images of their own authorial pasts. In this chapter, they present an integrative thematic secondary analysis of four of their published research papers, all examining cases of multimodal design, after which they critically reflect upon the value and limitations of this approach.

COMPLEX JUNCTIONS BETWEEN SELF AND OTHER

In the final grouping of chapters, we see a returned focus on language and intercultural learners but also criticality and awareness development on both the part of the researched and researcher in different contexts. The authors weave in and out from critical action research, to critical exploration of methods ('weaving' as a method) and critical dialogue between a researcher and a language teacher. Following Malinowski and Nelson's chapter, we observe that the authors continue to draw upon multimodal processes and hyper-reflexivity, in that they consider the intersections and junctions between self and other (the researcher/practitioner and research participants/language users) and how they (can) influence each other.

As such, the seventh chapter, by Eric Chauvier, 'Uses of Digital Text in Reflexive Anthropology: The Example of Educational Workshops for Out-of-School/Educationally Excluded Adolescents,' details the anthropologist's creation of a digital text with the student participants (in the form of a wiki) in attempts to encourage the intertwining of ethnographic observations and their resulting reactions. This collective, reflexive, and interactive text presents two seemingly important issues: First, it contributes to the adolescents' education by allowing them to express themselves, and, second, it allows for the deconstruction of a set of stereotypes concerning the socially excluded youth of Seine-Saint-Denis, in Paris, France.

In a similar vein, the eighth chapter, 'Reflexivity and Critical Language Education at Occupy LA' by Christian W. Chun, details a reflexive, multimodal perspective on the linguistic landscape (LL) constructed by the Occupy Movement in Los Angeles and the accompanying production of politicized space. In tracing how the Occupiers' LL discourses were resemiotized in their discussions during a workshop, Chun addresses how these specifically located LL discourses interconnect with global actions and discourses of revolt. Examining his own self-reflexivity as a participant and organizer of the workshop, as well as the reflexivity displayed by the workshop participants, Chun concludes by exploring the implications of the Occupiers' transforming and resemiotizing formerly 'neutralized' and commodified public spaces into a dynamically infused critical language/multimodality in action.

In the ninth chapter, 'Weaving a Method: Mobility, Multilocality, and the Senses as Foci of Research on Intercultural Language Learning,' Ulrike Najar argues for a rethinking of postmodern methodology based on reflexivity in order to follow the multiple traces of intercultural language learning and its flowing, mobile, and networked aspects. In this rethinking, she proposes weaving as a method, illustrating an aimed synchronization of everyday multicultural realities with a range of methodological tools and implying a criticism of method understood as more or less rigid steps connected to singular disciplinary research paradigms. Najar presents this methodological assemblage in relation to addressing intercultural learning processes of international learners of English in Australia, going beyond merely cognitive realms of meaning making by following concrete practices and journeys of language learners in actual everyday environments instead. The researcher also shares, reflects upon, and weaves in and out of her own intercultural places of significance.

In the final chapter, Chapter 10, 'Everyday Practices, Everyday Pedagogies: A Dialogue on Critical Transformations in a Multilingual Hong Kong School,' Miguel Pérez-Milans and Carlos Soto reflect upon a reflexive dialogue between a researcher and one of his focused participants, a teacher involved in critical pedagogy, in the course of a critical sociolinguistic ethnography carried out in Hong Kong. On the basis of these interactional dynamics, the researcher and his focused teacher engage in a collaborative reflection on what 'critical' means to them under those everyday circumstances, with an emphasis on the potentials of a collaborative reflection like this for both critical educators and sociolinguists interested in school spaces as sites for empowerment.

Following this, we (Julie and Fred) offer a brief concluding chapter to share reactions to some valuable points made in the volume and to propose some considerations for future research and practice. Our goals in this volume have been to provide new research insights on reflexivity in language and intercultural education, particularly concerning future research and pedagogical practice. Reflexivity, as a complex process and social construct, as presented in this introduction, offers important implications. First, reflexivity offers us the potential to reexamine interpretations (our own and others'), as well as our ideological positionings, self–other relations, previous writings, engagements with participants in our research, engagements with learners in our language classrooms, and it could help us move beyond others' constructions of us (as well as our own). Through our interactions with one another, reflexivity enables us to see how difference is constructed. As such, reflexivity could not only help us to become aware that we are all social actors trying to make meaning in this social world, but, more importantly, reflexivity has the capacity to illuminate some of the irony (and inequality) surrounding the ways in which we invest in hierarchical categories. For example, how, when, and why do 'we' begin to think we're better and/or less than others? How and why do certain people get to be recognized as gods, film or TV actors, gurus, and the like, while others don't become regarded that way, and what are the opportunities and consequences of such identifications in either case? Second, reflexivity through multimodality offers both researchers and language educators some innovative ways of incorporating multimodal practices in their work and of understanding *new* forms of belonging and performativity as well as overlapping tensions between structure and agency. Reflexivity can allow more space for creative strategies in providing us possibilities to understand new forms and uses of language and literacy/ies, different ways of seeing groups or looking at cultures, and bridging space for creative writing to be included in academic writing. Reflexivity as a construct and a process could take us to deeper levels by providing us the openness, imaginative resourcefulness, and flexibility that one needs for attempting to get at the complexities, thinking about the social processes and consequences of our practices, becoming other, and engaging with self–other relations in order to give a fairer, more meaningful image of who and what

Introduction 35

we are researching. More importantly, reflexivity could lead to meaningful action rather than being stuck and/or overwhelmed by the complexities, instabilities, and exceptions. Finally, reflexivity, in this sense and as shown in this volume, could also serve to make one aware of or at least provide one the opportunity to engage with the vulnerabilities and blind spots of both the researcher and participants' power and representational systems. Although reflexivity cannot provide a universal cure for all the dilemmas of conducting research, it offers the potential of bringing these dilemmas to the forefront, which (we hope) could lead to a multidimensional transformation, both in research and in pedagogical practice.

Our volume concludes with a reflective and insightful commentary from Claire Kramsch.

NOTES

1. Western University, jbyrdcla@uwo.ca
2. University of Helsinki, fred.dervin@helsinki.fi
3. The field of intercultural education is very complex. In this volume, when we refer to it, we mean any subfield that takes the intercultural, the international, or the global as its central emphasis in educating or training individuals. Examples of such subfields are international business, general education, language education, health education, and the like.
4. In other words, reflexivity is not something that one can truly observe because the observer has an impact on this reflexivity. Therefore, researchers must work on what is referred to as 'discourses of reflexivity' or 'representations of reflexivity' in order to reflect this messiness and complexity.
5. 'We' here means people but also researchers.
6. That being said, our intentions are not to criticize and laud other researchers for their various critical and/or non-reflexive stances, but rather to demonstrate how reflexivity has been understood, construed, and taken up by researchers, particularly ethnographers, in the fields of applied linguistics, sociolinguistics, and intercultural communication.
7. Julie with Italian (San Fratedani) and English and Fred with German, French, and English.
8. For example, one of us (Julie) studied at a prestigious language school at the undergraduate level in the summer of 1988 (thanks to a U.S. government student loan!), she had difficulty 'fitting in', feeling very much 'out of her element' at the school, but ended up befriending the Director of the school's teenage daughter, Clarice, who was about 14 at the time. Upon receiving a scholarship in 1995, Julie returned to this language school for graduate study, and ran into Clarice, who at 19, was studying at one of the other language intensive schools. Upon meeting Clarice, Julie sensed that she seemed disappointed, asking why Julie had not returned or waited so long to return to the school. When Julie explained that she had to work during summers as well as throughout the academic year in order to attend university, Clarice appeared unable to understand or fathom that Julie had to work and couldn't afford to come back to this intensive summer program each year as an undergraduate. Please note that we are drawing upon this one representation (from Julie's interpretation) to demonstrate the diversity of experience(s) in our journeys of becoming 'multilinguals'.

9. While in Sweden, Julie was able to get by communicating in simple everyday interactions because of my understanding and use of German.
10. We will expand upon a critical perspective in the upcoming section, called 'Criticality or Critical Reflection: Getting at the Complexities'.
11. The Frankfurt School was a school of neo-Marxist interdisciplinary social theory.
12. Praxis represents the practical application of theories. Some would argue that it is the combination of theory and practice as well as practice and theory.
13. Norton has since written a reflective article about her former positioning, along with Margaret Early. See Norton & Early (2011).
14. In Buddhism, awakening and/or awareness has to do with 'seeing into one's true nature,' in other words, to 'have woken up and understood' meaning that one has understood a particular form of knowledge. This knowledge has led the person to an understanding of how sentient beings come into existence, as well as the operations of the mind that keep sentient beings imprisoned in craving, suffering, and rebirth. Awakening, then, is the way to liberate oneself from this imprisonment. For Habermas, enlightenment has a more romantic meaning. It has become synonymous with self-realization and the true self, being regarded as a substantial essence that has been covered over by social conditioning. Habermas's emphasis on enlightenment was on the potential for transforming the world and arriving at a more humane, just, and egalitarian society through the realization of the human potential for reason.
15. Even in ethnography!
16. Intersectionality here refers to using a reflexive approach as regards the assignment of categories (conceptual, social), particularly when the relevance of any one dimension of identity is "fluid and context-dependent, with saliencies that change and shift over settings and time" (Brekhus 2008:1071). For example, a reflexive approach that gives precedence to intersectionality can be useful not only in resisting the assignment of a "master status" (Brekhus 2008), but also in thinking through how multiple dimensions of identity could be relevant to the research relationship.
17. The subaltern, in this case, refers to the most powerless people who live within colonial confines; in Spivak's writing, this would mainly represent Indian women from the lower classes with little or no access to cultural imperialism. According to postcolonial theory, the subaltern's abandonment of his and her culturally customary ways of thinking—and subsequent adoption of Western ways of thinking—is necessary in many postcolonial situations. Subordinated men or women can be heard by their oppressors if they speak the language of the oppressor.
18. See on languaging (e.g., Shohamy, 2006), polylingual languaging (e.g., Moller, 2008), plurilanguaging (e.g., Makoni & Makoni, 2010), metrolingualism (e.g., Otsuji & Pennycook, 2010), translanguaging (e.g., Creese & Blackledge, 2010), and translingual practice (e.g., Canagarajah, 2013).

REFERENCES

Abdallah-Pretceille, M. (2003). *Former et éduquer en context hétérogène. Pour un humanisme du divers*. Paris: Anthropos.

Aikman, S. (2012). Interrogating discourses of intercultural education: From indigenous Amazon community to global policy forum. *Compare*, 42(2), 325–257.

Alim, S., Ibrahim, A., & Pennycook, A. (2009). *Global linguistic flows: Hip-hop cultures, youth identities and politics of language*. London: Routledge.

Andreotti, V. (2011). *Actionable postcolonial theory in education*. London: Palgrave.
Aull Davies, C. (2010). *Reflexive ethnography: A guide to researching selves and others* (2nd ed.). London: Routledge.
Bayart, J. P. (1996). *L'illusion identitaire*. Paris: Fayard.
Beacco, J. C., & Byram, M. (2003). *Guide pour l'élaboration des politiques linguistiques éducatives en Europe de la diversité linguistique à l'éducation plurilingue*. Strasbourg: Council of Europe.
Becker, H. 1967. Whose side are we on? *Social Problems*, 14(3), 234–247.
Behar, R. (1993). *Translated woman: Crossing the border with Esperanza's story*. Boston: Beacon Press.
Bensa, A. (2010). *Après Lévi-Strauss, pour une anthropologie à taille humaine*. Paris: Textuel.
Bergson, H. (1906). *L'évolution créatrice*. Paris: Félix Alcan.
Beverly, J. (1999). *Subalternity and representation*. Durham, NC: Duke University Press.
Blackledge, A., & Creese, A. (2010). *Multilingualism: A critical perspective*. London: Continuum.
Block, D. (2003). *The social turn in second language acquisition*. Washington, DC: Georgetown University Press.
Block, D. (2005). Convergence and resistance in the construction of personal and professional identities: Four French modern language teachers in London. In S. A. Canagarajah (Ed.), *Reclaiming the local in language policy and practice* (pp. 167–196). Mahwah, NJ: Lawrence Erlbaum.
Block, D. (2007). *Second language identities*. New York: Continuum.
Block, D. (2010). Speaking Romance-esque. In D. Nunan and J. Choi (Eds.), *Language and culture: Reflective narratives and the emergence of identity* (pp. 23–29). Cambridge: Cambridge University Press.
Blommaert, J. (2006). *Discourse*. Cambridge: Cambridge University Press.
Blommaert, J. (2012). Debate on linguistic ethnography. Retrieved September 15, 2012, from www.jiscmail.ac.uk/cgi-bin/webadmin?A0=LING-ETHNOG.
Boas, F. (1928). *Anthropology and modern life*. New York: Norton.
Boas, F. (1940). *Race, language, and culture*. New York: Macmillan.
Bohman, J. (1996). *Public deliberation: Pluralism, complexity and democracy*, Cambridge: MIT Press.
Bourdieu, P. (1977). *Outline of a theory of practice*. R. Nice (Trans.). Cambridge: Cambridge University Press.
Bourdieu, P. (1982). *Ce que parler veut dire*. Paris: Fayard.
Bourdieu, P. (1990). *Choses dites*, 1987 Eng. *In other words: Essays toward a reflective sociology*. Stanford, CA: Stanford University Press.
Bourdieu, P. (1991). J. B. Thompson (Ed.), G. Raymond & M. Adamson (Trans.). *Language and symbolic power*. Cambridge, MA: Harvard University Press.
Bourdieu, P., & Wacquant, L. (1992). *An invitation to reflexive sociology*. Chicago: University of Chicago Press/Polity.
Braud, W., & Anderson, R. (1998). *Transpersonal research methods for the social sciences: Honoring human experience*. New York: Sage.
Brekhus, Wayne H. (2008). Trends in the qualitative study of social identities. *Sociology Compass*, 2(3), 1059–1078.
Budach, G., Roy, S., & Heller, M. (2003). Community and commodity in French Ontario. *Language in Society*, 32(5), 603–627.
Burawoy, M. (2003). Revisits: An outline of a theory of reflexive ethnography. *American Sociological Review*, 68(5), 645–679.
Butler, J. (1990). *Gender trouble: Feminism and the subversion of identity*. New York: Routledge.
Butler, J. (1997). *Excitable speech: A politics of the performative*. New York: Routledge.

Byram, M. (2010). Linguistic and intercultural education for Bildung and citizenship. *The Modern Language Journal*, 94, ii, 317–321.
Byrd Clark, J. (2008). So, why do you want to teach French? Representations of multilingualism and language investment through a reflexive critical sociolinguistic ethnography. *Education and Ethnography*, 3(1), 1–16.
Byrd Clark, J. (2009). *Multilingualism, citizenship, and identity: Voices of youth and symbolic investments in a globalized world*. London: Continuum.
Byrd Clark, J. (2010). Making some 'wiggle room' in French as a second language/français langue seconde: Reconfiguring identity, language, and policy. In S. Lamoureux & N. Labrie (Eds.), Special issue. *Canadian Journal of Education*, 33(2), 379–406.
Byrd Clark, J. (2012). Heterogeneity and a sociolinguistics of multilingualism: Reconfiguring French language pedagogy (invited/commissioned submission). *Language and Linguistics Compass—Blackwell Online Journal*, 6(3), 143–161.
Byrd Clark, J., & Labrie, N. (2010). La voix de jeunes canadiens dans leur processus d'identification: Les identités imbriquées dans des espaces multiformes. In S. Osu (Ed.), *Construction d'identité et processus d'identification* (pp. 435–438). Berlin: Éditions Peter Lang.
Canagarajah, S. (1996). From critical research practice to critical research reporting. *TESOL Quarterly*, 29(2), 320–330.
Canagarajah, S. (2004). Language rights and postmodern conditions. *Journal of Language, Identity, and Education*, 3(2), 140–145.
Canagarajah, S. (2005). Rhetoricizing reflexivity." *Journal of Language, Identity, and Education*. 4(4), 309–315.
Canagarajah, S. (2013). *Translingual practice: Global Englishes and cosmopolitan relations*. New York: Routledge.
Castellotti, V. (2008). Au delà du bilinguisme: Quelle place en France pour une éducation plurilingue ? In J. Erfurt, G. Budach, & M. Kunkel (Eds.), *Écoles plurilingues—Multilingual schools: Konzepte, Institutionen und Akteure. Internationale Perspektiven* (pp. 169–189). Frankfurt am Main: Peter Lang.
Cenoz, J., (2013). Defining multilingualism. Special issue: Topics in multilingualism. *Annual Review of Applied Linguistics*, 33, 3–18.
Chauvier, E. (2011). *Anthropologie de l'ordinaire*. Toulouse: Anacharsis.
Clifford, J., & Marcus, G. E. (1986). *Writing culture: The poetics and politics of ethnography*. Berkeley: University of California.
Cook, V. J. (2002). Background to the L2 user. In V. J. Cook (Ed.), *Portraits of the L2 user* (pp. 1–28). Clevedon, UK: Multilingual Matters.
Coste, D. (2002). Compétence à communiquer et compétence plurilingue. In *Notions en questions*, 6 (pp. 115–123). Lyon: ENS Éditions.
Creese, A. (2008). Linguistic ethnography. In K. A. King & N. H. Hornberg (Eds.), *Encyclopedia of language and education: Vol. 10* (2nd ed., pp. 229–241). Springer Science and Business Media LLC.
Creese, A., & Blackledge, A. (2010). Translanguaging in the bilingual classroom: A pedagogy for learning and teaching. *The Modern Language Journal*, 94(1), 103–115, ISSN: 0026-7902.
Cummins, J. (1996). Empowering minority students: A framework for intervention. In T. Beauboeuf-Lafontant & D. Smith Augustine (Eds.), *Facing racism in education* (2nd ed.). Reprint Series No. 28, *Harvard Educational Review* (pp. 349–368). Cambridge, MA: Harvard Educational Review.
Davies, A. (2003). *The native speaker: Myth and reality*. Clevedon, UK: Multilingual Matters.
Davies, C. A. (1999). *Reflexive ethnography. A guide to researching selves and others*. London: Routledge.
Day, S. (2012). A reflexive lens: Exploring dilemmas of qualitative methodology through the concept of reflexivity. *Qualitative Sociology Review*, 8(1), 60–85.

Dervin, F. (2008). *Métamorphoses identitaires en situation de mobilité*. Turku, Finland: Humanoria.
Dervin, F. (2011). A plea for change in research on intercultural discourses: A "liquid" approach to the study of the acculturtion of Chinese students. *Journal of Multicultural Discourses*, 6(1), 37–52.
Dervin F., & Badrinathan, V. (2011). *L'enseignant non-natif: Identités et légitimité dans l'enseignement-apprentissage des langues étrangères*. Liège: Editions EME.
Dervin, F., Gajardo, A., & Lavanchy, A. (2011). *Politics of interculturality*. Newcastle, UK: Cambridge Scholars Publishing.
Dervin, F., & Risager, K. (2014). *Identity and interculturality*. New York: Routledge.
Duchêne, A., & Heller, M. (2007). *Discourses of endangerment: Interest and ideology in the defense of languages*. London/New York: Continuum.
Duchêne, A., & Heller, M. (2012). *Language in late capitalism: Pride and profit*. New York: Routledge.
Duranti, A. (2009). *Linguistic anthropology: A reader* (2nd ed.). Malden, MA: Wiley-Blackwell.
Edwards, D. (1997). *Discourse and cognition*. London/Beverly Hills, CA: Sage.
Edwards, D. (2007). Managing subjectivity in talk. In A. Hepburn & S. Wiggins (Eds.), *Discursive research in practice: New approaches to psychology and interaction* (pp. 31–49). Cambridge: Cambridge University Press.
Ewing, K. P. (1990). The illusion of wholeness: Culture, self, and the experience of inconsistency. *Ethos*, 18(3), 251–278.
Fairclough, N. (1995). *Critical discourse analysis*. London: Longman.
Fairclough, N. (2006). *Language and globalization*. London/New York: Routledge.
Fairclough, N., & Wodak, R. (1997). Critical discourse analysis. In T. Van Dijk (Ed.), *Discourse studies: A multidisciplinary introduction*, Vol. 2 (pp. 258–284). London: Sage.
Gadamer, H. G. (1976). *Philosophical hermeneutics*. Berekely: University of California Press.
Gadamer, H. G. (1997). *Gadamer on Celan: "Who am I and who are you?" and other essays*. R. Heinemann and B. Krajewski (Trans. & Eds.). Albany: SUNY Press.
Gallagher, S. (2011). A philosophical epilogue on the question of autonomy. In H. Hermans & T. Gieser (Eds.), *Handbook of the dialogical self theory* (pp. 488–496). Cambridge: Cambridge University Press.
Garfinkel, H. (1967). *Studies in ethnomethodology*. Englewood Cliffs, NJ: Prentice-Hall.
Giddens, A. (1984). *The constitution of society: Outline of the theory of structuration*. Berkeley: University of California Press.
Gillespie, A. (2006). *Becoming other: From social interaction to self reflection*. Greenwich, CT: Information Age Publishing.
Goffman, E. (1963). *Stigma: Notes on the management of spoiled identity*. New York: Simon & Schuster.
Goffman, E. (1967). *Interaction ritual: Essays on face-to-face behavior*. New York: Doubleday Anchor.
Gramsci, A. (1971). *Selections from the prison notebooks*. New York: International.
Gumperz, J. (1982). *Discourse strategies*. Cambridge: Cambridge University Press.
Habermas, J. (1962, Trans 1989). *The structural transformation of the public sphere: An inquiry into a category of bourgeois society*. Cambridge: Polity.
Habermas, J. (1974). On social identity. TELOS 19 (Spring 1974).
Hall, S. (2006). The future of identity. In S. Hier & S. Bolaria (Eds.), *Identity and belonging: Rethinking race and ethnicity in Canadian society*. Toronto: Canadian Scholar's Press.
Hall, J. K. (2002). *Teaching and researching language and culture*. London: Pearson Education.

Hall, S. (1992). The question of cultural identity. In S. Hall, D. Held, & T. McGrew (Eds.), *Modernity and its future* (pp. 274–316). Cambridge: Polity Press.

Hammersely, M. (2007). Reflections on linguistic ethnography. *Journal of Sociolinguistics*, 11(5), 689–695.

Hawkins, M., & Norton, B. (2009). Critical language teacher education. In A. Burns & J. Richards (Eds.), *Cambridge guide to second language teacher education* (pp. 30–39). Cambridge: Cambridge University Press.

Heller, M. (1994). *Crosswords: Language, education, and ethnicity*. Berlin: Mouton de Gruyter.

Heller, M. (1999). *Linguistic minorities and modernity: A sociolinguistic ethnography*. London/New York: Longman.

Heller, M. (2006). *Linguistic minorities and modernity: A sociolinguistic ethnography* (2nd ed.). London: Continuum.

Heller, M. (2008). Doing ethnography. In L. Wei & M. Moyer (Eds.), *The Blackwell guide to research methods in bilingualism and multilingualism* (pp. 249–262). Hoboken, NJ: Wiley-Blackwell.

Heller, M. (2011). *Paths to post-nationalism: A critical ethnography of language and identity*. Toronto: Oxford University Press.

Holliday, Adrian. (2010). *Intercultural communication and ideology*. London: Sage.

Horkheimer, M. (1937, 1972). *Traditional and critical theory*. New York: Herder and Herder.

Hornberger, N. (2005). Opening up and filling up implementational and ideological spaces in heritage language education. *The Modern Language Journal*, 89, 605–609.

Jaffe, A. (2009). *Stance: Sociolinguistic perspectives*. Oxford: Oxford University Press.

Jovchelovitch, S. (2007). *Knowledge in context: Representation, community and culture*. London: Routledge.

Kapoor, I. (2004). Hyper-self-reflexive development? Spivak on representing the third world "other." *Third World Quarterly*, 25(4), 627–647.

Karsenti, T., Raby, C., & Villeneuve, S. (2008). Compétence professionnelle des futurs enseignants du Québec en regard de l'intégration pédagogique des technologies de l'information et de la communication (TIC). *Formation et pratiques d'enseignement en questions*, 7, 11–28.

Kelly, M., & Grenfell, M. (2004). European profile for language teacher education: A frame of reference. www.lang.soton.ac.uk/profile

Kramsch, C. (2005). Post 9/11: Foreign languages between knowledge and power. *Applied Linguistics*, (26)4, 545–567.

Kramsch, C. (2006). From communicative competence to symbolic competence. *The Modern Language Journal*, 90(2), 249–252.

Kramsch, C. (2011). The symbolic dimensions of the intercultural. *Language Teaching*, 44, 354–367.

Lahire, B. (2008). De la réflexivité dans la vie quotidienne: Journal personnel, autobiographie et autres écritures de soi. *Sociologie et sociétés*, 40(2), 165–179.

Lakoff, R. (1990). *Talking power*. New York: Basic Books.

Lin, A. M. Y. (2004). Introducing a critical pedagogical curriculum: A feminist, reflexive account. In B. Norton & K. Toohey (Eds.), *Critical pedagogies and language learning* (pp. 271–290). Cambridge: Cambridge University Press.

Mahboob, A. (2005). Beyond the native speaker in TESOL. In S. Zafar (Ed.), *Culture, context, & communication* (pp. 60–93). Abu Dhabi: Center of Excellence for Applied Research and Training/The Military Language Institute.

Maffesoli, M. (1996). *Ordinary knowledge: Introduction to interpretative sociology*. Cambridge: Polity Press.

Malinowski, B. (1927). *Sex and repression in savage society*. London: Kegan Paul, Trench, Trubner & Co.

Malinowski, B. (1944). *A scientific theory of culture and others essays*. Chapel Hill: University of North Carolina Press.
Makoni, B., & Makoni, S. (2010). Multilingual discourses on wheels: A case for vague linguistique. In J. Maybin and J. Swaan (Eds.), *Routledge companion to English language studies* (pp. 25–38). London: Open University Press.
Marcuse, H. (1964). *One-dimensional man: Studies in the ideology of advanced industrial society*. New York: Beacon Press.
Mead, M. (1928). *Coming of age in Samoa: A psychological study of primitive youth for Western civilization*. New York: William Morrow.
Merton, R. (1948, 1982). "The self-fulfilling prophecy? In A. Rosenblatt & T. F. Fieryn (Eds.), *Social research and the practicing sessions* (pp. 248–267). New York: Abt Books.
Meyerhoff, B. (1978). *Number our days*. New York: Simon & Schuster/Touchstone Books.
Minh-ha, T. T. (1989). *Woman, native, other: Writing postcoloniality and feminism*. Bloomington: Indiana University Press.
Moller, J. (2008). Polylingual performance among Turkish-Danes in late-modern Copenhagen. *International Journal of Multilingualism*, 5(3), 217–236.
Moore, D., & Gajo, L. (2009). French voices on plurilingualism and pluriculturalism: Theory, significance and perspectives. *International Journal of Multilingualism and Multiculturalism*, 6(2), 137–153.
Mondada, L. (1998). Technologies et interactions dans la fabrication du terrain du linguiste. *Cahiers de l'ILSL (Institut de Linguistique et des Sciences du Langage*, 10, 39–68.
Moscovici, S. (Ed.). (1984). *Psychologie sociale*. Paris: PUF.
Moustakas, C. (1990). *Heuristic research: Design, methodology, and applications*. London: Sage.
Moustakas, C. (2000). Heuristic research revisited. In K. J. Schneider, J. F. T. Bugental, & J. F. Pierson (Eds.), *The handbook of humanistic psychology: Leading edges in theory, research, and practice* (pp. 263–274). Thousand Oaks, CA: Sage.
Norton Pierce, B. (1995). Social identity, investment, and language learning. *TESOL Quarterly*, 29(1), 9–31.
Norton, B., & Early, M. (2011). Researcher identity, narrative inquiry, and language teaching research. *TESOL Quarterly*, 45, 3, 415–439.
Norton, B., & Toohey, K. (Eds). (2004). *Critical pedagogies and language learning*. New York: Cambridge University Press.
Otsuji, E., & Pennycook, A. (2010). Metrolingualism: Fixity, fluidity and language in flux. *International Journal of Multilingualism*, 7(3), 240–254.
Pavlenko, A. (2003). The privilege of being an immigrant woman. In C. Casanave and S. Vandrick (Eds.), *Writing for scholarly publication: Behind the scenes in language and multicultural education* (pp. 177–193). Mahwah, NJ: Lawrence Erlbaum.
Pennycook, A. (1994). *The cultural politics of English as an international language*. London: Longman.
Pennycook, A. (1999). Introduction: Critical approaches to TESOL. *TESOL Quarterly*, 33, 329–348.
Pennycook, A. (2001). *Critical applied linguistics*. Mahwah, NJ: Lawrence Erlbaum.
Pennycook, A. (2005). Performing the personal. *Journal of Language, Identity, and Education*, 4(4), 297–304.
Pennycook, A. (2010). *Language as a local practice*. London: Routledge.
Pillow, W. (2003). Confession, catharsis, or cure? Rethinking the uses of reflexivity as methodological power in qualitative research. *International Journal of Qualitative Studies in Education*, 16(2), 175–196.
Potter, J. (1996). *Representing reality: Discourse, rhetoric and social construction*. London: Sage.

Rampton, B. (1995). *Crossing: Language and ethnicity among adolescents.* London: Longman.
Rampton, B. (2005). Identity in sociolinguistics. Presentation given at first Programme Workshop, January. www.open.ac.uk/socialsciences/identities/Ben%20 Rampton.doc
Rampton, B., Tusting, K., Maybin, J., Barwell, R., Creese, A., & Lytra, V. (2004). UK linguistic ethnography: A discussion paper. www.ling-ethno.org.uk
Reisigil, M., & Wodak, R. (2001). *Discourse and discrimination: Rhetorics of racism and antisemitism.* New York: Routledge.
Risager, K. (2007). *Language and culture pedagogy: From a national to a transnational paradigm.* Clevedon, UK: Multilingual Matters.
Said, E. (1978). *Orientalism.* New York: Penguin.
Sen, A. (2006). *Identity and violence.* New Delhi: Penguin.
Shi-xu. (2001). Critical pedagogy and intercultural communication: Creating discourses of diversity, equality, common goals and rational-moral motivation. *Journal of Intercultural Studies*, 22(3), 279–293.
Shohamy, E. (2006). *Language policy: Hidden agendas and new approaches.* New York: Routledge.
Sole, D., & Wilson, D. (2002). Storytelling in organizations: The power and traps of using stories to share knowledge in organizations. Harvard Graduate School of Education. www.providersedge.com/docs/km_articles/storytelling_in_organizations.pdf
Spivak, G. (1988). Can the subaltern speak? In C. Nelson & L. Grossberg (Eds.), *Marxism and the interpretation of culture.* Basingstoke, UK: Macmillan Education.
Thomas, W. I., & Thomas, D. S. (1928). *The child in America: Behaviour problems and programs.* New York: Knopf.
Visweswaran, K. (1994). *Fictions of feminist ethnography.* Minneapolis: University of Minnesota Press.
Volkart, E. H., & Thomas, W. I. (1951). *Social behavior and personality: Contributions of W. I. Thomas to theory and social research.* New York: Social Science Research Council.
Weber, J. J., & Horner, K. (2012). *Introducing multilingualism: A social approach.* New York/London: Routledge.
Wikan, U. (2002). *Generous betrayal. Politics of culture in the new Europe.* Chicago: University of Chicago Press.

1 The Process of Becoming Reflexive and Intercultural
Navigating Study Abroad and Reentry Experience

Jane Jackson

> We do not learn from our experience. We learn from reflecting on experience. (John Dewey)

INTRODUCTION

Study abroad can have a profound impact on students, and it is not unusual for returnees to claim that their international experience has been life altering. Many, however, find it very difficult to articulate what this actually means. 'It broadened my horizons' is a well-worn phrase that offers little insight into sojourn learning. Further, although study and residence in an unfamiliar linguistic and cultural setting have the *potential* to be transformative, there is no guarantee that this will happen (Vande Berg et al., 2012). Individuals who find it challenging to make sense of international experience may return home with reinforced stereotypes of host nationals, identity misalignments, and a myriad of questions about their intercultural interactions (Block, 2007; Jackson, 2008, 2010).

Although much has been written about the benefits of adequate presojourn preparation and strategic sojourn interventions (e.g., Bennett, 2004; Jackson, 2006, 2008, 2010; Lou & Bosley, 2012; Vande Berg et al., 2012), this chapter underscores the importance of helping returnees (as well as incoming exchange students) deepen, integrate, and extend sojourn learning. It is based on the premise that structured reflection can enhance the immediate and long-term impact of international experience. As well as fostering the habits of critical thinking and self-analysis, this approach can nurture a more open mind-set and encourage interaction with people from diverse backgrounds.

At the Chinese University of Hong Kong (CUHK), I designed Intercultural Transitions, a credit-bearing course for students with recent or current international experience (Jackson, 2013). Before focusing on an illustrative case study of Endora, a participant in the first offering, I provide an overview of the course (theoretical foundation, rationale, core elements), describe my multifaceted roles, and explain the importance of a reflexive approach in projects of this nature.

MAKING SENSE OF INTERNATIONAL EXPERIENCE

Intercultural Transitions draws on multiple theories including poststructuralist notions of identity (Norton, 1997; Weedon, 1997), experiential learning theory (Kolb, 1984; Passarelli & Kolb, 2012), transformational learning theory (Mezirow, 1994, 2000), and intercultural (communicative) competence (Bennett, 1993; Byram, 2012; Deardorff & Jones, 2012).

Poststructuralist Notions of Identity

Early identity scholars tended to portray identity as unitary and fixed by the time one reaches adolescence (Erikson, 1968). In contrast, poststructuralists stress the dynamic, fluid, relational, and sometimes contradictory nature of identities, recognizing that many dimensions are context dependent and may change or evolve over time (Byrd Clark, 2009; Dervin, 2012; Hall, 1992; Norton, 1997). People may give little thought to their ethnicity and other facets of their identities until they travel or study abroad and perhaps become a visible minority for the first time. This experience can serve as a powerful stimulus for reflection on multiple dimensions of one's self (e.g., cultural, ethnic, linguistic, religious, national, regional).

How sojourners define and express themselves is only part of the picture because people they encounter abroad may choose to view and label them in a different way. One's avowed identity refers to the particular identity (or dimension of one's identities) that we wish to present or claim in an interaction, whereas an ascribed identity is one that others give to us (or we give to someone else) (Oetzel, 2009). When students venture abroad, their preferred identities may not be recognized. This unsettling experience can heighten awareness of the personal meaning of their identities and lead to a questioning of their place in the world (Jackson, 2010, 2013; Joseph, 2004).

In some situations, student sojourners may embrace both local and global identities that afford them a sense of belonging in their home environment and the wider world. Those who acquire a multicultural identity may experience a 'psychological state of not owning or being owned by a single culture' (Ryan, 2012: 428). In other words, they may develop transnational, hybrid, or mélanged identities that integrate diverse linguistic and cultural elements (Bhabha, 1994; Byrd Clark, 2009, 2012; Dervin, 2011; Kramsch, 2009).

EXPERIENTIAL LEARNING AND INDIVIDUAL TRANSFORMATION

Experiential learning entails 'a dynamic view of learning based on a learning cycle driven by the resolution of the dual dialectics of action-reflection and experience-conceptualization' (Passarelli & Kolb, 2012: 138). Put another way, knowledge is derived from 'the combination of grasping and transforming experience' (Kolb, 1984: 41). This 'holistic approach to student learning' (Passarelli & Kolb, 2012) may be linked to the work of Jack Mezirow and other scholars who view experience as a potential impetus for individual transformation.

Mezirow's (1994, 2000) transformational learning theory posits that individuals who engage in critical self-analysis may experience profound personal change during key moments in their lives, such as moving to an unfamiliar linguistic and cultural milieu. When observing and interacting with people who have been socialized in a different cultural environment, newcomers naturally encounter modes of thinking and acting that differ from what they are accustomed to. Although some border crossers feel under threat and retreat from cultural difference, others question their usual ways of being. Through the act of engaging in deep, critical reflection, individuals may revise their initial interpretations of their experience and develop new understandings. As they negotiate their identities in intercultural interactions, they may gradually develop more appreciation of different perceptions and practices.

This experiential-reflective process has the potential to bring about life-altering transformation, including the restructuring of one's identities (Kolb, 1984; Mezirow, 1994). Border crossers who embrace an open stance may develop a more broadened sense of self, incorporating elements from diverse cultures. Thus, this transformational theory is in accord with poststructuralist perceptions of identity as dynamic, complex, and multiple (Block, 2006, 2007; Hall, 1992; Kramsch, 1993; Norton, 2000).

INTERCULTURAL (COMMUNICATIVE) COMPETENCE AND CRITICAL REFLECTION

Intercultural competence may be defined as 'the intentional integration of culture-sensitive knowledge, open-minded attitude, and adaptive communication skills in an intercultural encounter' (Ting-Toomey & Chung, 2012: 304), whereas the term 'intercultural communicative competence' draws attention to the use of a second language when interacting with and building a relationship with people who have been socialized in a different linguistic and cultural environment (Byram, 2012).

To help students develop an intercultural perspective, many interculturalists (e.g., Alred et al., 2003; Bennett, 2008; Byram et al., 2001; Guilherme, 2012; Jackson, 2006, 2008, 2012; Marginson & Sawir, 2011, Najar, this volume) advocate intercultural education coupled with experiential learning, with critical reflection as a core element (Byrd Clark & Dervin, this volume; Jackson, 2011; Kohonen et al., 2001; Kolb, 1984; Savicki, 2012). When thoughtfully planned and executed, this combination has the potential to nurture 'transformative learning' (Mezirow, 1994, 2000). Through critical reflection, individuals can develop a deeper awareness of themselves as cultural beings and become more attuned to the ways in which their behavior and mind-set influence their intercultural interactions. This can help them reign in the natural tendency to rush to judgment when encountering unfamiliar ideas and actions.

INTERCULTURAL TRANSITIONS: CURRICULUM DESIGN AND DEVELOPMENT

With these theories in mind, I aimed to incorporate elements into the Intercultural Transitions course that would encourage participants to reexamine their international experience and take further steps toward intercultural (communicative) competence. When designing the curriculum, I began by considering student needs, drawing on a review of the literature, and my ethnographic and mixed-method investigations of Hong Kong sojourners (e.g., Jackson, 2008, 2010, 2012). This enabled me to identify specific learning aims. By the end of this 14-week (42-hour) course, I expected that the participants should be able to:

- Articulate how their international/intercultural experiences have impacted their sense of self and worldview.
- Describe and test theories and models of Intercultural Transitions, drawing on their own international/intercultural experience and those of others (e.g., published sojourner accounts).
- Critically assess their cultural self-awareness and communication style(s) and set realistic goals for further enhancement of their intercultural (communicative) competence.
- Integrate their international/intercultural experiences into their academic/social lives and future plans.
- Enhance their English language skills (e.g., reflective writing, oral skills).

For this course, I decided to adopt a 'practice-to-theory-to-practice' pedagogy (Jackson, 2013; Meyer-Lee, 2004), a version of experiential learning (Kolb, 1984; Passarelli & Kolb, 2012). In this approach, the students are prompted to describe and share their international, intercultural stories before being exposed to intercultural transition theories and research reports. Through structured reflection (e.g., guiding questions and probes both in class and online), the participants then take a more critical look at their personal narratives (oral and written) and consider multiple interpretations of critical incidents, taking into account their own actions and affective states.

Learning activities and modes of assessment were carefully selected to foster student engagement and critical thinking. In addition to in-class participation, the following elements would be assessed: online reflection (forum postings and blog entries on Moodle, an e-learning course management system), a reflective writing portfolio (three reflective essays[1] and peer reviews), and an end-of-term oral presentation (open to any students interested in studying abroad). For most elements, I designed rubrics to further clarify and emphasize notions of critical reflection and reflexivity. Throughout the semester, students would be encouraged to include photos or video clips to enrich their narratives (e.g., online posts, reflective essays, oral presentations).

FOREGROUNDING THE ILLUSTRATIVE CASE STUDY: THE SELECTION OF THE CASE PARTICIPANT

Instead of briefly touching on the experiences of multiple participants, this chapter takes a closer look at one young woman's journey. When I reviewed the oral and written narratives of the 18 students in the first offering, I was drawn to Endora's story because her data is rich in detail and she appeared to become much more introspective and open-minded by the end of the course. With her permission[2], Endora's recent and varied international experience is scrutinized to offer insight into the multifarious factors that can influence the path to interculturality, self-reflexivity, and mélanged identities in multilingual sojourners. As she re-stories herself, we gain a better understanding of the potential impact of guided, structured reflection.

FIRST-PERSON NARRATIVES

We learn about Endora's journey largely from her perspective, that is, through her oral and written narratives and digital images, which are highly personal in nature. When processing first-person data, it is essential to bear in mind that this material presents *versions* of reality (Pavlenko, 2007). Each telling of a story or incident is 'never complete self-understanding on the part of the narrator . . .' (Ochs & Capps, 1996: 91); rather, these accounts are 'partial representations and evocations of the world' (21), as seen through the eyes of the individual at a particular point in time in a specific location. When reminiscing about past interactions, individuals are constrained by their memory, level of self-awareness, and contextual elements (e.g., status of interviewer, location of interview, the target audience of writings, concerns about assessment, etc.). Therefore, the analysis of sojourner accounts must consider the context and 'linguistic, rhetorical, and interactional properties' of these 'discursive constructions' (Pavlenko, 2007: 180–181).

Although the grading of some sources of data (e.g., online Forum entries, reflective essays) might have affected Endora's comments, this did not seem to be the case because she offered both positive and negative opinions. In her interview, which took place after the course ended, she candidly shared her views with my Hong Kong Chinese research assistant who was close to her age.

Endora was open about aspects to improve and did not appear to feel pressured to give positive comments about the course and her learning. At that point, no grades were involved, and I did not see her after the course ended.

REFLEXIVITY AND THE RESEARCHER'S VOICE

In research of this nature, it is also important to acknowledge elements of the researcher's background, biography, and identities that could impact the framing of questions, the type of information collected, and the interpretation of data. This project is no exception. A native speaker of English, I am a female Canadian (Caucasian) professor of applied linguistics. I have taught university students in Hong Kong for more than 15 years. Since 2001, I have been investigating the developmental trajectories of students from Hong Kong and Mainland China who participate in an education abroad program (e.g., faculty-led sojourn, semester-abroad, or year-abroad program) through ethnographic and experimental design studies. As an undergraduate, I majored in French and participated in a junior-year-abroad program at a French Canadian university. I have also worked in several countries or regions (e.g., Canada, the United States, Oman, Egypt, China, Hong Kong SAR). On my home campus in Hong Kong, I have developed and taught both undergraduate and intercultural communication courses, including the Intercultural Transitions course described in this paper. For this project, I served as both teacher and researcher.

Many scholars (e.g., Alvesson & Sköldberg, 2000; Bourdieu & Wacquant, 1992; Byrd Clark & Dervin, Holmes, this volume) advocate reflexivity in qualitative research, and this was borne in mind throughout this teaching development project. As noted by the authors in this volume, researchers who continuously reflect on their attitudes and positioning throughout the research process can become more mindful of assumptions and behaviors that might be influencing data collection and the meaning-making process. By cultivating the habit of critical self-reflexivity, researchers are more apt to consider elements from multiple perspectives rather than limit themselves to a single orientation.

A NARRATIVE LENS

For this case study, I elected to interpret Endora's international and reentry experience through a narrative lens, drawing on the work of Clandinin and Connelly (2000) and Dewey (1938), who observe that new understandings can emerge through the critical analysis of personal and social narratives in context. In narrative inquiry, reflexive researchers are mindful of multiple interpretations of oral and written narratives and sensitive to 'the perceptual, cognitive, theoretical, linguistic (inter-)cultural circumstances that form the backdrop to—as well as impregnate—the interpretations' (Alvesson & Sköldberg, 2000: 7).

DATA COLLECTION AND ANALYSIS

All of the material related to Endora's case was brought together with the help of NVivo 9, a qualitative software program. The data consisted of weekly online forums (discussions on Moodle), longer blog entries, multiple surveys, three reflective essays about her sojourn/reentry experiences, her oral presentation materials (PowerPoint file), interview, and my field notes. The postcourse interview, which took place in Cantonese and lasted more than two hours, was translated and transcribed.

As part of my larger investigation of international exchange students (Jackson, 2011), I was also able to review the application essay Endora wrote about her motivation to join an academic yearlong exchange program in North America. Her oral and written narratives were very detailed and candid, offering a window into her second language use, (inter)cultural learning, self-identities, and depth of reflection at different stages.

To make sense of the hypermedia data (e.g., interview transcript, open-ended survey responses, online Forum comments, digital images, blog entries, reflective essays, my field notes), I employed an 'open coding' approach (Grbich, 2007; Richards, 2009), devising codes to reflect what I saw in the narratives and images rather than restricting myself to preconceived notions (Clandinin & Rosiek 2007; Dicks et al., 2005). Triangulating this multimodal data helped me to understand how Endora made sense of intercultural, international experience and readjusted to Hong Kong. The analysis allowed me to track changes in her degree of critical reflection and intercultural sensitivity and drew attention to the ways in which she negotiated her identities in multiple languages in various contexts. As I also questioned my own understandings of Intercultural Transitions throughout this process, I gained more awareness of the complexity involved and the ways my assumptions may impact the inquiry.

ENDORA'S PROFILE

I begin this young woman's story by briefly describing her presojourn family life, education, social networks, language proficiency/use, and intercultural/international experience.

When Endora joined the Intercultural Transitions course, she was a 22-year-old, fourth-year English major in a bilingual (Chinese-English) university in Hong Kong. Born and raised in the city, she spoke Cantonese as a first language. Like most of the local students in the Transitions course, her family knew very little English and used Cantonese at home. A multilingual speaker, Endora also spoke Putonghua (Mandarin) fairly fluently and knew basic German. She had attended an English-medium secondary school and considered herself to be quite fluent in the language. She received a B in her A-level Use of English examination just before joining the university. As an English major, she took literature and applied linguistics courses, as well as general education electives in other subject areas (e.g., German language, journalism). She did well in her coursework and had a grade point average (GPA) of 3.3 when she joined the Intercultural Transitions course.

Before gaining international experience at the end of her second year of university studies, all of her friends were Cantonese-speaking Hong Kong Chinese. Although there were many international students on campus from different parts of the world, she did not socialize with any. Endora lived in a hostel on campus and shared a room with a local student. In Hong Kong, her use of English was largely confined to formal classroom settings; outside of class, she switched to Cantonese or code-mixed (Cantonese-English).

When she joined the university, she had never ventured outside Asia; however, by the time the Intercultural Transitions course got underway, she had international educational experience in Canada and Germany and had completed a sojourn in Mainland China. She had also spent several weeks traveling around the United States as a tourist.

Endora's first academic sojourn took place at the end of her second year of university studies. It consisted of an eight-week summer internship in Guangzhou, a city in Southern China, less than a two-hour train ride from Hong Kong. This global internship program was arranged by her home university, but no special preparation was provided. Endora worked as a trainee in a government office, where she conducted library research and helped analyze survey data. Although the primary language of the workplace and community was Cantonese, she primarily used Putonghua with her roommate, a Mainland Chinese intern from CUHK. Endora found Guangzhou to be 'unexpectedly old and dirty.' Suffering from 'severe homesickness,' she 'blacklisted' the city, and escaped to Hong Kong every weekend. At this time, her social networks still largely consisted of Hong Kong Chinese.

Two weeks after the internship program ended, Endora packed her bags and traveled to Vancouver, a multicultural city in Western Canada, where she joined an academic yearlong exchange program. Because she had been in Guangzhou in the summer, she was unable to attend the brief predeparture sessions organized for outgoing exchange students by the Office of Academic Links at CUHK. In her second year of studies, she had also opted not to enroll in the elective intercultural communication course that was offered by the English Department. Consequently, she had no formal presojourn orientation or intercultural education prior to her stay in Canada.

During her nine-month sojourn in Vancouver, Endora took a full load of courses in literature and applied linguistics at the host institution, a large, comprehensive university. The medium of instruction was English, and, for the first time in her life, she found herself in very diverse classes where the majority spoke English as a first language. On campus, she shared an apartment with three roommates: two Canadians and a Hong Kong exchange student from CUHK. Endora used English to converse with the Canadians, and Cantonese or code-mixing (Cantonese-English) with her Hong Kong roommate when they were alone.

Throughout her stay in Vancouver, all of her closest friends were from Hong Kong or other parts of Asia (e.g., Mainland China, South Korea). During the break between semesters, Endora traveled to the West Coast of the United States with international students from Hong Kong and South Korea. In late April and early May, after her studies ended, she toured the East Coast of Canada and the United States with Hong Kong Chinese friends.

After her sojourn in Canada, Endora returned to Hong Kong for only five days before embarking on yet another international experience. With a few students from CUHK, she flew to Düsseldorf, Germany, to take part in a summer language immersion program. During this short-term sojourn, Endora attended basic German language and culture classes with students of different ages and nationalities. During her month long stay, Endora lived with a German host family and an American PhD student who was fluent in the host language. Endora returned to Hong Kong in July and began the Intercultural Transitions course in early September.

UNPACKING INTERNATIONAL/REENTRY EXPERIENCE

The analysis of Endora's oral and written narratives and my field notes identified multiple gains from this semester-long period of intense introspection: more understanding of the nature and impact of Intercultural Transitions, recognition of the ways her attitudes and behaviors might influence intercultural communication, a heightened awareness of her self-identities and others' perceptions of her, and new understandings of what it means to be interculturally competent. By the end of the course, Endora appeared to understand and recognize multiple benefits of critical reflection as evidenced by her narratives, comments in class, and postcourse interview.

Understanding the Nature and Impact of Intercultural Transitions

When she returned to Hong Kong to resume her studies, Endora was still quite confused about why she had experienced a range of conflicting emotions during her sojourns, especially in Guangzhou and Düsseldorf. As she learned more about the natural ups and downs of cross-cultural adjustment through lectures, readings, and discussions, she discovered that the emotions she had experienced were not unique to her:

> After listening to others' stories and reading their writings, you realize that what everybody has experienced is actually quite similar so you'll be less inclined to enlarge your own feelings as much when you are in these situations in the future. For example, I think everybody who has had international experience has had some uncomfortable moments so you don't have to see these moments as if the sky is collapsing! (Interview)

Candid sharing sessions (both in class and online) exposed Endora to different ways of handling the challenges of international transitions.

READJUSTING TO HONG KONG

Early in the course, similar to many returnees, Endora disclosed that she was feeling very unsettled and finding it difficult to reconnect with friends and family. She was surprised that she felt so out of place in her home environment:

> When I first returned home, I felt like there was a big gap between my friends and me. Although we had contact while I was away, there was still a feeling that we're not the same as before. When we were together in a group I felt like I was the only one who didn't share their collective experience and I felt really isolated. (Interview)

As she developed more understanding of her emotions and experimented with various coping strategies, she began to feel more at ease in her academic and social life. In the postcourse interview with my Chinese research assistant, she stated:

> When I first came back, I was quite unhappy but I learned that this is normal so I won't be like, 'Oh, why am I so down all of a sudden?' The course gave me a new approach to handling things when I face difficulties. For example, I learned how to get along with the people around me. . . . Through this course, I gradually learnt to find my own way.

INADEQUATE PREPARATION FOR STAYS ABROAD

Before venturing abroad, Endora did not feel it necessary to join an intercultural communication course or take part in presojourn orientations. After experiencing difficulty building satisfactory relationships with people who have been socialized in a different linguistic or cultural milieu, her views changed. In her interview, she acknowledged the value of adequate preparation for stays abroad:

> I didn't expect it would be so hard to adapt to another place especially when I was only going to Guangzhou. But after taking this course, I know, actually, it's because of this and that, and the simplest reason is I didn't prepare well enough. Though the language the people use is the same as in Hong Kong, and Guangzhou's very close to us, its culture is very different from ours and I didn't expect that. Realizing this is one of the gains from the course.

UNREALISTIC EXPECTATIONS AND VAGUE AIMS FOR SOJOURNS

Before entering university, Endora had yearned to travel and study outside Asia and harbored rather romantic notions about distant lands:

> I am hungry for traveling as I did not have the chance before going to university. One of my childhood dreams was to travel and study abroad. I envied those having annual or seasonal overseas trips, enjoying the beauty of nature, appreciating those famous tourist attractions while I could only enjoy the scenery in picture books. This reinforced my determination to go abroad. (First reflective essay)

Her idealistic stance was also evident when she discussed her expectations for her academic yearlong stay in Canada. In her first essay, she wrote:

> Participating in the exchange programme gave me the golden opportunity to spend two semesters in Vancouver, Canada. Happiness, excitement, anxiety and worries alternately dominated my heart before my departure. I dreamed of lying on the grass, reading Jane Austen with the glittering sun shining; I looked forward to meeting many new friends but was worried if I would be accepted by natives; I hoped to become a totally new person, mature and independent, but I didn't exactly know how. Still, I was determined to open the door to Canada.

Like many exchange students, she aspired to transform into a 'totally new person,' even though she had no idea how this might come about. Similar to her summer internship in Guangzhou, she was very vague about aims for her stays in Vancouver and Düsseldorf. Because inadequate preparation and unmet expectations can lead to sojourner dissatisfaction and withdrawal from the host community (Kim 2012; Ward et al., 2001), it is significant that Endora demonstrated more awareness of the benefits of setting realistic goals and expectations for sojourns by the end of the course: 'If I can go on exchange again, for example, to a European country that is new to me, I won't be expecting that it's a place where everywhere is vintage, or very elegant. Instead of holding onto these stereotypes, I'll look at things more objectively' (Interview). Although there is no guarantee that she would put her new understandings into practice, this increased awareness was a positive development.

ATTITUDES, AGENCY, AND SOJOURN OUTCOMES

As she learned about the sojourns of her peers and became adept at unpacking her own international experience, Endora displayed more understanding of how her attitudes (e.g., judgmental stance, negative perceptions) impacted the quality of her stays abroad, including her social networks and second language/culture learning.

> When I listened to others and read their stories, I realized that in the same intercultural situation, I might have had a negative attitude, while they approached it with a positive and optimistic attitude, and the results were totally different from mine. I realized that by changing my mindset I can actually feel happier and the whole experience can be different. (Interview)

During the semester, I observed a considerable shift in Endora's level of self-awareness and sense of responsibility as evidenced in the following excerpt from a survey completed near the end of the semester:

> The most important thing I learnt is how I should adjust my attitude—to be open-minded to differences in culture, beliefs, and personality. Attitude is the major element in deciding how I feel and think towards a certain incident. It can also greatly influence the enjoyment level of my international experience.

Later, in her interview, she added: 'I now realize that if I have the chance to go abroad again, I'll need to change the way I approach things. My attitude shouldn't be so negative and I shouldn't think only from my perspective.' Again, she displayed more understanding of how one's attitudes and actions can influence the way intercultural interactions unfold.

DEVELOPING THE HABIT OF CRITICAL REFLECTION

Likening herself to a 'cross-cultural athlete' in her final reflective essay, Endora compared her journey toward a more open-minded perspective as replete with obstacles that she was overcoming through perseverance:

> I see myself as a cross-country athlete, running up and down mountains after mountains. Be it gentle or steep, rocky or muddy. The intense and intensive climbs smoothed my edges while I still managed to appreciate the scenery with increasing openness and more comprehensive understanding of cultural differences.

Similar to many of her peers, critical reflection did not come easily to Endora, as she explained in her interview:

> When I began the Intercultural Transitions course, I viewed my year-long exchange experience as one large memory but the course required us to dissect some of the experiences and reflect on a certain period of time or specific incidents. You have to break up the issues into smaller

parts and think about each of them . . . In the beginning, I sometimes found it difficult to choose the most relevant experience to share and discuss online or during class but now I understand that this makes you think more deeply about things and see how everything is related to each other. In this way, I became aware of things I'd overlooked in the past.

This semester-long period of introspection helped Endora become more attuned to her personal development (e.g., second language/intercultural learning, recognition and acceptance of linguistic and cultural diversity). In her interview, she declared: 'I think I now have a better understanding of my international experience and my reactions to it.'

NEGOTIATING IDENTITIES AND STEREOTYPES ON STAYS ABROAD

As she revisited critical incidents, Endora realized that she had become more aware of the impact of identity and stereotypes in intercultural interactions. In particular, she had acquired a deeper grasp of the complex, sometimes emotive, identity negotiation process that can occur when interacting with individuals who do not understand or recognize one's preferred self-identities. Because this was a major element in her sojourns, near the end of the course, she opted to do a presentation that explored the avowed and ascribed nature of identity as well as self-expansion (e.g., the development of hybrid, multicultural selves). In her interview, Endora also discussed identity issues:

> When I was in Germany, the Japanese said I was Korean, the Koreans said I was Japanese, and the Mainland Chinese wouldn't say I was Chinese. I felt, well, a bit helpless . . . I simply said, 'No, I'm from Hong Kong, a Chinese student'. Living abroad and taking this course have made me think more about my identity. At first, I didn't think much about it but the people around me would ask me lots of questions about it. And, while answering their questions, I began to think about whether I see myself as a Hong Konger or as a Chinese. Now, I'd say I'm a Hong Kong citizen but if you ask about my nationality, I'll say I'm Chinese . . . Foreigners can't really distinguish between Hong Kongers and Chinese people unless they already know about the one country–two systems situation. Besides, I don't think Hong Kongers are that hugely different from the Chinese people. For example, there are many daily living habits that are similar. Also, in terms of traditional beliefs, we are all under the influence of the same culture . . . Before I went abroad, I used to think that I'm a Hong Konger and that I'm very different from the Mainlanders. This changed after I went abroad. Actually, I'm also

a Chinese. After all, even in the U.S., not all Americans have the same practices so it's the same feeling.

Compared with her initial revelations about her sojourn in Guangzhou, there was a discernible shift in her attitude toward Mainland Chinese and more awareness of diversity *within* cultures. She was much less hostile and no longer referred to 'those people' in a disparaging tone. Endora recognized that she had 'felt superior to the local people' during her stay in Guangzhou and had harbored 'a lot of stereotypes about Mainlanders' (Third reflective essay).

As her self-identities were frequently contested, Endora began to think more deeply about what elements were central to her sense of self. Through readings and sharing sessions (online and in-class), she discovered that being misidentified is a common occurrence, which often stems from a lack of knowledge rather than malice. She began to realize that she, too, sometimes did not acknowledge the preferred identities of others. These discoveries helped her to deal with negative emotions related to identity misalignments.

BENEFITS OF SHARING AND REFLECTIVE WRITING

In her postcourse interview, Endora identified several benefits of reading about the experiences of others, as well as sharing stories with her peers. These practices helped her to make sense of critical incidents and the emotions that accompanied them: 'Reading the blogs and essays of others who've studied abroad, you realize that many of their feelings are like your own. This is quite useful coz when you talk about some problem you had abroad others understood you and empathized with you.' In a survey, she remarked: 'Both classroom discussions and blogging helped me learn the concepts better and develop a deeper understanding of my own experience. I also learned a lot from my classmates' sharing and how I can better react to my difficulties.'

Endora also wrote about the benefits of writing and ongoing reflection to apprehend international experience: 'Writing reflective essays allows me to evaluate my experience, both happy and unhappy. I can then better prepare myself for similar incidents in the future and put what I have learnt into practice' (Survey). Later, in her interview, she offered more insight into what she gained from the process of reflective writing:

> Although some classmates think that writing a blog each week is a lot, I think that it's necessary 'cause if you don't write about your experience, you may not be aware of your own feelings about things that happen. Also, you have different ways of looking at things when you learn to write and reflect. Your thoughts at the beginning of the course are quite

different from those at the end. For example, what I'm thinking at this moment is already different from what I was thinking when I was writing my last essay so I think the reflective writing part is necessary.

Being 'forced to think' pushed Endora to go beyond mere descriptions of international experience: 'Blogging requires you to analyze your experience critically and not just discuss your emotions . . . In the course, you're forced to think, and to evaluate your feelings. I think you learn to go deeper in this way' (Interview).

INTERNATIONAL AND INTERCULTURAL ASPIRATIONS

Critical reflection also raised Endora's awareness of the importance of intercultural (communicative) competence and the sociopragmatic dimension of second language use in intercultural interactions. In her interview, she said:

> It may sound superficial but I think language is important for sojourners, not just the skills or knowledge of the language but also how to use the language appropriately in different contexts. I think it's an important factor for an intercultural communicator. Now, I hope to become more and more advanced as an intercultural communicator. Speaking many languages well is a must.

Along with a shift in attitude, Endora had become more willing to interact and build friendships with people who have been socialized in a different linguistic and cultural environment. This was significant because her social networks had largely consisted of Hong Kong Chinese people before the course got underway. She now appeared to value the multicultural dimension of intercultural friendships and stated that she was determined to seek out more opportunities to expand her social circle:

> As for my future social life, my international experience and this course have made me much more motivated to get to know people from different nationalities. I no longer like to hang out or communicate with only Hong Kong or Chinese people. When I chat with others about simple things like family life and friendship, the things they say reveal some of their values, These values and some of their perceptions were developed under the influence of their culture so I want to understand different cultures through this mode. (Interview)

With more self-awareness and confidence, Endora began to make concrete plans for more international, second language experience. She appeared to be keen to put into practice what she had just learned:

> Before taking this course, I planned to do another intensive German course in Germany. What I originally planned was to stay in a student hostel in a single room with a private kitchen and bathroom after the not-so-successful communication with my host mom last summer. However, taking this course has inspired me with the idea of living with another host family to see if I can make a better experience through interacting more with the family members. Then, I could make full use of the opportunity to improve my language skills and learn more about German culture. (Survey)

Inspired by the international stories of her peers and other sojourn writers, Endora aimed to optimize future stays abroad by learning more about local practices through intercultural interactions:

> After going on exchange and taking this course, I want to go to explore more. I realized that my previous sojourns focused too much on vacationing, the sight-seeing part, and I didn't have much contact with locals. Now I want to stay in a place for a longer time and really come to understand more about the local culture. Also, maybe later I'll pursue further studies, and, ideally, go abroad, for example, to Britain. (Interview)

Interestingly, she also resolved to seek out intercultural interactions in both her social and work spheres in Hong Kong:

> Ideally, I want to work next year after graduation. I hope the nature of the work will allow me to have contact with people from different countries. I also want to keep in regular contact with my international friends and find more opportunities in Hong Kong to have contact with foreigners. (Interview)

ADVICE FOR FUTURE SOJOURNERS

Near the end of the course, the participants gave oral presentations that were open to any students interested in study abroad. Endora and Zoe (a pseudonym) gave a presentation entitled 'Who Are We?' In it, they drew on their personal experience of identity misalignments and self-expansion, as well as related literature. Endora's concluding remarks and advice to future sojourners offered insight into her current thinking about international and intercultural experience, suggesting gains in self-awareness and maturity:

> Step out of your comfort zone!
> Stay open-minded.
> Get prepared to be challenged . . .
> What you have always taken for granted *will* be challenged.

Have a positive attitude.
Be ready to construct a new intercultural self. [Emphasis in original]
(Excerpt from PowerPoint presentation, 'Who Are We?')

Endora's remarks brought an end to a semester of guided, critical reflection and seemed to indicate that she had taken steps toward a more reflective, open mind-set. Although it was unclear whether she would implement these ideas, at least she had become more aware of the role that her attitudes and actions can play in intercultural interactions.

CONCLUSION

Throughout this intense period of guided, critical reflection, Endora unpacked the emotions of her 'lived experience' through class discussions (online and in class), visually enhanced blogs, essays, and an oral presentation. This rich data offered insight into her language and (inter-)cultural learning/adjustment, identity negotiation/reconstruction, and degree of openness to other ways of being. Her case study raises awareness of the subjective dimension of the international/reentry experience and the affective, agentive, social, and historical dimensions of interculturality and multilingualism.

Before her international experience, Endora was confident about her ability to interact successfully with people who have been socialized in a different linguistic and cultural environment, even though she had had very little intercultural experience. Consequently, similar to many of her peers, she devoted little time and energy to sojourn preparation. During her stays abroad, she suffered identity misalignments and homesickness and found it challenging to accept new practices; her social networks also included very few host nationals. When intercultural interactions did not go well, she tended to attribute it to discrimination, overlooking the possibility that her own attitudes and behaviors may have been contributing factors.

When the Intercultural Transitions course got underway, Endora claimed that international experience had broadened her horizons, but she was unable to articulate any specific gains, and much of her discourse was critical of other practices and worldviews. After a semester-long period of structured, critical reflection, she displayed more awareness of gaps in her intercultural communicative competence and recognized that her own actions and mind-set had contributed to unsatisfactory intercultural encounters. In particular, her oral and written narratives suggested that she realized that unrealistic expectations and negative attitudes had hampered her sojourn experiences, limited the diversity of her social networks, and curtailed her personal growth.

A review of Endora's narratives suggests that she had acquired a much deeper understanding of what it means to be self-reflexive and open-minded. Although it was not possible for me to observe her after the course ended, this awareness, at minimum, serves as a good foundation for building intercultural relationships. Her attitude toward intercultural interactions had become noticeably more positive, and she was more enthusiastic about international experience. To determine the actual long-term impact of a course like this, however, future research is needed that tracks participants long after the course has ended (e.g., longitudinal studies that involve annual interviews and surveys for five or ten years postcourse).

Although this chapter largely centers on the storied life of a multilingual Hong Kong student, her trials and tribulations are apt to resonate with sojourners and returnees in other parts of the world. Endora's case study and the experiences of her peers have implications for the structuring of education abroad programs and for the timing and design of intercultural education programming. Ideally, students should gain more understanding of intercultural communication and cross-cultural adjustment *before* going abroad. The reality is, however, that even when elective intercultural communication courses are available presojourn, students may not enroll because they may not realize they need guidance or support until they are actually in an international setting.

As this case study illustrates, students can benefit from the opportunity to unpack their intercultural, international, and reentry experience in a supportive environment. The learning cycle should not end when they return to home soil. In addition to helping them make sense of critical incidents and identity shifts/misalignments, structured reflection can promote self-reflexivity and encourage more intercultural interactions both at home and abroad.

Students are the not the only ones who can benefit from a reflective stance. Although most of this chapter focused on Endora's developmental trajectory, the act of shaping her story helped me to acquire new insights into the complexity of Intercultural Transitions and what it means to be reflexive and interculturally competent. This iterative process also raised my awareness of course elements that should be modified to prompt more critical engagement and self-reflection earlier in the course. For example, more critiques of study abroad essays in the first few weeks should help the participants to better understand what is meant by critical reflection and self-analysis without putting them under too much pressure at this stage. A more profound grasp of the nature and benefits of reflection may potentially bring about deeper insights earlier in the course. In the next offering, I aim to investigate the impact of this adjustment.

Critically reflecting on one's work can alert researchers and teachers to assumptions that may be limiting their views. It can raise awareness of multiple interpretations of events and help to problematize current theories and practices. Ultimately, this process can lead to the development of new ideas and frameworks. In particular, reflexivity can enable us to become more aware of the multifarious factors influencing student learning and provide direction for improvements in the way we teach and guide learners. In this way, students can truly benefit from new understandings. In sum, reflexivity can be instructive and deeply rewarding for educators, researchers, and students.

ACKNOWLEDGMENTS

This research has been supported by a General Research Fund (444709) from the Research Grants Council of Hong Kong and a Teaching Development Grant (4170338) from the Chinese University of Hong Kong (CUHK). This case study would not have been possible without Endora's willingness to share her story. I would also like to thank the editors for their insightful comments and helpful suggestions to enhance this chapter.

NOTES

1. A reflective essay is a type of writing that requires the author to describe how an experience (e.g., critical incident, intercultural interaction) has impacted him or her. In addition to descriptive elements, the writing includes self-analysis, providing insight into the author's personal growth.
2. Following the ethics guidelines for my university, the students in the intercultural transitions course were asked in writing if they would be willing for me to analyze their work/surveys and be interviewed after the course ended. They were assured that their participation (or nonparticipation) would not affect their grades and that pseudonyms would be used in subsequent reports. All agreed to allow their written work to be evaluated; only one declined to be interviewed. The students were offered the option of withdrawing their consent at any time. None did.

REFERENCES

Alred, G., Byram, M., & Fleming, M. (2003). *Intercultural experience and education*. Clevedon, UK: Multilingual Matters.
Alvesson, M. & Sköldberg, K. (2000). *Reflexive methodology: New vistas for qualitative research*. London: Sage.
Bennett, J. M. (2004). Turning frogs into interculturalists: A student-centered developmental approach to teaching intercultural competence. In R. A. Goodman, M. E. Phillips, & N. A. Boyacigiller (Eds.), *Crossing cultures: Insights from master teachers* (pp. 312–442). London: Routledge.
Bennett, J. M. (2008). On becoming a global soul: A path to engagement during study abroad. In V. Savicki (Ed.), *Developing intercultural competence and transformation: Theory, research, and application in international education* (pp. 13–31). Sterling, VA: Stylus.
Bennett, M. J. (1993). Towards ethnorelativism: A developmental model of intercultural sensitivity. In R. M. Paige (Ed.), *Education for the intercultural experience* (pp. 21–71). Yarmouth, ME: Intercultural Press.
Bhabha, H. (1994). *The location of culture*. London: Routledge.
Block, D. (2006). *Multilingual identities in a global city: London stories*. London: Palgrave Macmillan.
Block, D. (2007). *Second language identities*. London: Continuum.
Bourdieu, P., & Wacquant, L. J. D. (1992). *An invitation to reflexive sociology*. Cambridge: Polity Press.
Byram, M. (2012). Conceptualizing intercultural (communicative) competence and intercultural citizenship. In J. Jackson (Ed.), *Routledge handbook of language and intercultural communication* (pp. 85–97). London: Routledge.

Byram, M., Nichols, A., & Stevens, D. (2001). *Developing intercultural competence in practice*. Clevedon, UK: Multilingual Matters.
Byrd Clark, J. (2009). *Multilingualism, citizenship, and identity: Voices of youth and symbolic investments in an urban, globalized world*. London: Continuum.
Byrd Clark, J. (2012). Heterogeneity and a sociolinguistics of multilingualism: Reconfiguring French language pedagogy. *Language and Linguistics Compass Blackwell Online Journal*, 6(3), 143–161.
Clandinin, D. J., & Rosiek, J. (2007). Mapping a landscape of narrative inquiry. In D. J. Clandinin (Ed.), *Handbook of narrative inquiry* (pp. 35–75). Thousand Oaks, CA: Sage.
Clandinin, D. J., & Connelly, F. M. (2000). *Narrative inquiry: Experience and story in qualitative research*. San Francisco: Jossey-Bass.
Deardorff, D. K., & Jones, E. (2012). Intercultural competence: An emerging focus in international higher education. In D. Deardorff, H. de Witt, J. D. Heyl, & T. Adams (Eds.), *The SAGE handbook of international higher education* (pp. 283–304). Thousand Oaks, CA: Sage.
Dervin, F. (2011). A plea for change in research intercultural discourses: A 'liquid' approach to the study of Chinese students. *Journal of Multicultural Discourses*, 6(1), 37–52.
Dervin, F. (2012). Cultural identity, representation and othering. In J. Jackson (Ed.), *Routledge handbook of language and intercultural communication* (pp. 181–194). London: Routledge.
Dewey, J. (1938). *Experience and education*. New York: Touchstone.
Dicks, B., Mason, B., Coffey, A., & Atkinson, P. (2005). *Qualitative research and hypermedia: ethnography for the digital age*. London: Sage.
Erikson, E. H. (1968). *Identity: Youth and crisis*. New York: Norton.
Grbich, C. (2007). *Qualitative data analysis*. London: Sage.
Hall, S. (1992). The question of identity. In S. Hall, D. Held, & A. McGrew (Eds.), *Modernity and its futures* (pp. 274–316). Cambridge: Polity Press.
Jackson, J. (2006). Ethnographic preparation for short-term study and residence in the target culture. *International Journal of Intercultural Relations*, 30(1), 77–98.
Jackson, J. (2008). *Language, identity, and study abroad: Sociocultural perspectives*. London: Equinox.
Jackson, J. (2010). *Intercultural journeys: From study to residence abroad*. Basingstoke, UK: Palgrave Macmillan.
Jackson, J. (2011). Cultivating cosmopolitan, intercultural citizenship through critical reflection and international, experiential learning. *Language and Intercultural Communication*, 11(2), 80–96.
Jackson, J. (2012). Education abroad. In J. Jackson (Ed.), *Routledge handbook of language and intercultural communication* (pp. 449–463). London: Routledge.
Jackson, J. (2013). The transformation of 'a frog in the well': A path to a more intercultural, global mindset. In C. Kinginger (Ed.), *The social turn in study abroad research* (pp. 179–204). Amsterdam: John Benjamins.
Joseph, J. (2004). *Language and identity: National, ethnic, religious*. New York: Palgrave Macmillan.
Kohonen, V., Jaatinen, R., Kaikkonen, P., & Lehtovaara, J. (2001). *Experiential learning in foreign language education*. London: Pearson Education.
Kolb, D. A. (1984). *Experiential learning*. Englewood Cliffs, NJ: Prentice Hall.
Kramsch, C. J. (1993). *Context and culture in language teaching*. New York: Oxford University Press.
Kramsch, C. J. (2009). *The multilingual subject*. Oxford: Oxford University Press.
Lou, K. H., & Bosley, G. W. (2012). Facilitating intercultural learning abroad. In Vande Berg, R. M. Paige, & K. H. Lou (Eds.), *Student learning abroad: What our students are learning, what they're not, and what we can do about it* (pp. 335–359). Sterling, VA: Stylus.

Marginson, S., & Sawir, E. (2011). *Ideas for intercultural education*. New York: Palgrave Macmillan.

Meyer-Lee, E. (2004). Follow-up courses for study abroad returnees' problems and possibilities. Presentation at the Council for International Education (CIEE) Conference, Santa Fe, New Mexico, November 11, 2004.

Mezirow, J. (1994). *Transformative dimensions of adult learning*. San Francisco: Jossey-Bass.

Mezirow, J. (2000). *Learning as transformation: Critical perspectives on a theory in progress*. San Francisco: Jossey Bass.

Norton, B. (1997). Language, identity and the ownership of English. *TESOL Quarterly*, 31(3), 409–429.

Norton, B. (2000). *Identity and language learning: Gender, ethnicity, and educational change*. London: Longman.

Ochs, E., & Capps, L. (1996). Narrating the self. *Annual Review of Anthropology*, 25, 19–43.

Oetzel, J. (2009). *Intercultural communication: A layered approach*. New York: Vango Books.

Passarelli, A. M., & Kolb, D. A. (2012). Using experiential learning theory to promote student learning and development in programs of education abroad. In M. Vande Berg, R. M. Paige, & K. H. Lou (Eds.), *Student learning abroad* (pp. 137–361). Sterling, VA: Stylus.

Pavlenko, A. (2007). Autobiographic narratives as data in applied linguistics. *Applied Linguistics*, 28(2), 163–188.

Richards, L. (2009). *Handling qualitative data*. Thousand Oaks, CA: Sage.

Ryan, P. (2012). The English as a foreign or international language classroom. In J. Jackson (Ed.), *Routledge handbook of language and intercultural* communication (pp. 422–433). London: Routledge.

Savicki, V. (2012). The psychology of student learning abroad. In M. Vande Berg, R. M. Paige, & K. H. Lou (Eds.), *Student learning abroad* (pp. 215–238). Sterling, VA: Stylus.

Ting-Toomey, S., & Chung, L. C. (2012). *Understanding intercultural communication* (2nd ed.). Oxford: Oxford University Press.

Vande Berg, M., Paige, R. M., & Lou, K. H. (Eds.). (2012). Student learning abroad: Paradigms and assumptions. In M. Vande Berg, R. M. Paige, & K. H. Lou (Eds.), *Student learning abroad* (pp. 1–28). Sterling, VA: Stylus.

Weedon, C. (1997). *Feminist practice and poststructuralism theory* (2nd ed.). Oxford: Blackwell.

2 'Or, Just It's My Fault, Right?'
Language Socialization through Reflexive Language Writing Feedback

Jérémie Séror

Throughout the world, language instructors devote innumerable hours responding and providing feedback to students' written assignments. Widely recognized as a means of accelerating and scaffolding learning (Hounsell, 2007; F. Hyland, 2010), feedback is also, however, a controversial literacy practice (Carless et al., 2011). Indeed, the search for the mode and medium of feedback that can best support second language (L2) writing development remains an issue of considerable discussion in the field (Bitchener, 2008; Ferris; 2010; Truscott, 2007). Studies, for instance, have stressed surveyed students' dissatisfaction with instructor feedback (Carless, 2006; Crisp et al., 2009; Mustafa, 2012; Weaver, 2006) and highlighted tensions between the perceived pedagogic benefits associated with feedback and the seeming inability to fully capitalize on this means of scaffolding student learning and literacy development (Séror, 2009; Hounsell, 2007). In this chapter, I will explore how a reflexive approach to feedback practices that draws on the language socialization framework can facilitate our understanding of this powerful but complex literacy practice and its significance for the (co-)construction and representation of writing development and multilingual writers.

Focusing on feedback as unique opportunities for students to receive personalized guidance from instructors, this chapter situates itself within a growing body of research on feedback practices that seeks to go beyond a traditional focus on feedback's role as a catalyst for grammar acquisition in order to also address the interactive and contextual dimensions of feedback interactions and the interpersonal dynamics in which they are embedded (Hyland & Hyland, 2006b; Parr & Timperley, 2010).

This research orientation benefits greatly from the inclusion of a reflexive gaze on literacy events and scaffolding processes and their links to the intentions and identities of the actors involved in these practices. For instance, explorations of instructors' reflections on feedback practices have revealed the importance of their time-consuming nature (El Ebyary & Windeatt, 2010), the need for substantive formal training (Ferris et al., 2011), and the impact of institutional forces (Séror, 2009; Bailey & Garner, 2010). Focusing on learners' perspective, this approach has been critical to understanding students' active engagement with literacy practices such as feedback as they search for understandings that will guide the creation of their texts as well as their interpretation of academic literacies (Lea & Street, 2006; Pérez-Milans, this volume) and themselves as writers (Ivanič et al., 2000; Sutton, 2012).

To further illustrate the value of this approach, this chapter reports on a study that drew on a language socialization framework to investigate feedback practices' impact as locally produced, ideologically inscribed acts of languaging (Byrd Clark & Dervin, this volume; Suzuki, 2012; Swain, 2006), which, in addition to promoting students' awareness of a reader's response to their texts and specific linguistic forms, can also reify for students particular beliefs and norms.

EXPLORING FEEDBACK FROM A LANGUAGE SOCIALIZATION PERSPECTIVE

Rooted in anthropological linguistics and drawing on ethnographic and discourse analysis traditions, language socialization research explores the relationship between individuals' acquisition of linguistic, pragmatic, and cultural knowledge and their participation in a community's language-mediated activities (Duff & Talmy, 2011; Kulick & Schieffelin, 2004; Ochs & Schieffelin, 2008). In the field of L2 acquisition, this paradigm has been made significant contributions to our understanding of the impact of everyday language practices, both in and out of the classroom, on students' identities and negotiated participation in communities of practice (Duff, 2010; Mökkönen, 2012; Zuengler & Cole, 2005). Significantly, L2 socialization research has helped underscore the unpredictable and conflicted nature of language learning (Kulick & Schieffelin, 2004; Morita, 2009), as well as students' ability to renegotiate, resist, and even subvert language-mediated activities and the dominant ideologies and norms these help promote (Evaldsson & Cekaite, 2010; Talmy, 2008).

STUDY DESIGN

To investigate the discursive and interactional nature of feedback and its role in the language socialization of L2 learners, this study employed a longitudinal multiple case study design (Duff, 2008, 2012; Stake, 2006) focusing on five Japanese international students participating in an exchange program at a large Canadian university.

In L2 writing research, case studies have been identified as an important means of studying the complex interactions of local knowledge and sociopolitical forces that shape texts and language development (Casanave, 2003). Moreover, their ability to gather an extensive amount of information about a phenomenon in a detailed, context-sensitive manner (Yin, 2003) made this methodology aptly suited to produce 'thick' descriptions (Geertz, 2003) of feedback practices as the phenomenon of interest for this study.

The five focal participants (three males and two females) were Japanese undergraduate students from Nihon Daigaku University (NDU) and its sister campus Nihon University International (NUI), participating in their second year of an exchange program with Blue Mountain University (BMU).[1] The participants stemmed from a cohort of approximately 100 Japanese students who had come to spend a maximum of two academic years in Canada. During the duration of their study abroad experience, these students took both language and content courses in English with the objective to develop English academic skills, gain discipline specific knowledge, and participate in cross-cultural learning activities.

The focal participants in this study were recruited from the smaller pool of exchange students who had opted to stay for a second year of study at BMU in self-selected courses based on their majors and interests. While none of the participants were my students at the time of the study, my decision to recruit from this pool of students originated in my own previous involvement with these students as one of their instructors during their first year of exchange at BMU. In designing the study, I hoped to benefit from the trust I had developed with many of them because I had asked them to share, over a period of eight months, their interpretations of the role feedback played in their evolution as multilingual writers. Moreover, in their second year of exchange, these students were largely expected to function independently with very little support as they participated in so-called regular courses designed for L1 students. Their experience was hence judged as representative of that lived by a growing population of international students pursuing studies in North American universities (Khoo, 2011).

This study drew on multiple data sources collected over a period of two academic semesters (fall and winter semesters from September to April). A principal data source involved biweekly semistructured interviews with focal students of approximately an hour in length (Merriam, 1998). These interviews were designed to elicit information about participants' experiences in their second year of study as well as their thoughts and reactions to the feedback received in their courses. Whenever possible, focal participants would bring to these interviews copies of their assignments and any feedback comments received. This allowed me to address specific details and elements in these documents during the interviews (e.g., 'You told me this feedback comment was useful. Can you tell me what specific part or words you found useful and why?').

In addition to gathering students' perspectives about the feedback they received, relevant documents associated with the students' courses and writing assignments (assignment descriptions, drafts of texts, feedback messages, course syllabi, etc.) were also collected to supplement the data analysis. Finally, field notes and informal communication with the participants, as well as in-class observations of three focal participants' classes and interviews conducted with four of the participants' instructors, were also used to help triangulate the data, thus enhancing the validity and credibility of the themes and categories identified through the data analysis (Johnson & Christensen, 2004; Silverman, 2004).

Throughout the study, data analysis was guided by principles of qualitative inquiry and drew on an iterative process to organize, code, and categorize the data (Creswell, 2007; Denzin & Lincoln, 2003). As patterns and relationships between key themes emerged, relevant literature was constantly reviewed, and participants were presented with preliminary reports of the findings to verify the degree to which the analysis accurately reflected their experiences (Thomas, 2006). Although admittedly nongeneralizeable to a larger population of international students, it should be noted that my analytical aims were to draw on the richness of the data collected to generate theory by building on existing constructs and propositions (Eisenhardt & Graebner, 2007; Firestone, 1993).

BEING POSITIONED BY FEEDBACK

In line with language socialization research, this study sought to reflect on the role feedback played in helping shape students' social identities, actions, and stances (Ochs, 1996). Findings for this study thus focused not only on the explicit advice and judgments on writing found in the feedback that students received but also on how these statements were interpreted and internalized by students. What emerged were repeated examples of feedback practices helping to position students, often in subtle but powerful ways that extended beyond the immediate surface-level meanings of the comments provided. Indeed, even when judged by students to be ineffective and less than ideal, feedback practices were shown to convey to students positions that were then adopted into identity statements and value judgments that students made about writing and themselves as writers.

To illustrate this positioning process, I will detail the case of Yoshimi, a male participant in the study, and his interpretation and reactions to feedback received on a major research paper written for a philosophy course. In what follows, a combination of interview excerpts, field notes, and feedback samples are used to reconstruct Yoshimi's interaction with and reflections on the feedback he received. Although the selection of this specific case reflects practical considerations linked to this chapter's space constrictions, it is also purposive in nature. First, this decision reflects a conscious attempt to take the time (and space) required to engage in rich descriptions of a social phenomenon from a participant's viewpoint. As is common with qualitative research in the field of language education, this strategy aligns itself with the belief in the importance of documenting and thus not overlooking the small yet crucial details and interactions that impact literacy processes and development (Duff, 2008). Moreover, this belief echoes the conviction that, despite the limits that stem from this commitment to 'the particular' (Stake, 1995), detailed descriptions and analysis of specific cases can contribute in important ways to investigations of complex educational phenomena and to the testing and generation of the theories and principles used to explain these (Flyvbjerg, 2006).

Second, my desire to focus on Yoshimi is linked to my desire to present this particular case in published form. Indeed, despite my belief in the value and strength of detailed cases, I have struggled to find ways to report the full story of each of the focal students who participated in this study while respecting the page limitations imposed by the genre of the journal article. Although the most complete version of the findings of this study can be found in the dissertation produced as a result of this research (see Séror, 2008), my attempts to give voice to the focal students in this study has resulted in a series of articles, each highlighting different themes and students. In so doing, I have sought to bring out the contribution of each student while staying true to the richness and power of the detailed insights these students so generously shared with me over the course of a year.[2] In the case of this particular chapter, I have thus chosen to highlight the case of Yoshimi not only because his case clearly illustrates in my mind why a reflexive approach to feedback is necessary but also because his case is one that I have not yet had the chance to make public in published form despite the fact that it stands out as a pertinent and moving illustration of how specific representations of academic writing and multilingual writers can be reflected and reinforced through the discourse of feedback with definitive, if unexpected, consequences for students' language socialization trajectories.

YOSHIMI'S CASE

Yoshimi was a 21-year-old economics major at the time of the study, who stood out for the seriousness with which he approached his studies. Goal-oriented, disciplined, and very deliberate in his approach to the challenges of studying abroad, Yoshimi planned things out in advance and made and kept schedules with detailed records of the hours devoted to various activities, including daily study sessions, regular gym workouts, and time spent volunteering at a seniors' home in his host city. Known among his peers as a 'good student,' Yoshimi was frequently consulted by his friends (both local and international students) for advice, especially with difficult concepts linked to the field of economics.

A memorable instance for me of the impact feedback could have on students occurred when Yoshimi received feedback on the first of two major research papers he composed for a two-semester, third-year History of Philosophy course. In this course, each semester, Yoshimi was required to submit a 2500-word paper on a major philosophical debate linked to influential thinkers presented during class lectures. These assignments were, according to Yoshimi, the longest texts he had ever had to write as a university student. They also represented a major obstacle for him because he had had little experience writing papers in Japan prior to coming to Canada and because most of his economics courses, both in Japan and at BMU, had generally relied more often on mathematical skills than on writing skills.

Despite the hard work that these papers called for, Yoshimi revealed he had deliberately taken this course to improve his writing skills and career outlook. Upon finishing his undergraduate studies, Yoshimi's goal was to work for a foreign securities company in Japan. Yoshimi and his family had had to make significant financial sacrifices to pay for his university studies, and Yoshimi had calculated that working for a foreign securities company would be the fastest way to repay the debts he had accrued.

It is worth noting that these professional goals were also at the heart of his decision to stay on for a second year of exchange at BMU. Yoshimi believed that developing his English communication skills would provide him with a considerable advantage on the job market in Japan. Indeed, throughout the study, in addition to choosing courses that would force him to develop his writing skills, Yoshimi worked actively to improve his English through activities such as keeping an English personal diary and creating and maintaining a public English blog.

'I AM NOT GOING BACK TO JAPAN'

When time came to meet with Yoshimi at the start of the second semester to discuss the feedback he had received on the first philosophy paper he had submitted in December, I was taken aback by his announcement that the feedback on this paper had 'shocked' him and that, as a result of this feedback, he had canceled an important trip to Japan originally scheduled during BMU's reading week in February. This trip to Japan was a topic Yoshimi and I had discussed in previous interviews. The trip would allow him to take an important securities exam administered only once a year in Japan. This exam, as well as the good score he hoped to obtain on it, would be invaluable for the job hunting he was planning to do upon his return from Canada. Yoshimi had demonstrated the importance of this exam by explaining that he had 'spent about 50 to 60 hours studying' over the holidays 'studying, all the time,' so that he 'didn't have an actual winter break.'

This sudden decision to cancel the trip truly surprised me. I knew the importance Yoshimi had assigned to this exam and that his flight had already been booked. I also knew that, prior to getting his feedback on the essay, Yoshimi had already been aware that he had not done well on the term paper (over the winter break, he had been able to check his final class average on the university computer system, thus allowing him to deduce that he had received a very low grade for the paper).

EXPLAINING THE WEAKNESSES IN ONE'S WRITING

To better appreciate the impact of the feedback Yoshimi received, it is important to note that I had asked Yoshimi, prior to his receiving his feedback on his essay, the reasons he felt might explain why he had not done well. In answering this question, Yoshimi listed his grammar and language difficulties as possible explanations. Significantly, he also mentioned that despite having had the paper read by three roommates, including one English major student, because they had little knowledge of the specific thinkers selected, he feared there might still be problems with the paper's content. He also stressed that, though he had spent many hours working on the paper, he regretted not having been able to talk more with his instructor to discuss the paper and its topic.

Yoshimi explained that on the only occasion he had spoken with his instructor, one week prior to the paper's due date, he had had to change his topic based on the face-to-face feedback from his professor. At the time, Yoshimi had brought with him an outline of his paper. The professor informed him that she felt his topic was too broad and strongly recommended a different topic, with specific readings and information sources he should look at. Although unhappy with the idea of completely changing his topic, Yoshimi complied with his instructor and collected the recommended references. For Yoshimi, this had meant restarting his draft from the very beginning with only one week left before the paper was due. In light of the difficulties he had finding readings and writing quickly, he felt these events had also contributed to the low mark that he knew he had obtained.

The interview excerpt that follows illustrates how some of these ideas were communicated by Yoshimi as we discussed how he might try to change things in the upcoming semester when he would once again have to write a paper in a similar style for the same instructor.

J: So what are some of the things that you will do differently this semester to be able to get a better grade?

Y: I am going to better grade? Ah yeah . . . like I am going to talk to my prof more often. Yeah, like, before, I made a draft, but I should have talked to her more, like otherwise, like last semester, like one week before the due date, I had to change my subject completely. Yeah . . . that's why I got a lower grade I think. So I try to talk and go visit her during office hours.

J: Did you do as well as you had expected?

Y: Uh, like, you mean, grade or effort? Depends, I did really like try to, like how to say, like study hard, yeah because like I spent so much time for only this course. Maybe, I took three [courses] right and maybe I spent 60% of the studying hours for this course.

In summary, Yoshimi's reflection on the difficulties that explained his unsuccessful writing assignment included references to the notions of effort, the actual series of events that surrounded the writing of the text, and the nature of the interactions that he had had with his professor and his peers. Notably, his predicted poor performance for this paper was linked not only to Yoshimi himself or to his language difficulties. This construction of writing as something complicated that one worked hard at but that, under the best conditions, required interaction with instructors and others and that was linked to contextual factors out of one's control was a recurrent theme in all focal students' interviews. What I would discover in the case of Yoshimi, however, is that the feedback received on papers could have a transformative impact on students' accounts of the challenges associated with L2 writing.

GETTING THE FEEDBACK AND REACTING TO THE INSTRUCTORS' ACCOUNT OF WHAT WENT WRONG

Again, as already noted, when Yoshimi received his feedback, he already knew it would be critical based on his knowledge of the low mark he had received. Prior to actually reading the feedback, however, this had not deterred him in any way from planning to go to Japan to write the exam for which he had studied so hard. Thus, when I learned Yoshimi had canceled his trip, I immediately asked why he had changed his mind. When explaining his decision, Yoshimi replied that he wanted to spend all his available time on the next essay for his philosophy class. In seeking to understand how receiving feedback on his paper could have had such an impact, we went over the comments he had received.

Yoshimi had obtained a final mark of 52% for the paper, along with a series of comments that included 13 separate marks (underlined words, inserted articles, etc., and no major feedback comment) on the first page of his paper, followed on the second page with the first substantive comment, which read, 'I'll stop correcting your grammar & your prose style, but it needs serious work.' Page two contained one inserted article and three underlined sections identified with question marks. Page three had one comment about the use of a long quote ('No need for this long quote') and a marginal 'AWK' written next to a paragraph. Three series of words/sentence structures had been struck out, and a mistyped word (low instead of law) was circled on page four. Page five had no comments; page six contained a single question mark next to one of Yoshimi's paragraphs, accompanied by the following statement in the margin: 'Not what is meant by these terms.' Finally, page seven had one final end comment:

> You have chosen good sources and show some understanding of the debates at issue, but your presentation of the ideas is very difficult to follow, bordering on being incomprehensible in places. I suggest you go to writing clinics and consider extra tutoring.

The final references page contained three check marks and a final comment: 'GOOD.'³

In analyzing the discursive features of the teacher's feedback, we can observe how its orientation is highly focused on an evaluation of Yoshimi's language skills, echoing a frequent complaint made by students in the study that the feedback received in content courses focused heavily on language while ignoring their ideas. We also find an extreme categorization of his writing as 'almost incomprehensible,' and the implied valuation of his writing as bad enough to justify the decision to limit further comments beyond the first page.

In talking with Yoshimi about this feedback, it became clear that the final comment was the element that had played a defining role in his decision to cancel his trip. The transcript of our conversation as we addressed this comment follows:

J: One question is how important do you think that final sen- paragraph is for you?
Y: uh most important
J: the most important
Y: yeah more than like grade
J: oh interesting, good . . . that was my second question. What do you look at first?
Y: [Points to the comment.]
J: uh . . . because?
Y: Because I am not sure . . . because I can get feedback right, even though I know the grade. I cannot tell like how much I did. Like yeah, if yeah like professor like says some comment. Yeah. It's more helpful to improve my skill right. Yeah . . . But this is not helpful
J: This is not help [laughter from both of us]
Y: Yeah no . . .
J: Because?
Y: Because like she's saying totally, like because of my grammar and skill, English skills. Yeah the reason. Yeah . . . Like, I can understand right. So it's not helpful because . . . because she's not evaluating my paper, or just it's my fault right, because I couldn't meet her expectation. Yeah that's why . . . She like couldn't evaluate my content yeah, yeah so . . . I think my fault yeah. So yeah I should improve my more writing skills.

In this excerpt, we find two general themes raised by all focal students in the study regarding their perceptions of feedback. First, students valued but struggled to make sense of feedback. Marks mattered, sometimes a lot, but so did the comments they received, even if they could be hard to decipher. Second, students valued a response to their ideas and content over comments on their language. As a result, in this specific case, this was clearly not the kind of feedback Yoshimi was looking for. Ideal feedback, he suggests, would have had the instructor orienting herself to something other than just his 'grammar and skills' and his 'incomprehensible' writing. We see this in how he comments explicitly on what the instructor has failed to address in her comment: the paper itself and its content, its ideas. She is not, in his opinion, 'evaluating my paper.' It is all 'totally' his grammar and skill. He can 'understand,' he suggests, but there is a strong sense that this is not what he would have desired.

From a socialization perspective, this excerpt illustrates a pattern of feedback that explicitly invokes and places precedence on L2 students' deficient linguistic skills as a feature of their writing over the validity or the originality of the ideas contained in their writing and the need to respond to these. This feedback establishes a specific image of writing development, that is, a process rooted in the writer's individual skills that is to be improved alone or at least separately from content courses. This construction stands in opposition to Yoshimi's earlier construction of learning to write that highlighted writing's more social, collaborative, and discipline-specific dimensions by referring to such factors as the disciplinary expertise of peer evaluators and issues of access to instructors.

The power of feedback to convey and legitimate this individual view of writing is seen in how Yoshimi rewords (in the preceding excerpt) the professor's account of his writing as problematic and in that this problematic nature is 'his fault.' This new explanation of the problems with his writing, offered as a direct reaction to the feedback he has received, is much simpler than the account originally offered prior to receiving his feedback. This time, he has not done well because he is a student who needs to 'improve his writing skills,' skills that are inferior to what had been expected by the instructor. Of interest is what is now missing in this second version of what has gone wrong. Now absent are any considerations of the unique series of events surrounding the creation of this paper: the effort and time invested in the paper, the fact that he was not able to talk to his professor as much as he would have liked, the fact that his topic was changed at her request at the last minute, and so forth. Rather, Yoshimi picks up the teacher's construction of writing as something linked exclusively to the writer's individual skills. It is up to him and him alone to 'improve his writing skills.'

This capacity for feedback to work as a force socializing students to see writing development as an individual act is also reflected in the discursive choices found in the advice the instructor gave Yoshimi regarding what can be done to deal with the problems found in this writing. The use of the second person singular 'you' reinforces a view that bases the evaluation of writing on those actions that he alone has taken or must take in the future. 'You' need to go to the writing clinics. 'You' need to get the extra tutoring. Absent as an actor in these recommended actions are references to the instructor or even aspects of the course itself as potential sources of support (or as components in the larger process of helping Yoshimi learn to write at BMU). Although it is very likely that the discursive choices made by his instructor in constructing her comments were unconscious ones, they did convey implicit messages regarding how writing was to be learned at BMU. Writing was something you might learn with others, through writing clinics and extra tutoring, but not necessarily, it seemed, with the content instructors of the courses you were writing for.

In summary, the feedback Yoshimi received did not include the dialogue or specific recommendations for improvement and interaction with his ideas that he and other students in the study had identified as key components of useful and effective feedback for writing development. On the contrary, in this case, though the feedback may have motivated him to work harder, it also appeared to exacerbate the distance between Yoshimi and his content instructor. Yoshimi was being made to view his own writing as 'incomprehensible' and unworthy of being commented on. As a solution to this issue, he was being asked to look for help, but in a manner that discouraged him from seeing his content instructor as a valid and legitimate source of this help. If he were going to improve, it would be something that he would have to do alone. Was it really a surprise that he judged it impossible, under the circumstances, to take the time to go to Japan?

REFLEXIVITY AND THE SOCIALIZATION POWER OF FEEDBACK

Yoshimi's case provides an important glimpse at the way in which feedback events can shape how multilingual students are socialized into various beliefs and norms linked to their sense of legitimacy as L2 writers and their understanding of the factors that might explain the success and/or failure of their texts. In so doing, these findings illustrate the value of language socialization research as a means of engaging in a more reflexive way with this popular yet often misunderstood literacy act.

Indeed, by stressing the discursive impact of feedback and its role in the positioning of both L2 students and writing, language socialization research aligns itself with the process of becoming reflexive, that is, seeking to better understand what feedback practices represent for instructors and students and how they might transform and adapt these to better control their impact.

In the case of Yoshimi, a few brief comments and the discursive quality of these comments were enough to alter in fundamental ways a students' understanding of his writing, his sense of where he could turn to for support and. at a larger level, what was or was not possible for him as an L2 writer (i.e., deciding that to take the time to go back to Japan was too risky to be worth it in the calculation of the effort and time required to be able to learn to write better). One is thus encouraged to acknowledge that, even when they are not deemed useful by students, feedback practices can reinforce discursively, in small but cumulative ways, the answer to such questions as: Who belongs in universities? What are the roles and responsibilities of L2 writers? What are the relationship and potential division of labor between language support and disciplinary teaching in content courses?

At an institutional level, language socialization research lends itself to being an integral part of a reflexive process concerned with how macro-level forces are echoed in micro-level interactions (Worthram, 2008). It thus challenges institutions to take seriously the relationship that exists between larger discourses surrounding the support and integration of multilingual students, local social structures (i.e., the perception of ESL students in a school), and micro-level discursive events (i.e., feedback practices in the classroom).

For instructors like myself, reflecting on how the discursive features of feedback can mirror, reproduce, and possibly transform students' understanding of themselves as writers leaves one with a greater appreciation that behind every symbol and/or comment made are indexed decisions, beliefs, and attitudes that can be transmitted to students even if unconsciously.

For myself, as well as the novice teachers I work with as a teacher educator, I am now more than ever convinced of the importance of questioning and seeking to make explicit the ideologies that feedback may be shaping and reproducing. The goal is to foster the habit of regularly reflecting on and gaining awareness of the 'apparently neutral and commonsensical premises' (K. Hyland, 2000: 178) that are found in one's feedback by developing a greater awareness of the discursive effects of specific word choices, modes (statements versus questions), tones (authoritative versus informal), and, as in Yoshimi's case, pronoun choices.

This reflexivity also better equips instructors with the ability to consciously select and design the messages they convey through their feedback through their understanding of the specific discursive choices that can most effectively promote rather than hinder their intended messages to students. I, for example, will remain, as a result of my work with Yoshimi, forever conscious of the powerful difference between the extreme categorization and individualized exclusion found in 'your writing is incomprehensible' versus the alternative of 'I find your writing hard to understand at this point in this essay.' Such realizations are essential to the larger work of identifying how feedback practices might be adapted to better support, resist, and redefine attitudes, hierarchies, and beliefs related to scaffolding multilingual writers in higher education

From the students' perspective, the benefits of reflecting and seeking to gain greater awareness of the way feedback can position and at times disempower them is just as important. Although this awareness cannot protect them from encountering feedback whose characterization of their writing and their identities as multilingual writers is negative, as suggested by research, processes that allow individuals to grasp how power, ideologies, and identities are negotiated, enacted, and (re)produced through discourse can help these same individuals better resist or selectively appropriate roles and values being imposed on them (Kasper & Omori, 2010; Luke, 2004). In this specific case, reflexivity hence becomes a powerful means of gaining insights into language's power to 'signify and act beyond all expectation' (Malinowski & Nelson, this volume) and to make sense of the struggles, tensions, and transformations experienced through language learning experiences such as international study abroad programs (Jackson, this volume).

Learning from my own experiences with Yoshimi, I have thus encouraged multilingual students to identify, question, challenge, and/or dismiss discourses that perpetuate the myth that learning to write is something they should do on their own in the proverbial sink-or-swim fashion.[4] Similarly, I have encouraged multilingual students to find ways to communicate with their instructors and administrators their frustration with feedback that exclusively focuses on the mechanics of their writing while offering little comment on their ideas, reinforcing the notion that their ideas are worth dismissing as long as they cannot produce an idealized (and often mythical) native-like text (Belz, 2003; McGroarty, 2010).

Hounsell has noted that, compared to other dimensions of teaching such as the delivery of content or assessment procedures, feedback has frequently been relegated to a 'Cinderella status' as a 'perfunctorily treated . . . sub silencio practice . . . begrudged . . . as an administrative chore rather than a pedagogical necessity' (2007: 110). As a result of this status, I would argue that feedback has not benefited to the same extent from work in applied linguistics that has helped highlight the multiple ways in which 'language is mobilized in the service of power, and how it shapes, frames, and privileges certain representations about the world' (Chun, this volume). The case of Yoshimi strongly suggests that this is a reality that must change. If one is to truly understand the relationship between feedback and the development of academic literacy, one must go beyond a simple appreciation of its nature as a potential catalyst for grammar acquisition and the development of decontextualized writing skills. Feedback, rather, must be seen as a literacy event connected to issues of power and access and to L2 students' desire to do more than produce language that is mechanically correct and native-like (Benesch, 2001; Canagarajah, 2002; Leki, 2000). In other words, Cinderella must step out of the shadows and be made the object of a reflexive process that can promote greater sharing, collaboration, and understanding of feedback practices as discursive sites where positionalities and their underlying ideologies are evoked and thus where the work of defining writing and writers takes place. As suggested by others in this volume, such efforts are but another example of how reflexivity can inform our understanding of how specific identities are made salient (while others are not) and how these can, in fact, be imposed and/or resisted by individuals as part of the daily, everyday struggles and negotiations that make up the difficult task of being a multilingual learner (see, for example, Byrd Clark & Dervin, Lamoureux, Frame, Pérez-Milans and Soto, this volume).

In conclusion, this chapter has sought to show that much can be gained by adding to discussions of the power of feedback a sense of its role as a socialization force that can convey specific representations of the nature of L2 writing and L2 writers. Indeed, most educators and students intuitively feel the power that feedback can have on L2 students' ability to integrate and participate meaningfully in educational contexts. The findings of this study strongly suggest that this intuition is correct. Feedback does matter and does influence students' academic trajectories and their socialization into discourses and communicative practices that make up academic literacies. It may not, however, always be in the ways imagined or intended as instructors. This underscores the need for a reflexive approach to the design of feedback that can be used to scaffold multilingual students' writing without negatively affecting their sense of themselves as valued and legitimate writers in their academic communities.

NOTES

1. Pseudonyms are used to refer to all institutions and participants of this study in order to ensure their anonymity.
2. Information about further findings based on the other focal students stemming for this study can be found by referring to Séror (2008, 2009, 2010, 2011a, 2011b).
3. Yoshimi did not fail to note that this positive response was to be expected in light of the fact that these were the very sources this instructor had assigned to Yoshimi when he had been asked to change his topic for his final paper.
4. See Kubota (2002) and Leathwood (2005, 2006) for insightful critiques of this discursive construction of the learner as an independent, autonomous individual who, to the great convenience of educational institutions, is solely responsible for his or her strengths as well as weaknesses and failures.

REFERENCES

Bailey, R., & Garner, M. (2010). Is the feedback in higher education assessment worth the paper it is written on? Teachers' reflections on their practices. *Teaching in Higher Education*, 15(2), 187–198.

Belz, J. A. (2003). Identity, deficiency and first language use in foreign language education. In C. Blyth (Ed.), *The sociolinguistics of foreign-language classrooms: Contributions of the native, the near-native and the non-native speaker* (pp. 209–248). Boston: Thomson Heinle.

Benesch, S. (2001). *Critical English for academic purposes: Theory, politics, and practice*. Mahwah, NJ: Lawrence Erlbaum.

Bitchener, J. (2008). Evidence in support of written corrective feedback. *Journal of Second Language Writing*, 17(2), 102–118.

Canagarajah, A. S. (2002). *Critical academic writing and multilingual students*. Ann Arbor: University of Michigan Press.

Carless, D. (2006). Differing perceptions in the feedback process. *Studies in Higher Education*, 31(2), 219–233.
Carless, D., Salter, D., Yang, M., & Lam, J. (2011). Developing sustainable feedback practices. *Studies in Higher Education*, 36(4), 395–407.
Casanave, C. P. (2003). Looking ahead to more sociopolitically-oriented case study research in L2 writing scholarship (But should it be called 'post-process'?). *Journal of Second Language Writing*, 12, 85–102.
Creswell, J. W. (2007). *Qualitative inquiry & research design: Choosing among five approaches* (2nd ed.). Thousand Oaks, CA: Sage Publications.
Crisp, G., Palmer, E., Turnbull, D., Nettelbeck, T., Ward, L., LeCouteur, A., et al. (2009). First-year student expectations: Results from a university-wide student survey. *Journal of University Teaching & Learning Practice*, 6(1), 11–26.
Denzin, N. K., & Lincoln, Y. S. (2003). *Strategies of qualitative inquiry* (2nd ed.). Thousand Oaks, CA: Sage.
Duff, P. A. (2008). *Case study research in applied linguistics*. New York: Lawrence Erlbaum.
Duff, P. A. (2010). Language socialization. In N. Hornberger (Ed.), *Sociolinguistics and language education* (pp. 427–454). New York: Multilingual Matters.
Duff, P. A., & Talmy, S. (2011). Language socialization approaches to second language acquisition. In D. Atkinson (Ed.), *Alternative approaches to second language acquisition* (pp. 95–116). New York: Routledge.
Duff, P. A. (2012). How to carry out case study research. In A. Mackey & S. M. Gass (Eds.), *Research methods in second language acquisition* (pp. 95–116). Malden, MA: Blackwell.
Eisenhardt, K. M., & Graebner, M. E. (2007). Theory building from cases: Opportunities and challenges. *The Academy of Management Journal*, 50(1), 25–32.
El Ebyary, K., & Windeatt, S. (2010). The impact of computer-based feedback on students' written work. *International Journal of English Studies*, 10(2), 121–142.
Evaldsson, A.-C., & Cekaite, A. (2010). 'Schwedis' He can't even say Swedish'—Subverting and reproducing institutionalized norms for language use in multilingual peer groups. *Pragmatics*, 20(4), 587–604.
Ferris, D. (2010). Second language writing research and written corrective feedback in SLA: Intersections and practical applications. *Studies in Second Language Acquisition*, 32, 181–201.
Ferris, D., Brown, J., Liu, H., Eugenia, M., & Stine, A. (2011). Responding to L2 students in college writing classes: Teacher perspectives. *TESOL Quarterly*, 45(2), 207–234.
Firestone, W. A. (1993). Alternative arguments for generalizing from data as applied to qualitative research. *Educational Researcher*, 22(4), 16–23.
Flyvbjerg, B. (2006). Five misunderstandings about case-study research. *Qualitative Inquiry*, 12(2), 219–245.
Geertz, C. (2003). *The interpretation of cultures: Selected essays*. New York: Basic Books.
Hounsell, D. (2007). Towards more sustainable feedback to students. In D. Boud & N. Falchikov (Eds.), *Rethinking assessment in higher education: Learning for the longer term* (pp. 101–113). London: Routledge.
Hyland, F. (2010). Future directions in feedback on second language writing: Overview and research agenda. *International Journal of English Studies*, 10(2), 171–182.
Hyland, K. (2000). *Disciplinary discourses: Social interactions in academic writing*. New York: Longman.
Hyland, K., & Hyland, F. (2006a). *Feedback in second language writing: Contexts and issues*. New York: Cambridge University Press.
Ivanič, R., Clark, R., & Rimmershaw, R. (2000). What am I supposed to make of this? The messages conveyed to students by tutors' written comments. In M. R. Lea &

B. Stierer (Eds.), *Student writing in higher education: New contexts* (pp. 47–65). Philadelphia, PA: Open University Press.
Johnson, B., & Christensen, L. (2004). *Education research: Quantitative, qualitative, and mixed approaches* (2nd ed.). New York: Pearson.
Kasper, G., & Omori, M. (2010). Language and culture. In N. H. Hornberger & S. L. McKay (Eds.), *Sociolinguistics and language education*, Vol. 18 (pp. 455–491). Bristol, UK: Multilingual Matters.
Khoo, S.-M. (2011). Ethical globalisation or privileged internationalisation? Exploring global citizenship and internationalisation in Irish and Canadian universities. *Globalisation, Societies and Education*, 9(3–4), 337–353
Kubota, R. (2002). Japanese identities in written communication: Politics and discourses. In R. T. Donahue (Ed.), *Japanese enactments of culture and consciousness* (pp. 293–315). New York, NY: Ablex.
Kulick, D., & Schieffelin, B. (2004). Language socialization. In A. Duranti (Ed.), *A companion to linguistic anthropology* (pp. 349–368). Malden, MA: Blackwell.
Lea, M., & Street, B. (2006). The 'academic literacies' model: Theory and applications. *Theory into Practice*, 45(4), 368.
Leathwood, C. (2005). Assessment policy and practice in higher education: Purpose, standards and equity. *Assessment & Evaluation in Higher Education*, 30(3), 307–324.
Leathwood, C. (2006). Gender, equity and the discourse of the independent learner in higher education. *Higher Education*, 52(4), 611–633.
Leki, I. (2000). Writing, literacy, and applied linguistics. *Annual Review of Applied Linguistics*, 20, 99–115.
Luke, A. (2004). Notes on the future of critical discourse studies. *Critical Discourse Studies*, 1(1), 149–152.
Merriam, S. B. (1998). *Qualitative research and case study applications in education* (2nd ed.). San Francisco: Jossey-Bass.
Mökkönen, A. C. (2012). Social organization through teacher-talk: Subteaching, socialization and the normative use of language in a multilingual primary class. *Linguistics and Education*, 23(3), 310–322.
Morita, N. (2009). Language, culture, gender, and academic socialization. *Language and Education*, 23(5), 443–460.
Mustafa, R. F. (2012). Feedback on the feedback: Sociocultural interpretation of Saudi ESL learners' opinions about writing feedback. *English Language Teaching*, 5(3), 3–15.
Ochs, E. (1996). Linguistic resources for socializing humanity. In J. J. Gumperz & S. C. Levinson (Eds.), *Rethinking linguistic relativity* (pp. 407–437). Cambridge: Cambridge University Press.
Ochs, E., & Schieffelin, B. (2008). Language socialization: An historical overview. In P. A. Duff & N. H. Hornberger (Eds.), *Language socialization: Encyclopedia of language and education*. Vol. 8 (pp. 3–15) (2nd ed.). Boston: Springer.
Parr, J. M., & Timperley, H. S. (2010). Feedback to writing, assessment for teaching and learning and student progress. *Assessing Writing*, 15(2), 68–85.
Séror, J. (2008). *Socialization in the margins: Second language writers and feedback practices in university content courses*. Unpublished doctoral dissertation. University of British Columbia, Vancouver.
Séror, J. (2009). Institutional forces and L2 writing feedback in higher education. *Canadian Modern Language Review*, 66(2), 203–232.
Séror, J. (2010). *Second language socialization for language learning and classroom management*. Paper presented at the TESL Ontario Conference, Toronto, Ontario, Canada.
Séror, J. (2011a). Alternative sources of feedback and second language writing development in university content courses. *Canadian Journal of Applied Linguistics (CJAL)/Revue canadienne de linguistique appliquée (RCLA)*, 14(1), 118–143.

Séror, J. (2011b). Exploring the contributions of second language socialization research for language teaching. *Contact Research Symposium Issue*, 37(2), 17–32.
Silverman, D. (2004). *Doing qualitative research: A practical handbook* (2nd ed.). Thousand Oaks, CA: Sage.
Stake, R. (1995). *The art of case study research*. Thousand Oaks: CA: Sage.
Stake, R. (2006). *Multiple case study analysis*. New York: Guilford Press.
Sutton, P. (2012). Conceptualizing feedback literacy: Knowing, being, and acting. *Innovations in Education and Teaching International*, 49(1), 31–40.
Suzuki, W. (2012). Written languaging, direct correction, and second language writing revision. *Language Learning*, 62(4), 1110–1133.
Swain, M. (2006). Languaging, agency and collaboration in advanced language proficiency. In H. Byrnes (Ed.), *Advanced language learning: The contribution of Halliday and Vygotsky* (pp. 95-108). London: Continuum.
Talmy, S. (2008). The cultural productions of the ESL student at tradewinds high: Contingency, multidirectionality, and identity in L2 socialization. *Applied Linguistics*, 29(4), 619–644.
Thomas, D. R. (2006). A general inductive approach for analyzing qualitative evaluation data. *American Journal of Evaluation*, 27(2), 237–246.
Truscott, J. (2007). The effect of error correction on learners' ability to write accurately. *Journal of Second Language Writing*, 16(4), 255–272.
Weaver, M. R. (2006). Do students value feedback? Student perceptions of tutors' written responses. *Assessment and Evaluation in Higher Education*, 31(3), 379–394.
Worthram, S. (2008). Linguistic anthropology. In B. Spolsky & F. Hult (Eds.), *Handbook of educational linguistics* (pp. 83–97). Malden, MA: Blackwell.
Yin, R. (2003). *Applications of case study research* (2nd ed.). Thousand Oaks, CA: Sage.
Zuengler, J., & Cole, K. (2005). Language socialization and second language learning. In E. Hinkel (Ed.), *Handbook of research in second language teaching and learning* (pp. 301–316). Mahwah, NJ: Lawrence Erlbaum.

3 Reflexivity and Self-Presentation in Multicultural Encounters
Making Sense of Self and Other

Alex Frame[1]

Reflexivity is a process underlying all interpersonal communication and one that appears particularly important in multicultural encounters due to its possible influence on the way individuals seek to play on different cultural identities, during such encounters, both consciously and unconsciously. On a first level of analysis, reflexivity will thus be considered in this chapter as a fundamental communication process. On a second level, reflexivity will be approached as a competence to be gained in a bid for communicative 'transparency' or 'efficiency,' thus echoing normative discourse about the concept often found in social science research (e.g., Tsai, 2012), particularly in literature dealing with second language acquisition (e.g., Turner, 2010) and intercultural competence training (e.g., Spencer-Oatey, 2009: 171–242; Jackson, Chapter 1 of this volume). When discussing reflexivity on this second level, I will thus be using the term in a sense close to what the editors of this volume define as awareness (as applied to second language acquisition and intercultural communication competence). On a third level, I will evoke the reflexivity inherent in the research process itself, both on the part of the researcher and the researched (cf. Holmes, Chapter 4 of this volume, for an excellent discussion of this), underlining the inherent subjectivity of any such undertaking. Understanding reflexivity as a basic communication process, I will argue, can help us apply it in practical terms on the second and third levels by showing its limits and by taking into account its specific importance in what we as academics describe as multicultural encounters but also in the ways we go about studying them.

To illustrate the processes at work, the chapter will cite examples and experiences from a field study I carried out as part of my PhD (Frame, 2008), looking at interpersonal interactions within the European student association AEGEE (European Student Forum). AEGEE is a pan-European student body, founded in 1980, that aims to promote European integration and cultural exchange. Its 13,000-strong network is made up of students and young adults in some 200 locals situated in university cities in 40 countries on and around the European continent.[2] In accordance with the dominant beliefs of its founding members about the political conditions necessary for the European ideal to succeed (Biancheri, 1996), the association has no national level. Rather, local satellites are coordinated directly by the executive committee (*comité directeur*), based in Brussels, and delegates regularly travel to meetings around the extended European continent in order to take part in network-wide projects, attend biannual congresses, to perform other functions. My interest in AEGEE was linked to this non-national philosophy since I was seeking, from a symbolic interactionist standpoint, to observe the degree to which members referred to different identities (both national and non-national) in trying to make sense of one another's discourse and behavior in interpersonal communication. One of my hypotheses when studying AEGEE was that national identities were important in this communication process, despite the ideological standpoint of the association's founders and leaders and the lack of a national level in its structure. My study was based largely on participant observation at congresses and so-called European events, as well as on interviews with informants of different nationalities. I will quote AEGEE to discuss how reflexivity and multimodality shape the way we represent, categorize, and communicate with others in multilingual or multicultural contexts. As with any context involving interactions between people carrying different group identities, whether based on gender, age, sexual preference, ethnic classifications, nationality, or other differentiating criteria, questions of power are never far below the surface (cf. Lamoureux, Chapter 5 in this volume). In this respect, AEGEE is no exception despite its espoused ideals of equality, solidarity, and European integration. Critical theory has taught us to reject universalizing discourse and value systems and has underlined the hegemonic power of linguistic and social norms; yet such norms and value-oriented representations are part and parcel of the way we go about experiencing the world and our interactions with one another. By focusing on reflexivity as a communication process, I will try to explain and illustrate just why this is the case, before trying to link these considerations, at the end of the chapter, to intercultural communication theories such as communication accommodation theory (Gallois et al., 2005; Giles & Ogay, 2007) or uncertainty and anxiety management theory (Gudykunst & Kim, 1992; Gudykunst, 1998). Finally, I will evoke ways in which I think these theories can be used to help students of intercultural communication to (1) gain a better understanding of the importance of reflexivity in the communication process and (2) increase their own critical distance and adopt a more reflexive stance in their communication practices.

REFLEXIVITY IN INTERPERSONAL COMMUNICATION

As a process, reflexivity underlies all human social interactions and can have an impact upon them. Much can be gained, in terms of understanding, by taking into account this process, not only in ethnographic research protocols, in the language classroom, and in intercultural competence training/education but also in many other social activities, such as job interviews, online interactions, or chess matches. Applied to social interactions, reflexivity refers to the capacity of people to reflect on what they are saying or doing, analyze the possible consequences, and attempt to adjust their behavior as a result. In his collected papers, published posthumously under the title, *Mind, Self and Society from the Perspective of a Social Behaviorist* (1934), George Herbert Mead indirectly explores this process, through the associated notions of self-consciousness and role taking. For Mead, communication is what makes the mind and thinking possible because humans learn to see the world in terms of symbols, by interiorizing gestures, through communication.[3] The faculty of reflexivity is thus a social product of human communication, as well as a key process underlying it. Role taking, for Mead, is what people do when they subconsciously project themselves into another person's social role or position within an interaction in order to assess their own actions or words 'through the eyes' of that person. It is an ongoing process, allowing each of us to anticipate and adapt our behaviors—our 'symbolic acts' in Mead's terminology—depending on the way we expect other people to react to them.

Arguably, role taking in itself is a *reflexive* process because, for Mead, normally socialized adults are thus continuously (yet not necessarily consciously) 'putting themselves in other people's shoes,' anticipating—with differing degrees of success—what they consider to be likely reactions to their words and deeds and endeavoring to adapt the way they communicate accordingly. From a symbolic interactionist standpoint, the fact that all interpersonal communication involves, to some extent, this process of consciously or unconsciously anticipating the reactions of others justifies the idea that the notion of reflexivity can be useful in conceptualizing human communication in general. However, since much role taking takes place subconsciously, such a broad definition of reflexivity, however helpful it may be to understand basic communication processes, is quite distant from the notion of reflexive awareness in intercultural encounters, whereby individuals consciously focus on differences they attribute to themselves and others. In this chapter, I will thus be using the notion of reflexivity, applied to interactions, to mean a more conscious, or mindful, (*infra*) form of role taking, in which individuals (stop and) think *consciously* about the possible impact of what they are doing and saying, depending on their representations of others, and adjust their communicative behavior accordingly[4]. This is not to suggest, however, that all reflexivity is conscious nor indeed that it is possible to establish empirically a clear distinction between conscious and unconscious forms of role taking in interactions. Indeed, the very process of soliciting representations and impressions from informants, by encouraging them to adopt a post hoc reflexive stance, can itself lead them to reconstruct many of the representations and thought processes they report, even when they are trying to do so in good faith and objectively.

Taking this narrower definition of reflexivity, we may be justified in asking how large a role (conscious) reflexivity/reflexive awareness plays in interpersonal communication. Writing about intercultural communication, Scollon and Scollon highlight the importance of social structure and preexisting identities in the way individuals behave socially:

> The idea of habitus is used to capture the idea of social practice. That is to say, our theoretical position is that *we do not* largely act out of conscious purpose and planning. We act as we do, not because we want to accomplish X, Y, or Z, but because we are the sort of person who normally does that sort of thing. (Scollon & Scollon, 2001: 169)

There seems to be little scope for reflexivity in such a vision of *normal* communication, where actors are seen to simply act out their social roles, at least in certain situations. Yet this does not exclude a certain degree of more or less conscious coordination, as interactional sociolinguist John Gumperz points out, underlining the way in which definitions of situations, identities, and meanings are negotiated intersubjectively:

> A successful interaction begins with each speaker talking in a certain mode, using certain contextualisation cues. Participants, then, by the verbal style in which they respond and the listenership cues they produce, implicitly signal their agreement or disagreement; thus they 'tune into' the other's way of speaking. Once this has been done, and once a conversational rhythm has been established, both participants can reasonably assume that they have successfully negotiated a frame of interpretation, i.e. they have agreed on what activity is being enacted and how it is to be conducted. (Gumperz, 1982: 167)

Interpersonal communication thus appears to involve both some degree of intersubjective negotiation and co-construction, but also semiautomated phases in which people subconsciously reproduce or refer to mental schemas and shared repertoires (Wenger, 1999: 82) of cultural and situationally grounded knowledge and representations, once certain basic choices have been made and mutually established. Until this 'frame of interpretation' evolves or is called into question and, depending on a whole host of contextual factors, including power relations, internal and external constraints, the nature of the situation, and the relationship between the individuals concerned, and the like, participants in the interaction may (but will not necessarily) content themselves to 'act out their roles' without worrying consciously about how to make a good impression, how best to get their point accepted, and so on. This is not to say that their behavior is dictated by social structure, simply that role identities, interaction rituals, internalized situational constraints and the like are commonly used to guide behavior and to comfort the impression of mutual predictability in the encounter in order to reduce participants' needs for conscious effort, both in understanding what is going on and in thinking about what to do or say next.

However, at times, participants can become conscious of this process and self-conscious,[5] thinking reflexively about their communicative behavior. This may notably be associated more particularly with three types of situation or behavior:

1. Managing face and accountability
2. Managing misunderstandings
3. Intended agency/'strategic' behavior

Erving Goffman's work on 'face' and 'facework' (1992, 1973) highlights the importance of reflexivity in situations where communication 'breaks down' and where perceived threats to one another's face lead people to focus consciously on the significance of what is being said and done in terms of identities and the intersubjective relationship.[6] Strategies dealing with 'face threatening acts' by trying to justify or account for communication behavior represent clear examples of reflexivity being used in everyday interactions, typically to subsequently analyze behavior deemed unsuitable or problematic. Participants seek to present narratives to explain or justify what they did or said, making them 'accountable'[7] in terms of their identities, interactional norms, the preceding conversation, and so on.

Reflexivity thus tends to surface in reaction to something happening that has been judged to be *abnormal* by one or all the parties involved. This may concern the relationship between the participants, but it may equally be linked to misunderstandings that crop up, which participants seek to resolve by going back over what was said and done and how they understood it. From an intercultural perspective, Jan Blommaert (1991: 24) analyzes a misunderstanding between himself and a Tanzanian colleague, surrounding the meaning of 'having a coffee.' For Blommaert, in the context of a semi-professional meeting between university colleagues in Belgium, this meant drinking a cup of coffee, whereas for his colleague, it meant chewing coffee beans, which was the tradition when welcoming a guest in Tanzania. Blommaert recalls that several exchanges were necessary to identify and resolve this lexical misunderstanding.

Yet reflexivity also comes into play in interpersonal communication when individuals actively seek to influence the course or the outcome of an encounter by consciously behaving in a certain way. Questions of structure and agency have been the source of many debates in sociology and elsewhere. It was suggested earlier that individuals very often tend to use social structure to guide their behavior and to show themselves to be predictable to one another during much of their communication. However, reflexivity is the faculty that allows them to attempt to adjust their behavior consciously in order to try to have an impact on the other people involved in the interaction—for example, to obtain agreement, to seek compliance, to work on improving a relationship, to reject an idea, and so on. This is not to suggest that individuals are able either to fully control their own behavior (let alone that of others) or to master the sheer complexity of all the factors affecting behavior during an interaction. Crucially, however, it suggests that they at least *try*. As Peter Burke points out:

> In light of [the nature of interactions], it seems to make little sense to speak of 'rational action' or 'planned behavior.' Instead we need to talk about the goal states that our behavior accomplishes in spite of disturbances, disruptions, interruptions, accidents, and the contrivances of others. . . . A variety of means is always available to accomplish some goal, and if one doesn't work, we try another. (Burke, 2004: 6)

In a similar way, George McCall and Jerry Simmons talk about long-term 'agendas' that give a general orientation to actions (McCall & Simmons, 1966: 241–248), goals that participants seek to obtain by trying to exploit perceived available 'opportunity structures,' themselves linked to the situation at hand, or what can also be defined as the 'figurative context' (Frame, 2013: 173–246). Intentionality and agency are thus limited here to conscious *attempts* by individuals, at a given moment, to influence an interaction in a certain way, based on their understanding and representations of the situation, the other people involved, and of the underlying context.

One of the ways in which reflexivity may be brought to bear on an encounter is when participants seek consciously to give a certain image of themselves (self-presentation strategies). Once again, the basic (reflexive) process is that which is at work in interpersonal communication in general, as people use role taking to produce behaviors that they expect to appear acceptable (or not) for others, in light of their salient identities in the context. However, this process may become more conscious when individuals actively try to highlight some identities rather than others. This may be the case, for example, when members of minority groups feel the need to position themselves in relation to the dominant majority identity (*infra*) and are more generally motivated by considerations of face. Identity Theory (Stryker & Burke, 2000; Burke et al., 2003) seeks to describe how people try to validate their different *social* (group) identities, *role* identities, or *person* identities in order to manage self-esteem and interpersonal predictability. By widening the scope of this theory and applying it to multiple identities (Burke, 2003; Frame & Boutaud, 2010), we are also able to account for 'strategic' performances of certain behaviors on the part of individuals in the way they seek to manage identities.[8]

During interactions, different identities are chosen and made salient for a variety of reasons. Very often, these include the situation (role identities), questions of predictability, and desires for inclusion or exclusion. People may also have identities 'forced' upon them either because they become salient in a given situation or because others insist on evoking them. As a Brit living in France, moreover as a scholar of interpersonal communication, I have become keenly aware of this process. On occasion, I consciously play on my national identity, for example, when seeking to appear legitimate in talking about the UK or when encountering a fellow expatriate. At other times, I tend to avoid drawing attention to this particular facet of my identity, for instance, during an anonymous discussion in the supermarket. In some circumstances, the identity becomes almost unavoidable, for example, in front of a France–versus-England rugby match. I may also choose to draw attention to my foreign identity if I'm aware of having made a syntactical error or of showing my ignorance about some element of French pop culture in order to avoid coming across as an *inculte*.[9]

It is important to note that, although we may reason in terms of identities, these are very often symbolized and conveyed by identity *traits*, which themselves are open to negotiation and interpretation. Identity traits can be defined as particular characteristics or attributes, discursive positions, speech styles, gestures, postures, expressions, clothing styles, and the like that are associated with particular identities. Thus, if I want to underline my Englishness (identity), I may play on my accent (identity trait), for example, by choosing an English pronunciation of English names or places when speaking French. Or I may attribute to myself a particular characteristic that I explicitly associate with this national identity, often in the form of a joke such as punctuality, reserve, strange humor, lack of culinary finesse, familiarity with dull weather, and so on.

Identity traits need to be approached multimodally, focusing on what is said but also on how it is said, with what tone, posture, expression, and so on. Indeed, when this is the case, an identity trait explicitly evoked may in fact be designed to suggest another, complementary trait that (we hope) will be associated with the same identity. For instance, I may make a joke about the English always being prepared for rain when offering an acquaintance my umbrella, while (vainly) hoping to appear gallant and organized! Of course, none of this is specific to national identities. The way we choose to dress is often designed to underline such and such an attribute of a particular (desired) social identity to which we may either belong or aspire to belong (age, sex, profession, ethnic group). In terms of intergroup stigmatization, as a civil servant in France, I often avoid disclosing my professional identity to people I don't know for fear of being represented in the light of negative media stereotypes, notably by people working in the private sector.

I carried out my PhD fieldwork studying interactions within the European student association AEGEE, based on the symbolic interactionist theoretical framework just described. Inspired by Identity Theory's vision of multiple social, role, and person identities and seeing the association as a collection of individuals with various shared and differentiating identities, I set about observing and trying to detect the ways in which members appeared to (consciously or unconsciously) employ various identities and identity traits in their interactions with one another. During the participant observation, I endeavored to remain sensitive to the multimodal aspects of communication, including accents (real or faked), gestures, facial expressions, and the

88 *Alex Frame*

like, as well as the power relations that seemed to be expressed through facework. I then discussed with informants certain examples of behavior I had observed, trying to link them to the context in which they were performed, in order to confront my interpretations with their own perspectives.

During this fieldwork, I often observed members referring explicitly to national identities because they sought to understand one another's behavior based on (foreign) national cultures. They would joke about or seriously discuss national identity traits attributed to one another or, more often, to absent third parties, who were presented as helping to understand or justify given behaviors or discourses or discourse styles. At other times, differentiating national identities seemed to fade into the background, replaced by salient common identities (student, associative, pro-European, . . .), which could be used as alternative sources of predictability and which underlined a sense of collective belonging. In situations in which the formal setting was clearly defined (e.g., plenary congress sessions) and/or in which the activity at hand gave each participant a set role as an association member (e.g., workshops), people appeared globally less likely to mobilize national identities, unless the person spoke with a strong accent, had a particularly marked national appearance, or did or said something that could plausibly be attributed to national culture, for instance.

Power relations were also apparent in the way members would play on certain identity traits, seemingly in order to give themselves legitimacy or to try to cultivate a particular image, often on an insider-versus-outsider basis. A person who had taken on responsibilities in the association might refer to them in passing, or members of a certain group might (consciously?) use jargon in a way that symbolically underlined their shared membership of one of the association's internal thematic working groups, for example, thus setting them apart from the other people present.

As I report in my PhD thesis (Frame, 2008: 513–515), I observed what I analyzed to be an instance of this type of power-related figurative behavior when taking part in an editorial team working on a news bulletin during an AEGEE congress in Istanbul. The editorial team was made up of about 10 people of different nationalities who had volunteered to produce a daily newsletter, entitled *M(Eye) Agora*, relating the events and providing opinion and reactions on what took place during the four-day congress. This anecdote concentrates on four figures:

1. Gunther,[10] the German-born editor in chief of the newsletter, an experienced oldie in the association, who worked as a professional magazine editor in Germany. He had been in charge of the recent 20-year anniversary publication of the association's annual review.
2. Jean, a contributor to the newsletter, also an oldie, of French nationality living in Germany and working as a business consultant.
3. Barbora, a contributor to the newsletter, having recently joined the association, a communication student of Hungarian nationality, hoping to become a journalist.

4. Myself, a contributor to the newsletter, having joined the association two years previously explicitly for the purpose of my PhD in communication, and a British-born university lecturer in English, living and working in France. I was also a member of the Culture Working Group and a workshop leader at the congress in question.

I had agreed to work on this newsletter after being approached by Jean, whom I had met at two previous congresses. Gunther and he were friends and well-known members of the network. Within the group, they worked closely together, often conversing in German despite the fact that English was very much the lingua franca of the association and the language of the publication and that they both spoke English fluently. At the first meeting, Gunther issued instructions to the group, distributing tasks and warning contributors of the importance of respecting deadlines and working efficiently. He identified me (the only native English speaker in the group) as a resource person who could reread and correct articles, along with himself, should the other contributors desire this. Jean spontaneously acted as a coordinator between the contributors because he already knew many of them. He reported back to Gunther, who concentrated more on the editing, layout, and integration of the different texts.

Barbora was the only other member of the 10-person group to speak German. She admitted feeling very nervous about writing articles that were going to be read by hundreds of people (there were over 800 attendees at the congress). She said she hoped that she would be able to contribute to other publications for the association because this was good work experience for her as a prospective journalist. Compared to the generally relaxed and friendly atmosphere in the association, she said that she found the editorial team 'very German' in their approach, explaining that by this she meant organized and serious and adding that this way of working did not bother her unduly. I myself felt slightly out of place in an environment where I could not understand the language spoken by the two leaders. I was happy to have been asked to join the group and wanted to be included in the decision making, yet I felt that the use of German was partly a way to exclude me from this. Different languages were frequently spoken within the association, but AEGEE etiquette usually required people to look for a language common to all those present in a conversation and to use English if no other lingua franca was found (Frame, 2009).

My misgivings were strengthened by an encounter with Gunther, when I presented him my first article, slightly after the deadline he had imposed. Although I had respected the word limit, he immediately shortened it by almost half, deleting or rewriting several sections, while voicing his (moderately favorable) opinion on its style and contents. I vainly referred to my experience of writing articles in an academic context (identity trait) in a conscious bid to defend my legitimacy (and pride!). He explained to me that he was used to this kind of writing in the context of the association (a reference to his status of oldie), that

Table 3.1 Identities, Identity Traits, and Behavioral Manifestations Associated with Gunther

Identity	Type of identity	Identity traits performed	Behavioral manifestations
AEGEE oldie	Social	Hierarchical Relationships + Seriousness + Professionalism +	• Little consultation • Use of German • Constraints imposed • Finished texts treated as material to be reworked
Professional editor	Social		
Editor of publication	Role		
German nationality	Social		

it took real professional experience (reference to his own professional identity), and that it was not at all like writing for an academic publication.

In this situation, Gunther seemed to be playing on several social and role identities, more or less consciously, in order to impact on the situation and the relationships with myself and other members of the group. The main identities and identity traits used by Gunther, according to my analysis of the situation, are shown in Table 3.1.

The combination of identities I attributed to Gunther was associated with certain identity traits that appeared salient in the context, themselves reflected in the behavioral practices performed. For example, the fact that he imposed strict guidelines (behavioral manifestation) was compatible with all of the identity traits listed here and could be justified by his role of editor (role identity) and possibly also by his experience in this domain and in the association (social identities).

This discussion raises three important points. First, it illustrates the importance and the limits of adopting a reflexive stance as a researcher attempting to carry out participant observation as a method. As described in Chapter 5 (by Lamoureux) and elsewhere in this volume, studies that employ this methodological can of worms are inevitably marked by our subjectivity as researchers and by our limits and sensibilities, even when we try to cross-check our analyses with several informants. These limits are possibly all the more powerful in a context we describe as 'intercultural,' though not simply because of the supposed cultural distance from the subjects we are studying because academics working in this field generally expect to encounter cultural differences. However, many studies in intercultural communication tend to focus solely on national cultures and identities, whereas other identities can often reveal themselves to be just as important to the subjects being observed (Frame & Boutaud, 2010).

Second, even if, from a symbolic interactionist point of view, we consider that Gunther's behavior as reported here involves role taking and strategies of self-presentation (Goffman, 1973), this discussion does not enable us to establish with any degree of confidence to what extent this behavior is *consciously* reflexive. It seems likely that even the people concerned, whatever their reflexive capacity may be, would be very hard-pressed to provide a categorical answer to this question. For instance, we might argue that Gunther's decision to speak German is the result of role taking (a reflexive procedure) in that we can assume that Gunther has thought (on some level) about the identities of the people present and has chosen his language according to their capacity to understand it. However, the conscious motivation for this, as well as its intended 'meaning,' is much less clear. Has Gunther thought consciously about the situation and planned his choice of language? Might he be wanting to make a point about the supposed expert in English not being able to speak another major European language? Maybe he has always had a habit of speaking German with Jean and does so because the conversation does not concern me? Or, indeed, maybe his choice is motivated by a combination of these factors, among others.

Third, even if we were to accept that my (extravagantly oversimplified) interpretation of the situation as presented here were relatively close to other participants' own interpretations of the encounter, it appears impossible to isolate identities and identity traits from one another and from the context in which they are performed or enacted. If we accept the hypothesis that Gunther is acting in a way that seeks to underline hierarchical distance between himself and the other members of the group, should this be attributed to his role identity of editor, his position of oldie, his professional status, or something else entirely? Indeed, some participants might attribute it to his individual character (a 'person identity' in the terminology of Identity Theory) and others to his national identity or his age, or other factors depending on their idiosyncratic representations and stereotypes. If the situation were to change, would Gunther exhibit the same behavior? Going one step further, it appears plausible that his actions are not governed by one particular identity but indeed by the combination of identities activated in the context. Hence this supposed trait of underlining hierarchy may be privileged precisely because it appears compatible (or at least not contradictory) with several of his salient identities in this particular context. The study I carried out into AEGEE culture underlines the idea that many cultural traits attributed to the association appear inherently contradictory. For example, although hierarchy, seriousness, and professionalism do appear to be espoused values in some contexts, conviviality, irony, fun, solidarity, and equality can be observed as central traits attributed to association culture in other circumstances (Frame, 2008: 527 et seq.). From a postmodern, poststructuralist point of view, such a fragmented conception of an incoherent, constantly evolving organizational culture, where the traits and values espoused depend heavily on the figurative context and the sets of identities activated simultaneously, is close to Joanne Martin's 'fragmentation perspective' of cultures in organizations (Martin, 1992). Furthermore, the idea that identity traits feed off one another dialogically, in their sometimes ambivalent, sometimes coherent relationship to an individual's various activated identities, can encourage us to reject approaches that limit themselves to considering one particular identity at a time in favor of analyses of individuals' self-presentation strategies and interactions based on the concept of *intersectionality* (Choo & Ferree, 2010; Walby et al., 2012). However, even here it would be important to underline the powerful influence of the figurative context on the way multiple identities and identity traits are performed simultaneously by subjects in different situations (Frame & Boutaud, 2010).

MULTIMODALITY AND REFLEXIVITY IN MULTICULTURAL CONTEXTS

Having asserted the fundamental importance of reflexivity in interpersonal communication, both through conscious reflection on communication behavior and subconscious role taking, I will now move on to discuss the particular ways in which this specifically affects situations involving individuals who represent different national, cultural, or linguistic groups. To do this, I will consider the way certain theories of intercultural communication refer, implicitly or explicitly, to intrasubjective reflexive processes. As an academic studying instances of what I define as intercultural communication, these theories contribute to structuring my vision of what I am analyzing and of the importance of reflexivity therein, and this subjective vision is necessarily inherent in both my research activity and in the following discussion.

During encounters with people of different nationalities, interpreting what is going on and trying to respect considerations of face and politeness (Spencer-Oatey, 2000) very often implies a conscious effort to try to interiorize, or at least to grasp in some form, what one sees as their point of view. Not surprisingly, reflexivity is frequently listed among those skills that favor a high level of intercultural competence (e.g., Spencer-Oatey & Franklin, 2009: 171–242; see Jackson Chapter 1 in this volume), and indeed many intercultural training programs explicitly seek to encourage the capacity of their students to take a step back and analyze not only their own behaviors and those of their partner(s) but also the ethnocentricity of their stances.

In their work on Anxiety and Uncertainty Management Theory (AUM), William Gudykunst and Young Yun Kim (Gudykunst & Kim, 1992; Gudykunst, 1998) insist on the importance of *mindfulness* in interactions. Mindfulness is characterized as the state of reduced uncertainty and anxiety that allows individuals to remain attentive to what is going on in order to be alert to the possibility of misunderstandings. From our point of view, the state of mindfulness appears particularly propitious to (conscious) reflexive processes because these may be hindered either by too little uncertainty and attentiveness or by too much anxiety, which further reduces our (already limited) subjective capacity to reason in a detached way. In this sense, we can read the central propositions of AUM as a theory based on the subject's capacity for reflexivity, *ceteris paribus*. AUM's insistence on 'communicating with strangers,' where 'strangers' covers both new acquaintances and foreigners, in turn underlines a link between acculturation and reflexivity. When an individual seeks to become accepted within a new group, not only does he/she not necessarily know what to expect ('predictive uncertainty') or how to interpret what is going on ('behavioral uncertainty'), he/she often attempts to fit in, to do the right thing, or at least not to stand out, and doing this very often entails a relatively high level of reflexivity. This is the case for people trying to understand, copy, and master foreign codes and communication rituals but also for new recruits to a company or organization, children in a new school, and such circumstances. This level of conscious reflexivity can be expected to gradually drop over time (though not necessarily in a purely linear fashion) because socialization occurs within the group and semiautomated reflexes develop, together with a specific *repertoire* of past actions and experiences, that the individual associates with (constantly evolving) group culture and upon which behavior and interpretations can be based.

However, differences between primary (absolute) and secondary (relative) socialization processes, between enculturation in children and acculturation in adults, can also have an impact on our capacity to mobilize culturally based identity traits for identity and facework purposes. Since ethnocentricity can be seen as a limit to reflexivity, then deeply ingrained, unconscious primary socialization behaviors, beliefs, and values would appear harder to call into question than cultural traits assimilated later in life, that is, those that are learned when an individual begins to frequent a new social group and that are perceived as different to previously taken-for-granted norms. Because the individual thus tends to have less conscious purchase on his or her primary socialization culture (Berger & Luckmann, 1991: 129), their *habitus* in Bourdieu's terms, reflexive behavior, becomes more of a challenge when the individual changes national contexts or encounters a group that does not share the dominant national doxa, *despite* the fact that he/she may be more *conscious* of the need for reflexivity in such situations. One of the reasons for this (along with affect, symbolic and ethical factors, among others) is the complexity of multimodal communication. Whereas verbal communication is generally perceived as the dominant mode and traditional education programs focus primarily on language acquisition (namely lexical, syntactical, and phonological codes), speakers are also attentive to other paraverbal and nonverbal aspects of communication. Prosody, intonation, extraverbal utterances (tutting, blowing raspberries, clearing one's throat, etc.), along with bodily codes, such as facial expressions, gestures, posture, proxemics, and bodily contact, and also peripheral codes, such as dress codes, are all taken into account when interpreting one another's behavior, along with the sociolinguistic knowledge and behavioral codes (protocols and rituals associated with specific situations and social categories and groups) that prescribe what is considered appropriate when. These elements all go to make up what interactional sociolinguists such as Dell Hymes (1984) or John Gumperz (1982) call 'communication competence,' not to be confused with 'intercultural communication competence.'[11] Thus, even when people are aware of the existence of cultural differences and of the reflexively adapt language and other codes of which they are more or less conscious, they are very likely unaware of other codes. Misunderstandings may arise on the basis of these unsuspected codes, although the people surprised or offended by their transgression may themselves be no more consciously aware of the reason why a particular behavior should be unexpected or deemed inappropriate. At times, divergences in codes may result in seeming contradictions or double binds, where what is said explicitly is reinterpreted depending on what is done, or vice versa. This may result in misunderstandings or value judgments that are often linked to stereotypes, but in other cases, incoherencies may well simply be seen as idiosyncrasies, attributed to the other person's character or foreign identity.[12]

This discussion inevitably raises questions of power once again because it underlines the way in which the negotiation of a linguistic and cultural frame of reference can advantage or disadvantage the different parties, both symbolically and semiotically, in terms of their communication competence.[13] Fredrik Barth (1969) evokes the importance of such choices, notably linked to underlying intergroup relations, and Carmel Camilleri (1990) describes the different 'identity strategies' that can be adopted, more or less consciously, by members of immigrant minorities in reaction to hegemonic identities and cultural practices of dominant groups. Through reflexively adopted postures or self-presentation strategies, explains Camilleri, members of minority national groups in society can thus seek to underline their national origins in a bid to gain recognition for that identity or to justify different behaviors or, on the other hand, to distance themselves from their 'migrant' identity by conforming actively to norms of the majority host culture and declaring a preference for this group. Such preference can be not only reflected in explicit declarations but also conveyed through adopted mannerisms, speech style, dress style, and other means. Furthermore, Camilleri also points out that individuals very often change strategies depending on the social context and perceived symbolic (self-esteem) or material gains, ranging from one extreme to the other, with a whole variety of intermediate positions.

Finally, Communication Accommodation Theory (CAT) also deals with questions of convergence and divergence between different (multimodal) communication styles, linked to considerations of intergroup and interpersonal relations (Gallois et al., 2005; Giles & Ogay, 2007). Once again, strategies can be more or less conscious, ranging from intentional mimesis or distancing snubs to unconscious reproductions of postures or gestures, or unwitting accentuation of differences in communication style. The theory describes different degrees and logics of accommodation (Gallois et al., 2005: 141), sometimes associated with a lack of reflexivity, which can have repercussions on the relationship between the different parties in an encounter. These include:

- *Overaccommodation,* whereby one party overadapts to the other's perceived lack of communication competence, for example, by adopting *foreigner talk* (Smith et al., 1991) when addressing a foreigner who speaks their language well enough to feel belittled by this 'good intention.'
- *Underaccommodation,* consisting of a failure to adapt one's communication style to that of the other person, which can sometimes be interpreted as showing a lack of interest or consideration toward them. Whereas overaccommodating consists in overcompensating for (imagined) cultural differences and can be interpreted as patronizing, underaccommodation may give the impression that a person cannot be bothered to make an effort to communicate clearly and to help a foreigner understand what is being said.
- *Counteraccommodation,* when an individual heightens the differentiation between their speech style and that of the other party, which can be interpreted as a put-down, especially between members of groups that occupy different places in the social hierarchy (such as in the case of class differences or minority/majority relations). For example, in the AEGEE newsletter situation, I interpreted Gunther's choice of language as an instance of counteraccommodation, designed to exclude me from conversations.

Such theories, often applied to intercultural communication, can help us to conceptualize and discuss the importance of reflexivity from an operational point of view, notably for educational and training purposes. By analyzing real-life situations with students, based on their own experiences as foreign nationals or minority group members, especially when they have felt disregarded (underaccommodation), have had the impression of being 'talked down to' (overaccommodation), or rejected (counteraccommodation), it is possible to encourage them to think about not only their own experience but also how they might have been perceived by other parties, as well as the behaviors they themselves might adopt in situations in which the roles were reversed. This can lead to a discussion of reflexivity and mindfulness as ideals, which can be aimed at in such situations, and of the factors that may encourage and inhibit them.

CONCLUSION

Interpersonal communication is a semiautomated, multimodal activity in which participants consciously and unconsciously negotiate a shared frame of reference in relation to existing and evolving cultural norms. Within this framework, they seek to give a certain image of themselves, based on multiple identities and a repertoire of shared knowledge and representations, while sometimes trying to influence others and the outcome of the encounter. The process of negotiation is all the more delicate and often more conscious in encounters involving individuals of different nationalities and cultural groups because participants may be more aware of differences in knowledge, representations, and communication codes.

Understanding the role of reflexivity in the communication process can help us to better apprehend its importance from the perspective of intercultural education or second language acquisition, both in the first and second degree. Thus students should be encouraged to be reflexive, that is, to think about the ways in which they are communicating, to push back the limits of their ethnocentricity, to be mindful and aware of differences in representations and communication styles. Yet besides simply being an aim or necessary precaution, developing an understanding of reflexivity can prepare students to approach an intercultural encounter as a socially situated activity, helping them to anticipate the reflexivity of the different parties involved, not only the differences in communication style but the way participants may try to adapt their communication styles based on their representations of the other parties. In the same way that an ethnographer needs to develop an understanding of the impact of his or her presence and interactions with the subjects under study, students of intercultural communication should be aware of the impressions they give to the people they meet, as well as how these impressions may have an impact on their behavior, for example, when both parties reciprocally *overaccommodate* one another. Or when, as Earley and Ang describe (2003: 101–102), a newly arrived manager on an overseas posting at first receives very deferential treatment from the local subordinates and then gradually, over the next few months, increasingly is treated much more like any local manager. Finally, an understanding of critical theory and the associated implications of language choices and communication styles can alert students of intercultural communication—as well as managers and negotiators—to both the symbolic (identity) and semiotic (meaning-construction) aspects of implicit or explicit power struggles during various types of encounters, as well as the suffering and resentment that they may provoke.

To go beyond the comparative approaches to intercultural communication, centered on national differences, there is an urgent need to focus on the inherently reflexive and multimodal communication processes underlying the interactions themselves. The concept of *mindfulness* (AUM) and different types of *accommodation* (CAT) associated with insights into intergroup power relations, affect, multiple identities, and individual presentation strategies can help complexify our own vision of intercultural encounters and that of our students. Indeed, existing theories of intercultural communication provide models and concepts with which we can approach questions of reflexivity and multimodality, seeking to come to grips with the reality

Reflexivity and Self-Presentation in Multicultural Encounters 97

of multicultural interactions in today's 'accelerating, complex and transnational spaces' (Introduction, this volume). Incorporating these theoretical elements into teaching and learning about interculturality can thus benefit future practitioners and all those who work with them.

NOTES

1. I am associate professor in English and communication science at the University of Burgundy in Dijon, where I have been teaching intercultural communication for the last eight years, from undergraduate to postgraduate level. My research in intercultural communication centers on the dialogical sensemaking processes used by individuals to apprehend and comprehend multicultural encounters.
2. Source: www.aegee.org/
3. Mead compares humans to animals that cannot think, yet can communicate. "Mind arises through communication by a conversation of gestures in a social process or context of experience—not communication through mind' (Mead 1934: 50).
4. In this sense, but also with the same proviso, the notion of reflexivity appears close to Mead's notion of self-consciousness, which he defines as '[t]he taking or feeling of the attitude of the other toward yourself' (1934: 171). However, self-consciousness is the instantaneous result of the ongoing dialectic relationship between I and me, which forms the process of the self, for Mead, whereas reflexivity, as used here, is a more far-reaching process, not exclusively centered on the self.
5. Mead makes the distinction when evoking human and animal communication: 'The conversation of gestures is not significant below the human level, because it is not conscious, that is, not *self*-conscious (though it is conscious in the sense of involving feelings or sensations)'(Mead, 1934: 81).
6. Stemming from Goffman and the symbolic interactionists, Identity Theory (infra), and notably Peter Burke's model of Identity Control (Burke, 1991: 838), provides a theoretical framework allowing us to better understand the processes involved here.
7. This notion of accountability comes originally from ethnomethodology (Garfinkel, 1967) and supposes that individuals are able to account for their actions.
8. It should be noted that reflexivity and multiple identities are being used differently here from the way they are used in Giddens' (1991) 'flexive project of the self' (see Adams, 2003, for a critique of this approach). Whereas the latter imagines individuals in post-traditional societies constructing their self by consciously choosing to pursue certain identities from one situation to another, this chapter places the emphasis on individual interactions and the way salient identities affect the relationship between participants.
9. Goffman describes such strategies for 'passing' or dealing with stigmatizing identities in *Stigma: Notes on the Management of Spoiled Identity* (1963).
10. The names used here are fictitious.
11. Gumperz defines communication competence as 'the knowledge of linguistic and related communicative conventions that speakers must have to create and sustain conversational cooperation' (1982: 209). Communication competence applies to multimodal communication in general, whereas intercultural communication competence concentrates on the affective, behavioral,

and cognitive qualities that specifically help someone deal with individuals from unknown national environments. The first is culture specific, whereas the second focuses on transcultural interpersonal communication skills adapted to contexts marked by cultural differences.
12. The classic solution, as far as intercultural communication competence is concerned, is to stress the need for tolerance, empathy, and a 'decentered' approach to the other.
13. This is not to suggest that 'native speakers' will systematically gain from imposing their language because their effectiveness, to some degree, depends on their capacity to establish conditions for mutual understanding, while both parties can play on ambiguity, feigned misunderstanding, and so on.

REFERENCES

Adams, M. (2003). The reflexive self and culture: A critique. *British Journal of Sociology*, 54(2), 221–238.
Barth, F. (1969). Ethnic groups and boundaries. *Nationality and nationalism: Area and period studies—modern Middle East, Asia, Africa, the Americas, Australia*, 3, 142.
Berger, P. L., & Luckmann, T. (1991). *The social construction of reality: A treatise in the sociology of knowledge* (new ed.). New York: Penguin.
Biancheri, F. (1996). *L'émergence des Eurocitoyens*. Paris: Prometheus-Europe.
Blommaert, J. (1991). How much culture is there in intercultural communication? In J. Blommaert & J. Verschueren (eds.) *The pragmatics of intercultural and international communication* (pp. 13–31). Philadelphia, PA: John Benjamins.
Blommaert, J., & Verschueren, J. (1991). *The Pragmatics of intercultural communication*. Philadelphia, PA: John Benjamins.
Burke, P., et al. (Ed.). (2003). *Advances in identity theory and research*. New York: Kluwer Academic/Plenum Publishers.
Burke, P. J. (1991). Identity processes and social stress. *American Sociological Review*, 56, 10.
Burke, P.J., 2003. Relationships among multiple identities. In P. Burke et al. (Ed.), *Advances in identity theory and research* (pp. 195–212). New York: Kluwer Academic/Plenum Publishers.
Burke, P. J. (2004). Identities and social structure. *Social Psychology Quarterly*, 67(1), 10.
Camilleri, C., et al. (1990). *Stratégies identitaires*. Paris: PUF.
Choo, H. Y., & Ferree, M. M. (2010). Practicing intersectionality in sociological research: A critical analysis of inclusions, interactions, and institutions in the study of inequalities. *Sociological Theory*, 28(2), 129–149.
Earley, P., & Ang, S. (2003). *Cultural intelligence: Individual interactions across cultures*. Stanford, CA: Stanford University Press.
Frame, A. (2008). *Repenser l'interculturel en communication: Performance culturelle et construction des identités au sein d'une association européenne*. Doctoral thesis. Université de Bourgogne, Dijon, France.
Frame, A., & Boutaud, J.-J. (2010). Performing identities and constructing meaning in interpersonal encounters: A semiopragmatics approach to communication. In *Constructing identity in interpersonal communication* (pp. 85–96). Helsinki: Société Néophilologique.
Gallois, C., Ogay, T., & Giles, H. (2005). Communication accommodation theory: A look back and a look ahead. In *Theorizing about intercultural communication* (pp. 121–148). Thousand Oaks, CA: Sage.
Garfinkel, H. (1967). *Studies in ethnomethodology*. Cambridge: Polity Press.

Giddens, A. (1991). *Modernity and self-identity*. Stanford, CA: Stanford University Press.
Giles, H., & Ogay, T. (2007). Communication accommodation theory. In B. B. Whaley & W. Samter (Eds.), *Explaining communication: Contemporary theories and exemplars* (pp. 293–310). Mahwah, NJ: Lawrence Erlbaum.
Goffman, E. (1963). *Stigma. Notes on the management of spoiled identity*. Englewood Cliffs, NJ: Prentice Hall.
Goffman, E. (1973). *La mise en scène de la vie quotidienne?: 1. la présentation de soi*. Paris: Editions de Minuit.
Goffman, E. (1992). *Interaction ritual*. New York: Anchor Books.
Gudykunst, W. (1998). *Bridging differences: Effective intergroup communication*. New York: Sage.
Gudykunst, W., & Kim, Y. Y. (1992). *Communicating with strangers: An approach to intercultural communication*. New York: McGraw Hill.
Gumperz, J. J. (1982). *Discourse strategies*. Cambridge: Cambridge University Press.
Hymes, D. (1984). *Vers la compétence de communication*. Paris: Hâtier.
Martin, J. (1992). *Cultures in organizations. Three perspectives*. New York/Oxford: Oxford University Press.
McCall, G. J., & Simmons, J. L. (1966). *Identities and interactions. An examination of human associations in everyday life*. New York: Free Press.
Mead, G. H. (1934). *Mind, self and society from the standpoint of a social behaviorist*. Chicago: University of Chicago Press.
Scollon, R., & Scollon, S. W.(2001). *Intercultural communication* (2nd ed.). Oxford: Blackwell.
Smith, S., et al. (1991). Foreigner talk revisited: Limits on accommodation to nonfluent speakers. In J. Blommaert & J. Verschueren, (Eds.), *The pragmatics of intercultural communication* (pp. 173–188). Philadelphia: John Benjamins.
Spencer-Oatey, H., & Franklin, P. (2009). *Intercultural interaction?: A multidisciplinary approach to intercultural communication*. Basingstoke, UK: Palgrave Macmillan.
Stryker, S., & Burke, P. (2000). The past, present, and future of an identity theory. *Social Psychology Quarterly*, 63(4), 13.
Tsai, K. (2012). Seeking affective spaces in cross-cultural research. In V. Carayol & A. Frame (Eds.), *Communication and PR from a cross-cultural standpoint. Practical and methodological issues* (pp. 85–95). Brussels: Peter Lang.
Turner, J. (2010). *Language in the academy: Cultural reflexivity and intercultural dynamics*. Multilingual Matters. Bristol, UK: Multilingual Matters.
Walby, S., Armstrong, J., & Strid, S. (2012). Intersectionality: Multiple inequalities in social theory. *Sociology*, 46(2), 224–240.
Wenger, E. (1999). *Communities of practice: Learning, meaning, and identity*. Cambridge; Cambridge University Press.

4 Researching Chinese Students' Intercultural Communication Experiences in Higher Education
Researcher and Participant Reflexivity

Prue Holmes

INTRODUCTION

Qualitative research, particularly ethnographic research, is a personal undertaking for both researcher and researched as they engage in fieldwork together. Jointly, they must negotiate the research context, the focus and topic of the research, the processes by which data is generated (e.g., through interactions between researcher and researched), and how each comes to know and understand the other as knowledge of the phenomenon under investigation is constructed. When multiple languages and intercultural communication are a part of the researcher/researched dynamic, these processes become all the more complex. Researchers must negotiate the multiple languages in use in the research site and communicate the purpose and focus of the research, often in language(s) unfamiliar to either researcher and/or researched.

In this chapter, my purpose is to show how the researcher and participants reflexively shape and are shaped by the research process and focus through their intercultural communication with one another and in a language they do not share. I revisit my own doctoral work—the intercultural communication experiences of 13 ethnic[1] Chinese students in a New Zealand university context—in order to reexamine my own researcher relationality and positionality vis-à-vis the participants, how we each managed intercultural communication in the research process, and the emergent challenges participants faced in having to use English in the research site. I draw on data neither published nor included in my doctoral thesis because, at the time, such data was not considered to be important in the thesis. Yet I was interested in knowing how my study was shaping participants' understandings in relation to both the research site and to me, the researcher. I explore how participants made sense of their relationship with and to me, the researcher, and the research topic. I discuss their reflexive and reflective recounts of their research experiences as knowledge generators and as intercultural communicators, as well as their emotional and cognitive responses to the research, all in a language that was not their native language—English. In postresearcher reflection, I too take a reflexive stance, focusing on what methodological and ethical issues I faced in managing the sampling, data collection, and writing up, as well as how my encounters with these participants impacted the research process and the data generated.

REFLEXIVITY IN THE RESEARCH CONTEXT

In describing my understanding of reflexivity, I align my position with that of the editors: Reflexivity can be seen as 'a multifaceted, complex, and ongoing dialogical process, which is continually evolving' (Introduction, this volume). Two aspects of the research process emerge as important: first, relationality, and second, the multilingual/intercultural spaces that the research occupies.

The first aspect, concerning relationality, explores who is involved, the function and purpose of the relationships in the research, and how these emergent relationships are constructed and negotiated, both interculturally and in terms of language choices. Research (especially ethnographic) may involve shared relationships with any of the following: supervisors, participants, sometimes translators and transcribers, examiners, funders, and publishers. Managing these relationships involves linguistic agency, the privileging of certain languages over others—in my research, English over the multiple languages spoken by my participants. It also involves negotiating trust, ethics, power, and face and addressing questions of who may enter the discourse, who speaks for whom, and how, when, and where (Krog, 2011). Where language is concerned, Scollon et al. (2012) note that language choice is also a matter of participants' face negotiation because what language they use indicates their relative statuses and their assumptions about these differences. The identities presented by those in the research also need to be negotiated. The identity I attempt to avow as I interact with participants may not be the one that they ascribe to me or that I wish to have ascribed to me (Collier, 2005). Identities are challenged and thus (re)constructed and (re)negotiated in intercultural communication throughout the research process. Thus, ethnographic research becomes an ongoing process of relationship building between the researcher and the researched.

The second aspect concerns the spaces of the research. Dacheva and Fay (2012) identified four research spaces that influence the construction of the research outcome(s): (1) the research phenomena under investigation (in this study, the intercultural communication experiences of international ethnic Chinese students in the academic and social context of a New Zealand university), (2) the research context (here, the classroom and social spaces on the university campus), (3) the research resources [e.g., the language and communicative resources of the researchers (me, a doctoral researcher)] and researched (the international ethnic Chinese students), and (4) the representational possibilities (e.g., how the linguistic resources and intercultural communication experiences of participants and researcher are understood, constructed, and represented in the writing up, in this case, of the doctoral thesis for examination at a university that accepts theses in English and Maori). Researchers need to develop awareness of these relational processes, along with intertwining and overlapping spaces, as they engage in multilingual, intercultural research (Holmes et al., 2013).

Through these relational and intercultural communicative processes, and within and beyond these representational spaces, the researcher and participants make sense of the research focus as they address the research questions, thus allowing 'knowledge' to emerge. Yet in this relational and dialogic activity of 'making' research, the intersubjectivities of the researcher and participants are also being shaped. Although the research activity can profoundly affect researchers' sense of the world and themselves (Canagarajah, 1999), so too can it profoundly affect the participants' understanding of their lifeworld and their place in it. By responding to an invitation to participate in the research, the participants enter into a new world of knowing and sense making with the researcher. My questioning prompted participants to think about their experience of living and studying, as ethnic Chinese students, in a New Zealand university. It also prompted me to think about how I should and do engage with the participants in ways that are ethical and appropriate, given our developing relationship and the research spaces we all occupy.

My research is framed by phenomenology, which is concerned with 'the world of everyday life [that] is the scene and also the object of our actions and interactions' (Schutz, 1973: 209). Schutz posited an intersubjective world, experienced and interpreted by others previously and now open to our experience and interpretation. Thus, meaning is particular and peculiar to individuals in the spaces they occupy as they construct and reconstruct social groupings. This focus means that the researcher must account for (1) the individual meanings that participants bring to the intercultural encounter, meanings that are socially constructed through communication with others, and (2) the multiple realities and identities that the participants construct and inhabit. Thus, knowledge is the result of each individual's unique experience, constructed in communication with others—and with the researcher. It is the researcher's task to come to know and understand the actors' own perspective (Weber's *verstehen*). Reflexivity, along with individuals' reflections or critical inspection of the unfolding of the research and what happens in the research spaces (Holmes et al., 2013), makes this sense making possible. Yet Altheide and Johnson remind us that this knowledge is incomplete, implicit, and tacit:

> Our subjects always know more than they can tell us, usually even more than they allow us to see; likewise, we often know far more than we can articulate. . . . [T]he key issue is not to capture the informant's voice, but to elucidate the experience that is implicated by the subjects in the context of their activities as they perform them, and as they are understood by the ethnographer. (2011: 592)

It is this coming to know that requires the researcher's active involvement of the sense making going on throughout the research process. Here I present participants' recounts of not only being researched but of becoming someone other through their intercultural communication with me, the researcher. The self and other are not separate but always in relation (or in dialogue) and situated (Hall, 1997). Self-reflexivity in my study is somewhere between Boas and Malinowski's understanding of the *native's* point of view—that is, of immersing oneself in the world of the native (Geertz, 1973)—and that of Bourdieu, where researchers must take into account the effects of their own position, their own set of internalized structures (or *habitus*), and how these might influence their sense making (Bourdieu & Wacquant, 1992).

These theoretical positions lead me to the following research questions, which I seek to answer by revisiting my participants' understandings of the research process:

R.Q. 1: How do I, as researcher, reflexively engage with the research and participants?
R.Q. 2: How do participants reflexively engage in the research [that is, how do they (re)construct and (re)negotiate their relationship with the researcher and research focus as a result of the research experience]?
R.Q. 3: What ethical and relational issues emerge between researcher and participants in the spaces of the research?

To address these questions, I now turn to my doctoral research. Although undertaken nearly 20 years ago, I revisit the researcher/participant experience with criticality and intentionality.

THE RELATIONALITY AND POSITIONALITY BETWEEN RESEARCHER AND RESEARCHED IN THE STUDY: MY POSITIONALITY AS RESEARCHER

As a researcher, then, I was not encouraged to interrogate relationality between researcher and participants, as well as the reflexive experiences of each as engendered by the research processes and outcomes. I was required by my supervisor to 'report' my 'findings' drawing on themes that illustrated rich, complex, common, and unique experiences, in common with standard approaches to thematic analysis (Braun & Clarke, 2006). Reflexivity was a section I was required to include in my methodology in order to show my 'examined' relationship between my research subjects and myself and the responsibility that that entails, for example, 'why we interrogate what we do, what we choose not to report, how we frame our data, on whom we shed our scholarly gaze, who is protected and not protected as we do our work' (Fine et al., 2000: 123). I also had to 'bracket' my own experience,

104 *Prue Holmes*

that is, to 'provide autobiographical or personal information' that somehow served 'to establish and assert [my] authority' to produce a text about the participants' experiences (Fine et al., 2000: 109). One of my supervisors validated my interest in the research. He believed that because, earlier, I had lived in China for a year as teacher and had undertaken a short intensive course in Mandarin, because I had then lived in Hong Kong a further three years as an English language teacher-educator, and because I also had experience tutoring and supporting international students in the school where the research was being undertaken, I was therefore satisfactorily positioned to undertake this research. I recall being shocked at that time at my supervisor's affirmation of my positionality and implied 'authority' in relation to the research site. At the time, I felt quite ill equipped—in my knowledge of the other—to engage with these students and then to interpret, make sense of, and write up their experiences.

THE PARTICIPANTS' POSITIONALITY

The study itself included an 18-month data collection of 13 ethnic Chinese students' intercultural communication experiences in a New Zealand university and the local community. The study focused on these students' everyday socially constructed intercultural interactions (Berger & Luckmann, 1966) and was underpinned by naturalistic inquiry (Lincoln & Guba, 1985), which included observation, interviews, and informal meetings, as well as ethnographic description and interpretation (Van Maanen, 1988). At that time, all international students needed a minimum 5.5 in the International English Language Testing System (IELTS) or equivalent TOEFL. The criteria for participant selection were that participants had been educated in a Chinese language (e.g., Mandarin or Cantonese) and had come from countries with systems of Chinese education (e.g., China, Hong Kong, Malaysia, Taiwan). Participants' profiles varied: Seven were undergraduates (ug), two were graduate diploma students, and four were graduate students (pg). Six were female and seven male. All had been educated in Mandarin Chinese, except for the one Hong Kong participant who had been educated in Cantonese. Some of the other participants spoke Cantonese, and many spoke other languages as their mother tongue or additional languages. Four of the undergraduates had come from a high school in their home country and then had undergone 6 to 12 months of language and/or university foundation study in New Zealand. Two Chinese Malaysians (WK and FO) were part of a cross-institutional twinning program and had therefore already completed two years of their degree in their home (private Chinese) university. One of the two diploma students (KZ) was a direct-entry student from China with no language or learning experience in New Zealand. All of the four graduate students were mature students, on government scholarships, and had completed their first degrees in China. These four had all undergone work experience in Chinese universities and were married. They had also completed a one-year diploma in the school.

Their profiles already indicate a disparate group of individuals, speaking multiple languages beyond the English language context of the research, yet tied, more tenuously, by my assumption that they shared an ethnic Chinese identity.

ETHNOMETHODOLOGICAL PROCEDURES

I realized early on in this study that I would need to build relationships with my participants. It would not be possible to invite them to my office for an extended interview; present them with a consent form to sign; explain ethical procedures of the right to withdraw, anonymity, and confidentiality; and expect them to answer my probing and deeply personal questions about how they were feeling as international sojourners, the nature of their intercultural communication experiences, and how they felt about them. This phenomenologically informed inquiry, I knew from my former experiences in China and Hong Kong, would require strong interpersonal relations between us. I would need to build trust before I could expect to engage with the participants. Therefore, I spent many hours in the research domain, especially in the initial months, meeting informally with participants on campus, inviting them to my home, and taking them on trips in an effort to establish friendship and trust. This seemed entirely appropriate to me at the time, and it was therefore a taken-for-granted action and one I did not think to explain to participants at the time, although, on reflection, it would have been ethically appropriate to do so. I recall the emotional effort required to make phone calls (the research preceded the social media era) to arrange meetings and so on. I was intruding upon their lifeworlds, yet I was bound to them in order for my research to happen—an inverse power relationship of which, I suspect, they were unaware.

The participants discussed the importance of relationship building. For example, midway in the research, WK explained his early reservation in interactions with me: 'Don't take much notice of what I said in the first few months.' And at the end of the research process another participant commented: 'The more we talk, the more I can know your personality . . . so I know you will not do some harm to me and so I can trust you' (KZ). Therefore, not just prolonged engagement in the field but careful relationship building were important aspects of the data collection process. To this end, I became known as 'the Godmother' by the other Malaysian/Chinese friends and classmates of WK and FO. Just as Frame (Chapter 3) mentions the importance of participants' need to develop self-preservation and identity strategies and to adopt strategic 'orientations' to their relationships with others, so did the participants in my study seem to exhibit these strategies as they sought to understand and negotiate their relationship with me, the researcher.

106 *Prue Holmes*

I spent observation periods of approximately one month in classrooms at the beginning and end of each of the three semesters (over the 18-month data collection period). These, along with informal discussions with participants in the research context and during social occasions, contributed to the construction of the in-depth interview protocols. In this sense, the participants were very much involved in the development and construction of the research process. Each participant was interviewed three times, and each interview lasted more or less 90 minutes. In total, I spent approximately 62 hours formally interviewing participants and about 500 hours in fieldwork. All interviews were audio-recorded and transcribed (amounting to 15–25 pages of typescript for each participant). Extensive field notes and memoranda documented the ethnographic observations. These handwritten notes were recorded in an exercise book, which became full over the study period.

POSTRESEARCH REFLECTIONS ON THESE PROCEDURES

No qualitative inquiry is value free (Lincoln, 1990). The data collection process enabled an exploration of participants' lifeworlds by drawing on and constructing meaning from data that is grounded and emergent in the social interaction of the participants (Glaser, 1992; Glaser & Strauss, 1967) and in gaining a 'thick description' (Geertz, 1973) of these students' encounters with others in the context in which communication is occurring. I drew on interview transcriptions and observations to identify both the shared and idiosyncratic experiences expressed by the participants in their intercultural communication with others. As much as possible, I wanted to preserve and give voice to their tellings as constructed in the context of the communication encounter and in accordance with the principles of naturalistic inquiry (Lincoln, 1990). Like Najar's work (in Chapter 9, this volume), I was interested in what she describes as a 'methodological assemblage,' a method that allows the researcher to focus on the concrete practices and journeys of the participants in their everyday lifeworlds and environments.

Yet in trying to be faithful to these procedures, I omitted important participant reflexivity that the participants shared with me at the end of the final interview concerning their own relationship to me, the researcher, and to the research phenomenon under investigation. I make an attempt to address that reflexivity in one of my publications on this study:

> My position as a New Zealand researcher meant that the data interpretation reflected to some degree the predispositions and parameters of a Western research tradition, as well as my knowledge of the research domain. As a doctoral student, a former teaching assistant in the school, an older student, and the occupant of an office with a computer, I may have been perceived by the participants as holding a position of power.

On the other hand, developing an empathy with the graduate student participants, at least, was facilitated by commonalities in our life experiences. (Holmes, 2005: 296)

This explanation acknowledges that researcher–researched reflexivity, the complexity of that dialogic engagement, and the spaces it entailed, but that experience is left unexamined, hanging.

Further, in my doctoral research and in my subsequent publications, I make no mention of the challenges in conducting research with participants who do not have the language of the researcher or the research context: English. I realized that the research focus and the interview questions required participants to engage in complex cognitive and affective processes in English. Yet I did not include any discussion of the multilingual dimension of my research, the challenges and possibilities that this might bring, or the participants' competence in English. To date, I am not entirely sure of how many languages the participants brought to the research context, although I know many had regional and local dialects and other languages that they spoke with their families; nor did I explore their experience of using English, the language of the researcher, to report their experiences. How did they deconstruct their interview experiences with me—either intrapersonally or with the other participants and friends? What possibilities may have arisen if I had considered the multilingual nature of the research? What if I had privileged focus groups (rather than one-to-one interviews), where participants might have shared their experiences in and through shared languages in a shared sense-making process (Hesse-Biber, 2012)?

Instead, as interviewer, I centralized my own role in the research as the 'interrogator' who directed and controlled the topics of conversation through my already scripted 'open-ended' interview protocol and through my prompting; I was privileging what got discussed, when, and how (Fine et al., 2000; Krog, 2011; Piller, 2011). Yet, ironically, in undertaking the data collection task that I draw on in this chapter, I was also acknowledging the importance of collaborative reflection between researcher and participants (as discussed by Pérez-Milans and Soto in Chapter 10) as a form of critical transformation (in my case, of self as researcher). Further, in privileging English throughout the data collection process and in choosing the interview as the key data collection instrument, I had unwittingly marginalized the participants' voices in hitherto unforeseen and unimagined ways. My recent investigation of multilingual processes in research methodology (Holmes et al., 2013, forthcoming) through the AHRC-funded Researching Multilingually project (http://researchingmultilingually.com/) has enabled me to realize, confront, and make sense of my own biases and predispositions and to acknowledge the challenges of conducting intercultural bi/multilingual research. I have become more aware, through this poststudy reflection, of the multidimensional, heterogeneous nature of language(s) as researcher and researched engage in intercultural encounters in interviews and field research. What further insights might have emerged if I had afforded participants the opportunity to discuss their experiences with one another first in an informal focus group and in the languages of their choice and then later to share their constructions with me (Ganassin & Holmes, 2013)?

As already noted, ironically, in closing my data collection, I included in the final interview a section on participant reflexivity that permits me here to engage in postreflexive analysis and to return to the data to present an in-depth analysis of this reflexive relationality and positionality of participants—vis-à-vis the research and researcher. Following Braun and Clark's (2006) thematic analysis guidelines, I analyzed solicited reflections on the research process and research topic by looking for common themes and multiple as well as singular instances of phenomena in the interview data. I also drew on communicative exchanges recorded in my researcher journal that I had had with participants in the field throughout the research period.

PARTICIPANT REFLEXIVITY VIS-À-VIS THE RESEARCH AND THE RESEARCHER

Several major themes emerge from this analysis. At the time of writing up the study, these themes seemed extraneous to the purpose of the study and so were omitted. Yet they allude to the importance of researcher reflexivity in intercultural ethnographic research. They include participants' motivation for participating in the research; how participants experienced relationship building and trust with the researcher; power; the ethics of data interpretation; language; and participant reflexivity.

MOTIVATION FOR PARTICIPATING IN THE RESEARCH

Participants chose to engage in the research for several reasons. They wanted to practice their English; some remarked that the interviews with me were their only source of contact with a local person outside of their international student social group. They wanted to make friends with a New Zealander, to learn more about New Zealand, and to find out what the researcher wanted to know about the participants. YR (female pg) wanted to learn about research processes: 'I learned how to ask questions, how to make a rapport with the interviewees from you,' and this entailed her behaving responsibly at my requests for interviews, even though she at times did not feel committed to the research goals: 'I should be cooperative, whatever difficulty I had, so that is why I never refused you . . . but I thought, oh, maybe waste my time.' FO (male ug), a classmate of WK (male ug), was motivated by WK's decision to participate. In FO's eyes, WK demonstrated enthusiasm to push himself out from the group, to engage in new experiences, and so FO was guided by this thinking. Conversely, M, a female first-year undergraduate student who had done a one-year preliminary language course, explained why she failed to answer my e-mails and phone calls at the outset when I was contacting potential participants. In this postanalysis interview at the end of the data collection period, she explained that she did not want to come or to participate in recorded interviews because she felt that, as a young student in her first year of study, she would have nothing to tell me; in other words, she felt that she was an unfit informant. Here she thanked me for taking care of her. Had I been aware of their motivations, I could have acknowledged their unique needs and contributions in how they perceived the data and their role in developing the study, as well as the meaning and importance of the study from their perspectives. However, these important reflections are missing in the implications section of the final chapter of my thesis.

RELATIONSHIP BUILDING AND TRUST

My experiences of living and working with Chinese people made me aware of the importance of building trust with my participants, but I did not realize that this trust was critical in gathering *authentic* data, as this postanalysis revealed: 'Initial data might not be very accurate because we were . . . self-conscious, getting the right answers for you' (WK, male ug). So in this case, WK felt that he should tell me things that put him, and perhaps my own research, in a positive light. He confided informally, 'Don't take too much notice of what I said in the first six months.' This shocked me at the time, as it does now. I had 'collected' all that data, analyzed it, and written it up, and perhaps it was useless! Perhaps I should have gone back to the initial data and rechecked it with the participants!

LJ talked of the importance of coming to know the other through communication and of the value of shared similarities and discovered meeting points:

> I don't think there . . . [is much] . . . difference in our culture, but I think . . . I feel much better and better when I communicate with you. Yeah, I mean, much more comfortable. When I first talk with you, probably because of my language problem, probably we don't know each other, you know, but today you can understand, get a far insight of my thought. You understand me now, to some extent. It's getting better and better. (LJ, male pg)

Sharing the experience of his newborn was one example. I visited LJ and his wife and gave a gift. I did this as an act of friendship and in recognition of the momentous occasion signaled by the arrival of a newborn. I had stepped out of my researcher role here. LJ felt that events like this, beyond the interview, helped to build trust within the interview. He made a comparison with China in that such behavior would be similar. Other participants expressed trust in terms of the need for self-protection against emotional harm:

110   *Prue Holmes*

> The more we talk, the more I can ... know your personality. The most important thing is the personality, so I know you will not do some harm to me and so I can trust you. (KZ, male pg).

> So like slowly, your influence, that I don't need to be afraid of you.... When I first came here I don't trust you. (WK, male ug)

YR spoke more in terms of reciprocity between researcher and researched: 'I think the researcher should be act as friends to the person being research[ed], that's one thing, and show concern for him or her.... Once you get trust from him or from her you can get the information' (YR, female pg).

Yet not all participants engaged with me in such a constructive way. With V (male ug), I felt I was struggling throughout the research to elicit his feelings and experiences. In the postresearch reflection interview, he concluded, 'I've been here almost three year, so all of my feeling is the same I think,' and of my questions over the 18 months, 'Sometimes it's very boring. You ask me the same question, and I answer you the same answer as well, similar answer. I told you already' (V). My doctoral thesis had less of V's voice in the findings, but, on reflection, what was lost by this lack of engagement with and commitment to the research? The research and interviews were some kind of abstraction, not an activity of interaction and sharing for V. I therefore had to rely on others' voices more for the data. I concluded that some relationships just don't work.

Outside the interview context, some participants reciprocated in this relationship building. Soon after the data collection, I was invited to a neighborhood barbecue where (local, international, and other Chinese) students and local families were present at a shared meal of neighborhood friendliness. I recognized my own biases because I felt surprised at how this shy and quiet participant (M, female ug) was socially networked to her neighborhood community in a way that I was not to my own neighborhood.

POWER

As much as I tried to minimize my own position, most participants perceived me as hierarchically superior to them: I had my own office, a computer, I was a doctoral student (not a master's or undergraduate student), I had been a lecturer, I was older (in most cases), and a mother (with two young children at the time), and these were all markers of my power and status. I recall one female student who seemed quite willing to come to interviews, but, while carrying out the data collection, I was never exactly sure how seriously she engaged with my questions or how comfortable she felt about participating. Yet in the following exchange, through what she perceived as my kindness, she demonstrated that she had always been open to engagement:

AS: It's just good to have a meeting time, lecturer, like you.
ME: I'm a student.
AS: No, you are lecturer before, so it's a good experience I think [for her to communicate with me, a 'lecturer']. . . . As I told you, I do well in this research and you try to look after all the research participants very well I think. Contact very well, and especially the dinner [I invited a group of them to my house], is unforgettable.

And then she went on to tell me, after eating lasagne at my house, about the challenges she faced in trying to make her own lasagne. And we laughed and shared tribulations about lasagne making. Why were these mundane everyday details, in which informants 'tell' their lives, so important in ethnographic research, missing in my write-up?

However, I had to work at minimizing this power distance: I had to show empathy and understanding of the challenges participants faced as students and sojourners. SX (male pg), who a couple of years after the research became my partner at bridge (the card game), spoke of how, through my interviewing approach and fieldwork, I encouraged his engagement in the research, which concomitantly, encouraged his growing interest and commitment:

At first, when you talked with me and I think, oh, you are a lecturer or you, I mean, you've got a high position, and I, yeah, I should I mean to follow you at every aspect. But gradually, gradually, I mean, yeah, this, I mean, something has been changed and now I mean, I know what's what I say at first I think I'm just a passive, passive role, and finally, I know actually both of us are . . . creating, yeah, so it's different. (SX, male pg)

Here SX demonstrates a postresearch critical self-awareness of his own agency in the shaping and emergence of the research data.

PARTICIPANTS' ETHICAL CONCERNS ABOUT DATA INTERPRETATION

Linked to issues of trust and power are participants' ethical concerns about presentation of the data. By way of member checking, I returned the interviews that I had transcribed myself to the participants to check. I also passed the findings chapters from the thesis to two postgraduate participants to read so they could check my interpretations and discussion of data.

Participants expressed concerns about the accuracy of my understanding and interpretation of their experiences and backgrounds and about ethical issues in reporting the data. Their comments indicate their own self-determination in the research process. One participant wanted to make sure that delicate matters discussed regarding his/her political positioning at the time of the Tiananmen Square situation in 1989 was not reported in the data. Another was concerned about how I would report his/her accounts of his/her intercultural/learning experiences in one of his/her classes. The class was taught by my supervisor who would then read about the episode in my thesis. A third was concerned about how I might misrepresent Chinese culture in my write-up:

> I'm quite interested in what you are thinking and doing and also I am . . . I want to give you some help . . . because, you know, the culture is very complicated thing. . . . Although you stayed in China or in Hong Kong for some, for a few years, but maybe I think you're not very well understand. You're not well understand about the culture in China, but I think the understanding of the culture is quite important in your research. So I think if I know what you are thinking and you are doing, maybe something I know, maybe you are not right, so I can tell you. (KZ, male ug)

KZ explained that he had read books written by famous Western authors on Chinese values and culture, 'but they don't really understand some simple things.' KZ's candid account suggests that the authority invested in me by my supervisors at the outset had always been open to question. And a fourth, AS (female ug), felt that the research itself was important because it enabled her to find out what international students are saying and thinking and that others too could learn from it. She acknowledged the political nature of the research—that it gave participants the opportunity to voice their lived experiences of internationalization and student mobility, perhaps outside of what they perceived as institutional constraints and pressures (such as the routine of preparing for and attending lectures and seminars, and assessment), all of which have the effect of silencing them.

Aside from demonstrating the importance of member checking, participants' feedback here indicates how they perceive the research as a political endeavor—where their voices are heard and represented and where the construction and representation of the research are truly co-collaborative endeavors (Collier, 2005; Pérez-Milans & Soto, Chapter 10 in this volume). Yet I now question whether I called on these voices and their positioning sufficiently throughout the fieldwork, analysis, and write-up.

LANGUAGE

The multilingual research practices at play impact the ways in which meaning is constructed and negotiated between researcher and participants (Andrews et al., 2013). The participants used complex cognitive and affective processes in describing and narrating their experiences: for example, they negotiated expression of perceptions and emotional experiences in

English; the researcher–researched relationship, which included deference to the researcher in some instances and participant agency in others; presentational strategies of the self (Goffman, 1969); and face strategies (Brown & Levinson, 1978). They were also negotiating the meaning of the interview questions vis-à-vis the research topic and aims, as well as the importance and significance of their own narratives and responses in meeting these aims. (For an analysis of the ways in which language learners mobilize their language resources multimodally to understand the transformations they experience, see Chapter 6 by Malinowski and Nelson).

My interview questions asked them to consider concepts like culture, values, social experience, communicative phenomena, and affective responses to encounters and interactions—not an easy task! FX (female ug) explained how the process worked: 'Sometimes I can't understand and can't express my idea exactly, but you can explain me and let me know what you want, are thinking, and what you want to know.' In other words, the multiple languaging techniques and strategies (recasting, reformulating, repeating) that I use as a researcher to convey the meaning of my questions help participants understand their meaning and intent. However, this interpretative process raised challenges that they expressed in multiple ways:

> I'm quite [a] slow thinker, I mean, I need time to think of the question. If interview straight away the question, I sometimes, when I, the answer that I give, [I] have to justify or change later when I think more about it. Or I might have something to add. (AS, female ug)

> I don't like to have interview because I feel uncomfortable, you know, because I have to speak English. . . . Sometime we have interview, I have, I don't understand. I think that difficult question also good for me, to think about it. (M, female ug)

In responding to questions about communication experiences, SX (male pg) reported that he knew the words in Chinese but could not find the words in English. FX (female pg) explained that some of the language in the interviews, such as words like 'values,' although easily translated into Chinese, she had not necessarily thought about; words like 'community,' a strange concept to her in Chinese, and 'intercultural communication' were unfamiliar and not easily translated. This uncertainty of the meaning of words caused her to question the quality of her responses. And YR (female pg), sighing in exasperation, commented, 'This question is quite abstract now!' For M (female ug), even the thought of having her voice recorded on a dictaphone was scary to her.

As a researcher, I too was negotiating language (word choice, sentence structure). I was also negotiating my relationship with participants, aware (I thought) of power issues, and the need to establish empathy and trust. Like all researchers, I share the concern of eliciting responses that contribute to the research objectives but simultaneously acknowledging participants' asymmetrical communicative competence when using other languages (Ganassin & Holmes, 2013).

THE INFLUENCE OF THE INTERVIEW EXPERIENCE ON PARTICIPANTS AS INTERNATIONAL STUDENT SOJOURNERS

For me, the most revealing aspect of the postreflection interview was how the participants had reflexively engaged with the interviews and research focus, an engagement I had been unaware of during the data collection. My questioning had prompted them to reflect on and make sense of their intercultural communication experiences with other students, teachers, and administrators in the university and with people in the community and even, in LJ's case, their reasons for choosing to study overseas:

> You has given me some information how to communicate with the other people. It's what I did not think before we made this programme. And after you talk with me about this question of course it forced me to thought about that, to think about that. (SX, male pg)

> Some questions I never thought about it, and when you ask me and I will start thinking about, yeah, it's a kind of self value . . . I quite enjoying this sort of self-evaluation. (KZ, male pg)

> I never think about, what about the value of my culture and what happen, because it's, I think it is very natural. I never think about the value, cultural value, in New Zealand, how they influence me. After the interview I think about this question. This is my first time to think about it. (M, female ug)

> Through this interview I can clear my mind and I'm thinking, 'Why I'm different from the other people, and why I come here?' and I can explain to you and I can also explain to myself as well . . . I can show my idea. I get feedback about my idea from another person. That's what I like. (LJ, male pg)

And WK explained that having to think about the interview questions over the three iterations encouraged him to think about everyday encounters, the mundane of ethnographic details; whereas once he would not have stopped to consider or question these things, his participation in the research encouraged him to reflect more:

> It makes me think whether I value [whether] coming here [to the interview] has had any impact on my life or not. . . . Initially, [it was] just

like [an] obligation because I agreed, but now I feel it's a contribution, it is a sort of pleasure, no[t] to say it's a pleasure, but it's good. I don't mind, I like it. (WK, male ug)

CONCLUSIONS

This postresearcher reflection and the recounts of the research participants in this study suggest complexities, hitherto unrecognized by myself as researcher, that need to be addressed in the data collection process and writing up of ethnographic research. Further, the analysis indicates that ethnographic intercultural/multilingual research does more than just generate knowledge: It can be a valuable, informative, formative, and cathartic experience for the researcher and participants as they each reflect on the research process and its implications for their life experiences and identities. And these reflections need to be written into all stages of the ethnographic account. More importantly, the discussion sheds deeper insights into how knowledge is constructed in the ethnographic endeavor. The outcomes of this analysis have implications for researchers and their research praxis.

First, in this study, participants' motivations for engaging in the research emerged in various ways. I realized that their motivations could influence their engagement in the field, and for some, this changed over time—from uncertainty and reluctance, to cartharsis, to an acknowledgment of the need for and value of the research. However, I had not foreseen other reasons for engagement. In the case of at least one participant, V, perhaps his role was one of obligation, having signed up to participate. This situation raises ethical issues of the validity of consent forms and indirectly of the quality and authenticity of the emergent data.

Second, my postresearch interviews illustrated to me the extent to which the participants engaged in reflexivity, which, in turn, led them to deeper understandings of their role and importance in the purpose and construction of the research. For example, they became aware of and began to explore a self that was in the process of becoming as they made sense of who they were through the research focus and in the research site. Through the research, they were also able to critically reflect on and make sense of their intercultural communication experiences and international student sojourn. Furthermore, they demonstrated an agency in constructing the research through their intercultural interactions with me, for example, in deciding what information they would reveal to me, when, and how. This power broker role is usually assigned to the researcher. In my initial analysis, I had not fully acknowledged the ways in which these participants reflexively experienced and managed the research process—and me, as the researcher—and thus these insights were omitted from my construction of their intercultural experiences in the write-up.

Third, the researcher is responsible for building relationships and trust with participants, as cultural informants, to ensure that the data is authentic and trustworthy (Lincoln & Guba, 1985). Ethical processes—beyond the use of consent forms and requirements of anonymity and the right to refuse to answer questions or withdraw from the study at any time—include a responsibility for the well-being and protection of participants' identities and experiences in the research site and an ethics of reporting: for example, what I should and should not disclose and the accuracy of my understanding and interpretation. Further, participants described the need to come to know the researcher first before projecting and exposing their inner selves. I was unaware of the ways in which they were exercising agency and power in their understanding of the research and in its unfolding. Had I been aware, I may have been able to explore this complexity further, along with its implications for their experiences and the research findings and outcomes.

Fourth, researchers, whether they are monolingual or working in their first language that is unshared by the participants, need to show sensitivity toward and be flexible about participants' language needs in the data collection process. Participants had to explain in English affective, cognitive, and behavioral aspects of their intercultural communication encounters. Deploying abstract terms like 'culture,' 'values,' and the like raises issues not only of translatability but also processes of sense making that resulted in participants developing a deeper self-awareness of their identities as they worked back and forth between the selves in their home countries and the selves they were creating through this research experience.

Fifth, the analysis highlights the 'outsider' position I inhabited. There is the need for researcher sensitivity in acknowledging the multiple interpretations participants ascribe to the research focus and process and how these diverse meanings contribute to the overall research outcomes. Through my questioning in interviews, and through my engagement with the participants in the field, they began to make sense of their intercultural encounters and (re)construct and (re)negotiate their multiple identities—as friends, as international student sojourners, as inhabitants of a particular country, and as members of certain groups with whom they may or may not share values. My perceptions of their identities and their multilingual/intercultural selves were shrouded by own researcher identity—of 'doing' research and 'being' a researcher. Therefore, researchers need to look beyond textual and thematic analysis of data—the words in the interview transcripts and researchers' treatment of them—for the meanings embodied in participants' reflexive experiences and how these insights might enrich and complement more traditional contextual and thematic analyses presented as 'findings' in the writing up of research.

Finally, this postresearcher reflection and analysis have illustrated to me that reflexivity needs to include the reflexivity of both the researcher and the researched in order to acknowledge the important role of the relationality that exists between them and to recognize researcher and researched agency in determining what gets reported by whom, how, and when. These aspects can be interpreted via the four research spaces outlined at the outset: (1) the research phenomenon under investigation, in this case, the international sojourn, and the ways in which researcher and participants make sense of it; (2) how researcher and researched build understanding of their research context; (3) how they make use of the language resources in their interactions and the extent to which these resources can generate knowledge and understanding; and (4) in representation of the research outcomes, the choices the researcher makes in consultation with the participants about what is included and excluded. As researchers engage with participants in their intercultural encounters, they need to be open to and investigate not just their own but also the participants' reflexive positions and lifeworlds and how they contribute to the construction of knowledge. The blind spots I have exposed here in my own understanding will hopefully guide me, and perhaps other researchers, toward a more dependable and authentic engagement with others and otherness in future intercultural and multilingual research endeavors.

NOTE

1. I use the term "ethnic" here to indicate that participants did not all share a Chinese national identity but were linked to one another by shared Chinese languages and, to some extent, shared ideas about what constitutes Chineseness.

REFERENCES

Altheide, D. L., & Johnson, J. M. (2011). Reflections on interpretive adequacy in qualitative research. In N. K. Denzin & Y. S. Lincoln (Eds.), *The Sage handbook of qualitative research* (4th ed.) (pp. 581–594). Thousand Oaks, CA: Sage.

Andrews, J., Holmes, P., & Fay, R. (in press). Researching multilingually. Special issue. *International Journal of Applied Linguistics*, 23, 3.

Berger, P., & Luckmann, T. (1966). *The social construction of reality.* London: Penguin.

Bourdieu, P., & Wacquant, L. (1992). *An invitation to reflexive sociology.* Oxford: Polity.

Braun, V., & Clarke, V. (2006). Using thematic analysis in psychology. *Qualitative Research in Psychology*, 3, 77–101.

Brown, P., & Levinson, S. (1978). *Politeness: Some universals in language use.* Cambridge: Cambridge University Press.

Canagarajah, S. (1999). *Resisting linguistic imperialism in English teaching.* Oxford: Oxford University Press.

Collier, M.-J. (2005). Theorizing cultural identifications: Critical updates and continuing evolution. In W. B. Gudykunst (Ed.), *Theorizing about intercultural communication* (pp. 235–256). Thousand Oaks, CA: Sage.

Dacheva, L., & Fay, R. (2012). An examination of the research and researcher aspects of multilingually researching one language (Ladino) through fieldwork in another (Bulgarian) and analysis and presentation in a third (English). *AHRC*

Researching Multilingually Seminar, School of Education, Durham University, UK, March 28–29.
Fine, M., Weis, L., Weseen, S., & Wong, L. (2000). For whom: Qualitative research, representations, and social responsibilities. In N. Denzin & Y. S. Lincoln (Eds.), *Handbook of Qualitative Research* (2nd ed.) (pp. 107–131). Thousand Oaks, CA: Sage.
Ganassin, S., & Holmes, P. (2013). Multilingual research practices in community research: The case of migrant/refugee women in North-East England. *International Journal of Applied Linguistics*, 23, 3.
Geertz, C. (1973). *The interpretation of cultures*. New York: Basic Books.
Glaser, B. (1992). *Basics of grounded theory analysis*. Mill Valley, CA: Sociology Press.
Glaser, B. G., & Strauss, A. L. (1967). *The discovery of grounded theory*. Chicago: Aldine.
Goffman, E. (1969). *The presentation of self in everyday life*. London: Penguin.
Hall, S. (1997). *Representation: Cultural representations and signifying practices*. London: Sage.
Hesse-Biber, S. N. (Ed). (2012). *Handbook of feminist research: Theory and praxis*. London: Sage.
Holmes, P. (2005). Ethnic Chinese students' communication with cultural others in a New Zealand university. *Communication Education*, 54, 289–331.
Holmes, P., Fay, R., Andrews, J., & Attia, M. (2013). Researching multilingually: New theoretical and methodological directions. *International Journal of Applied Linguistics*, 23, 3.
Krog, A. (2011). In the name of human rights: I say (how) you (should) speak (before I listen). In N. K. Denzin & Y. S. Lincoln (Eds.), *The Sage handbook of qualitative research* (4th ed.) (pp. 381–386). Thousand Oaks, CA.: Sage.
Lincoln, Y. (1990). The making of a constructivist. In E. Guba (Ed.), *The paradigm dialogue* (pp. 67–87). Newbury Park, CA: Sage.
Lincoln, Y., & Guba, E. (1985). *Naturalistic inquiry*. Beverly Hills, CA: Sage.
Piller, I. (2011). *Intercultural communication: A critical introduction*. Edinburgh: Edinburgh University Press.
Schutz, A. (1973). *Phenomenology and social reality: Essays in memory of Alfred Schutz: Collected papers I* (Vol. I). The Hague: Martinus Nijhoff.
Scollon, R., Scollon, S.-W., & Jones, R. (2012). *Intercultural communication: A discourse approach* (3rd ed). Chicester, West Sussex, UK: Wiley.
Van Maanen, J. (1988). *Tales of the field: On writing ethnography*. Chicago: University of Chicago Press.

5 Critical Reflexive Ethnography and the Multilingual Space of a Canadian University
Challenges and Opportunities

Sylvie A. Lamoureux

Drawing on fieldwork experiences and results of a mixed-method research project, as well as an ongoing autoethnography exploring language policy issues related to French in a minority context in Ottawa, Ontario, Canada, this chapter explores challenges and opportunities brought to light by reflexivity when conducting research in one's place of work. Power relations are at play on a variety of different levels: between the 'institution' and the primary researcher, an early–career, tenure-track academic; between researchers and participants; and even between researchers. As the chapter unfolds, supported by a few autoethnographic accounts (Holt, 2003), we navigate the many roles and preconceived notions of researcher and researched.

This chapter begins by setting the stage, that is, providing important information about the intersection of contexts that define the University of Ottawa (uOttawa) as a research setting and situating the narrator, the principal investigator of the project from which data for this chapter is drawn. This is followed by an overview of the research project and of my autoethnographic journey. Then, I delve into the challenges and opportunities that were highlighted through the reflexive lens of this research project.

SETTING THE STAGE: THE RESEARCH SITE

The city of Ottawa, Canada's national capital, is at the eastern edge of the province of Ontario. The University of Ottawa, North America's largest bilingual university (French-English), is located at the heart of the city, within walking distance of the Parliament, the downtown core, and embassies of the world's nations. It is situated against the backdrop of a national official bilingualism framework, within an officially unilingual (i.e., Anglophone) province (Ontario), bordering Canada's only officially unilingual Francophone province (Québec). This intersection of linguistic realities—communities within a space shared by several geopolitical borders and against the larger backdrop of Canadian multilingualism and multicultural reality—makes for a rather interesting laboratory in which to conduct research in general and critical reflexive ethnographic studies in particular. In this space, linguistic identity and issues relating to language are omnipresent in the daily negotiations of one's reality and place within this space.

Founded in 1848 by the Oblate Fathers, the University of Ottawa became a publically funded institution in 1965.[1] The university's nine faculties offer a wide array of undergraduate, graduate, postgraduate and professional programs, in English and in French. The institution has evolved as a city within the nation's capital, reflecting the evolution of Canadian society. In the fall of 2012, the university welcomed 42,000 students, of which 13,000 studied in French (Lamoureux & Malette, 2012). The university attracts students from across the province, the country, and internationally who wish to pursue studies in French medium-of-instruction programs, English medium-of-instruction programs, or our French immersion program. At the undergraduate level, 62% of students are registered in English medium-of-instruction programs, 30% in French medium-of-instruction programs, and 8% in French immersion programs.

About 55% of graduates from Ontario's French first-language secondary schools, who attend a university in that province, choose to attend the University of Ottawa (Labrie et al., 2009). It is not surprising, then, that Ontario students constituted 50% of the university's 2012 Francophone program first-year cohort. Students from Quebec's college system (cegep) accounted for 21%, while students from Canadian secondary schools accounted for another 13% (including Secondaire V graduates from Quebec). International students and or visa students accounted for 6% of this cohort. If we take a closer look at the provenance of students from the province of Ontario, we see the important impact of geography (Frenette, 2003) on postsecondary choice. Almost two-thirds of these students live within 150 kilometers of the university, in Eastern Ontario; 20 percent are from Northern Ontario and 15 percent from Southwestern Ontario (Lamoureux et al., 2013).

Linguistic and cultural heterogeneity is now the norm at the University of Ottawa. Massification of access to postsecondary education and evolving sociodemographic profiles of communities from which the university recruits have shifted the student body at this university from two largely monolithic linguistic groups, French and English, to linguistically and culturally diverse populations with blurred linguistic borders (Lamoureux & Malette, 2012). In 2008, 86% of students from Ontario who registered in a French medium-of-instruction program at the University of Ottawa identified French as their mother tongue, and a little over 5% identified a language other than French or English. By 2011, less than 80% of undergraduate students in French medium-of-instruction programs identified French as their mother tongue, and almost 10% of students identified a language other than French or English. A similar upward trend in linguistic heterogeneity is noted among students who register in one of the university's English medium-of-instruction programs (Lamoureux et al., 2013: 29). While striving to meet the needs of all students through its English and French medium-of-instruction programs, the university still retains its particular mandate[2] to serve Ontario's French language population through its 'commitment to the promotion of French culture' (University of Ottawa, 2012).

ONTARIO'S 'FRANCOPHONIE'

As previously indicated, Ontario is officially a unilingual Anglophone province. Its more than half a million Francophones represent about 4.5% of the province's population and is the largest Francophone community outside the province of Quebec.

They live across the province, in communities that are generally considered extreme minority regions, where Francophones represent less than 4% of the population, although in a few communities, Francophones represent the majority linguistic group, particularly along the border of Quebec, in Northern and Eastern Ontario. However, more than 70% of Francophones in Ontario live in communities where they represent less than 20% of the population (Lamoureux et al., 2013). It is important to note that, although 532,860 of Ontarians identified French as their mother tongue in the 2006 federal census, over 1,426,540 reported knowledge of French (Statistics Canada, 2006). In a country such as Canada that relies on immigration for demographic growth, we must look beyond mother tongue to have a true appreciation of both the diversity of members that make up communities of practice of French language speakers (Lamoureux, 2012) and of the numerous and complex multilingual spaces that represent a rich daily reality and that are too often hidden in an official bilingual framework (see Byrd Clark, 2012a).

Most communities in Ontario have access to the province's vast parallel network of publically funded French first-language K–12 schools. However, access to postsecondary education in French is much more regionalized. Students from a majority of communities in Northern and Southwestern Ontario must travel several hundred to well over a thousand kilometers to attend a French-language college or a bilingual university (Lamoureux, 2007). Although they stay within the province's borders, past research confirms that they do indeed cross linguistic borders because the communities closer to these Francophone and bilingual postsecondary institutions tend to have greater concentrations of Francophones and different identity markers than communities in regions where Francophones represent an extreme minority (Boisonneault, 2004; Byrd Clark, 2008, 2012b; Cotnam, 2012; Gérin-Lajoie, 2003; Labrie, 2012; Lamoureux, 2007; Turner, 2012).

SITUATING THE NARRATOR: THE PRINCIPAL INVESTIGATOR

Before presenting a quick overview of the research project that informed this chapter, I believe it is necessary for researchers to 'draw on their own experiences to extend understanding' of their object of study [Reed-Danahay

(1997), as cited in Holt, 2003:18]. In this case, I sought a deeper understanding of the student experience of Francophone youth from extreme minority regions, as they transition to universities in Ontario, particularly their experience of integration within the Francophone communities of bilingual universities (Lamoureux, 2007).

I firmly believe that linguistic and cultural identities are chosen and lived and that they are not necessarily tied to the first language they learn or to the language of one's parents. In this sense, I see linguistic identity tied to local communities of language practice (Pennycook, 2010). These differ from linguistic communities because communities of practice are not defined solely on the basis of mother tongue, but by all those who choose to speak a language, regardless of its status as an L1, L2, or L3.

I consider myself a Francophone; that is, although I speak French, English, and Spanish, I identify most linguistically and culturally with Ontario's Francophone communities of practice. Born in Sudbury, Ontario, prior to accepting my position at the University of Ottawa in 2008, I spent the majority of my adolescence and adult life living and working in Central Southwestern Ontario, in communities were Francophones are both extreme minorities (less than 2 percent of the population) and often extremely minoritized; that is, the French language and Francophone cultures can be marginalized by the larger community.[3]

As a child, we moved a lot. I became aware of the different linguistic varieties and registers of French, as we crossed municipal and regional borders and I attempted to integrate myself into Francophone communities and communities of practice in Eastern, Central, and Southern Ontario. I chose to pursue a career as a teacher in French first-language schools in Central Southwestern Ontario. As my first graduates pursued postsecondary education, I became increasingly aware of the challenges they experienced in their transition and integration to universities around the province. Despite a significant increase in the number of programs offered in French by the province's bilingual universities since the 1980s, many Francophone students I knew, graduates of French first-language secondary schools in Southwestern Ontario who had initially enrolled in French medium-of-instruction postsecondary program, would change to English medium-of-instruction programs or report difficulties integrating communities of French language speakers when relocating to regions in Central and Eastern Ontario where there are more Francophone communities than Francophone communities of practice.

The various testimonials that were confided to me spurred my pursuit of doctoral studies. My PhD project, a critical reflexive ethnography, tracked 15 French first-language secondary school students from Southwestern Ontario over 18 months as they graduated secondary school and transitioned to university in Ontario. Moving from an outsider to an insider status requires time, observation, and trust, and sometimes it is not achievable over 24 months.

As Chun states, 'an integral aspect of the critical is reflexivity in the form of a heightened awareness of how things (including oneself) are presented' (Chapter 8 this volume: 175). Reflexivity as a process of personal and professional growth has thus been a part of my journey for most of my life, helping me define my sphere of influence and opportunities for learning or action. Through this reflexive journey, I have come to identify myself in part as a *border dweller*, being at ease on the margins, the periphery, as well as at the center, as relationships form and strengthen and one is recognized and welcomed as part of a community. I am from here and there, what Turner [1967, as cited by Mahdi et al. (1987) in Preston (2011): 13] might refer to as 'betwixt and between.' I identify myself as Francophone and multilingual, generally being able to cross seamlessly and for the most part unnoticed, from one official language group to another, in a minority context. This also extended to my dual simultaneous realities within my research/work space: uOttawa. Reflexivity has always been an important part of my research toolkit. However, for this project, it was essential because the research experience and my professional daily experience as a professor were intertwined. I choose to do most of my research through a tridimensional critical reflexive ethnographic lens, supported by some quantitative tools to help inform my analysis of the qualitative or situate my findings in a broader context.

The critical lens enables me to include the 'political' dimensions to ethnography, revealing and questioning the power relations that belie the observed and shared realities of the various actors participating in the research projects (Simon & Dippo, 1986), as well as 'lead to disruptions in the status quo and empowerment of disenfranchised groups' (Baumbusch, 2011: 184), in this case to Francophone youth and their increased persistence and success in French language postsecondary education.

The reflexive lens applies to the researcher's process in identifying, confronting, and making explicit her biases and preconceived notions as they relate to the object of study (Aull-Davies, 2010, cited in Lamoureux, 2011a), in all phases of the study pre-, in- and postfieldwork, including the writing of results. However, in my research endeavors, reflexivity also applies to the participants, whom I generally view as co-researchers participating in the co-construction of the research data because they are called upon to position themselves and reflect upon their journeys of transition from *élève* to *étudiant*, from secondary school to university. This lens enables me to capture what Najar (Chapter 9, this volume: 193) refers to as the "messiness"/ impact of [the] process' on all actors and sites, including the researcher and the research process.

In this sense, the autoethnographic lens enriches the reporting of research findings. As Tenni, Smyth, and Bochner state:

> We must write about what we really prefer not to write about. It is not about presenting ourselves in a good light—in charge, competent, controlled, organised and so on, or how we might like to be seen. Rather

it is about writing rich, full accounts that include the messy stuff—the self-doubts, the mistakes, the embarrassments, the inconsistencies, the projections and that which may be distasteful. It is about writing all of it. (Cited in Preston, 2011: 110)

More than mere autobiography, autoethnographic anecdotes based in the reflexivity shared in this chapter allow me to fully present the challenges and opportunities that arose in the process of conducting critical reflexive ethnography in the multilingual space that is the University of Ottawa, a process that mirrored my path from junior academic to tenure. As Jackson (Chapter 1, this volume) reminds us, for Dewey (1929: 367), learning comes not from experiencing but from 'reflecting on experience.'

FROM OBSERVATION TO ACTION

In November 2009, I was approached by the Associate Registrar–Recruitment at uOttawa, who had stumbled upon my publications. He was surprised to realize that I was a faculty member at the university. We met to discuss my research findings, including the results of my doctoral research, which demonstrated that the four participants in my study, who had transitioned to uOttawa in 2003–2004, had experienced significant difficulties integrating the Francophone community at the university. This experience had impacted not only their academic success but also their linguistic identity and social integration.

Participants who had studied at Laurentian University in Sudbury, the province's other large bilingual university, had reported similar experiences. Interestingly, participants who chose to study at English medium-of-instruction universities were also not perceived by peers and professors as legitimate Francophones when experiencing language-related academic challenges.

BEYOND THE OTTAWA VALLEY

As our first meeting drew to a close in late November 2009, I invited the Associate Registrar to join me that weekend, when I would be meeting with a group of grade 12 secondary school students from Southwestern Ontario who were visiting the university prior to submitting their applications for admission. I explained that graduates of their school board, currently studying at uOttawa, would serve as informal 'ambassadors,' helping the grade 12 students imagine a possible postsecondary future at the university by sharing their own recent experiences of transition. My role was to address the linguistic shock that often arises during the transition to university when trying to integrate a setting where the French language is more dominant than in their home communities. Using some examples lived by the 'ambassadors' and the participants from my doctoral project that were from the same area, I identified and explained the concept of linguistic insecurity, hoping to help students move to a sense of linguistic security prior to their arrival on campus. The Associate Registrar accepted my offer, and with the Manager of the Student Support Unit, despite our varied backgrounds and disparate work responsibilities at the university, we worked toward a common goal: to ensure that all students have a successful university experience.

Working collaboratively with three Ontario French first-language school boards in regions where French is highly minoritized, we hired second-year university students originally from these boards, whom administrators had identified as former school leaders. I trained these students to conduct focus groups and do thematic discourse analysis, and over the course of five months in 2010–2011, we met with over 250 undergraduate Francophone students from regions where the French language is in an extreme minority context. The focus groups were student led from recruitment to analysis, following one clear directive: the university needed to hear the good, the bad, and the ugly regarding students' experiences of transition to and integration into the university's Francophone community. Turnout exceeded our expectations, and we had to limit participation.

Analysis of the focus group transcripts revealed four overarching themes, regardless of region:

1. Students struggle with linguistic insecurity, particularly during their first year of university. Their linguistic and cultural capitals are reported as having little or no value in their new habitus or setting.
2. Students from extreme minority regions are often not recognized as legitimate Francophones by their monolingual Francophone peers and professors or Francophones from regions where the French language is not in an extreme minority context. They are subjected to numerous accounts of symbolic violence[4] from both their peers and their professors (including lecturers and teaching assistants).
3. Students have difficulty accessing information about university services, let alone accessing student support services, until well into their third or fourth year.
4. Students felt ill prepared for the challenges of their first-year French foundational language course.

Based on these findings, the registrarial team and the then vice president academic decided to launch a pilot peer-mentoring program for French language students from extreme minoritized regions, in collaboration with our contacts from three French first-language district school boards. The pilot program would be documented by a mixed method research project, conducted by a collaborative research team initially comprised of myself, the Associate Registrar–Recruitment and the Manager of the Academic Support Unit.

The research project benefited from funding from the Higher Education Quality Council of Ontario (HEQCO), which allowed us to include graduate students as coresearchers and research assistants, as well as the associate vice president for undergraduate programs, the associate vice-president Institutional Research and Planning, and the Assistant Director Institutional Research and Planning. The project was launched just as I was submitting my application for tenure and promotion.

SOMEBODY LIKE ME: REGIONAL PEER MENTORING AT UOTTAWA

The regional peer mentoring program implemented in 2011–2012 targeted 264 Francophone first-entry undergraduate students from four regions where French is highly minoritized and/or in an extreme minority context. Peer mentors were asked to design the program based on the premise 'somebody like me,' informed by the results of the focus groups they led in 2010–2011. The project would adopt a 'for students by students' approach. Four students worked during the summer months, and a total of seven mentors welcomed and accompanied students during the university year, reporting directly to the associate registrars (recruitment and operations).

The regional peer mentoring initiative differs from other peer mentoring programs at uOttawa in that it (1) is proactive in nature and (2) targets specific students who share a common geolinguistic experience. In May 2011, mentors initiated e-mail contact with all incoming students from their region and created dedicated Facebook pages. Two hundred students joined these pages, and, over the course of 12 months, 100 students met with their mentor (in single and multiple visits), and another 25 were referred to and met with their faculty-specific peer mentor for academic support.

Mentors communicated with their students through e-mail, text messaging, and calls, but Facebook was by far the most used communication tool, in both public and private spaces. Mentors met with students alone or in groups, visited their home region for meetings with students and their parents just prior to the start of the academic year, and helped incoming students navigate the course registration website. Finally, mentors organized several group social activities on campus throughout the year. This initiative can be summarized as follows: a regional, proactive service that acts as a stepping stone or guide to facilitate social and academic integration into the university's Francophone community through personal contacts and networking (Cotnam, 2012).

A mixed-methods research design, with an established critical reflexive ethnographic component, was chosen to document and assess the impact of this initiative from both the participants' and the mentors' perspectives. The project drew inspiration from numerous research findings and methodologies.

Mentoring in postsecondary institutions is a growing field of study. Though the majority of sources consulted[5] demonstrated the importance and impact of mentoring programs on student success in postsecondary institutions, Terrion and Leonard's (2007) taxonomy of key characteristics of peer mentors to ensure successful program and student outcomes guided our work in selecting mentors and developing our data collection and analytical tools.

Although access, transition, persistence, and student experience are often presented as distinct areas of study within higher education, my previous work (Lamoureux, 2007, 2010, 2011a, 2011b) demonstrated the need for our research to address them within one study and to focus on the perspective of language minority students.[6] This perspective is oftentimes overlooked in studies that perceive students as a linguistically and culturally homogeneous (Anglophone) student body.

Language in general is another concept that is often overlooked in previous studies on student success and student experience in postsecondary education. We chose to address the concept in terms of university literacy[7] in order to help us identify gaps between students' literacy practices at the end of secondary school and the literacy requirements of work at the university level. Ongoing research in Francophone universities in Belgium since the early 1990s (Parmentier, 2011) was particularly useful in conceptualizing our analytical framework.

Finally, we drew on Bourdieu's notions of habitus, capital, and symbolic violence (1991), as well as Goffman's notion of stigma (1975) to justify the proactive nature of the peer mentoring program and its objective to help students feel linguistically secure in their new environment, despite being othered by Francophones from linguistically dominant or nonminoritized areas based on their accents, vocabulary, syntax, or even names. Bourdieu's and Goffman's concepts were an essential part of our conceptual and analytical frameworks and led to a better understanding of students' accounts of their experiences of transition and academic success, as well as how prevailing linguistic ideologies on campus (and students reactions to these) impacted not only their linguistic identity but also their academic and social integration.

All Facebook, e-mail and text messaging artifacts were analyzed thematically, including email exchanges between mentors and members of the university administration and the research team. Participants were invited to complete two surveys, one just before the start of the fall semester and one at the beginning of the winter semester, and to participate in two focus groups, one in early January 2012 and the other in May 2012, held in five regional cities once students had completed their first year of study. The research team participated in all regional visits, focus groups, and social activities.

Mentors played a dual role in this project. On the one hand, they formed part of the 'researched.' They were invited to participate in three focus groups. Furthermore, we asked them to keep a reflexive field journal, in which they could document their journey as mentors, as well as reflect upon their experiences and the impact of their work, as they integrated their new roles as mentors and performed this identity.

128 *Sylvie A. Lamoureux*

Finally, reflexivity was central in pre-, in- and postfieldwork to ensure that methodological rich points (Hornberger, 2006) related to the research relationships that could/would be formed during the study and to the experiencing of fieldwork by researchers and participants were not relegated to the margins (Lamoureux, 2011c). These rich points provided insight into the challenges and opportunities of conducting critical reflexive ethnography in the multilingual space that is the University of Ottawa.

CHALLENGES

> The committee asked me to meet with you. They feel your French is incomprehensible and unacceptable. They request that from now on, you submit your proposals in English. (Personal notes, December 2008)

> I came to the University of Ottawa to preserve and improve my French yet I'm always being told that my French isn't that bad for an Anglophone. (Participant focus group 1)

> My professor [fourth-year Français seminar] started the class by informing us she was perplexed by an expression she came across in one of our assignments. She was happy that we had an Anglophone in our class she could call upon to explain this term. I was surprised upon hearing this because I didn't realise there was an Anglophone in our class. I then realized she was talking about me, as she asked me to explain to her what 'douchebag' meant'. (Personal exchange with mentor, fall 2011)

As Jackson (Chapter 1 this volume) indicates, 'study and residence in an unfamiliar linguistic and cultural setting has the potential to be transformative' (??). The results of the analysis of the pilot project data demonstrate that the students where ill prepared for their new habitus because they did not anticipate that the Francophone community at uOttawa would in fact be an unfamiliar setting. More importantly, however, the results highlight the overwhelming success of the regional peer mentoring program in helping students from highly minoritized areas integrate themselves into this new habitus, academically and socially. Participants strongly feel that regional mentors are crucial in accessing essential information, resources, and services that positively impact their transition to university. Furthermore, they believe that social networking between Francophones and access to an insider perspective are necessary to a successful transition to postsecondary education (Cotnam, 2012; Lamoureux et al., 2013).

However, the research process and the data analysis revealed two major themes that presented particular challenges to various actors associated with the research project: (1) Linguistic and lexical insecurity abounds; and (2) furthermore, students participating in the peer mentoring program struggle in university programs reflecting dominant monolingual ideologies, as demonstrated in the previous three excerpts. These findings confirm the findings of the preliminary focus groups in 2010–2011 yet demonstrate how widespread these phenomena are experienced, not only during the transition to university but throughout a student's career as an undergraduate student and beyond.

The last two excerpts at the beginning of this section are representative of the experience of the vast majority of participants in the regional peer mentoring pilot project. They reveal how participants, first-entry students and mentors alike, were not recognized as legitimate Francophones and discouraged from performing and assuming Francophone identities, by peers and university personnel. Mentors found it particularly challenging as they became aware of the pervasiveness of these ideologies and felt the tensions embedded in the power relationships that traversed their 'work,' 'research,' and 'student' realities.

Symbolic violence poses two challenges because oftentimes the perpetrators are not aware of the impact of their words or actions and the victims believe that the identity reflected by the other is more legitimate than their own performed identity. Mentors recognized that they could intervene with students from a critical perspective to help them react to these statements from a position of linguistic security rather than succumb to the symbolic violence embedded in statements made by individuals unaware of the realities and the difficulties of ensuring the vitality of French in extreme minoritized regions. However, they found it difficult to reconcile their personal and their students' social experience as Francophones within the university's Francophone community with the university's mandate to serve Ontario's Francophone population.

Life transitions are moments filled with moments of instability, providing individuals with an opportunity to redefine themselves, as they adapt to new situations (Zittoun & Perret-Clermont, 2001). This holds true for the transition to university, where youth take on the new identity of university student. During these transitions, individuals may experience what Mezirow (2000) calls a 'disorientating dilemma' that can be a trigger for change, the transformative potential referred to earlier by Jackson (Chapter 1, this volume). For Francophones from extreme minority regions, these moments of disorientation caused by the linguistic shock experienced during those first few weeks at university do not necessarily lead to transformative learning but negatively impact their identity. The challenge, then, is to provide youth with positive role models that have experienced these dilemmas and help stem off linguistic insecurity. A closer look at our data did not reveal any incidences where students experienced other forms of insecurity. This is perhaps due to the linguistic nature of the study.

In the first six weeks of the fall semester, a linguistic crisis of sorts was gripping students because they were confronted by the gap in their literacy practices and those valued at university. As one student shared in a survey:

> One of my biggest challenges was [the] French [language at the University of Ottawa]. In Barrie, we all have the same slang and teachers understand. It's very different here. It's more of an academic French. (Survey 2, January 2012)

The mentors' journals for the fall semester abound with the struggles their students faced in foundational language courses. The following excerpt, from a Southwestern Ontario mentor's journal, is representative of her colleagues:

> The student had many problems with FRA1710. The teaching assistant in her course would constantly make negative remarks about her French language skills: 'are you in the right program? [Suggesting the student should switch to English] Your level of French will not help you succeed in this course.' I then had to reassure the student and to explain to her that she wasn't the only one in this situation. (Fall 2011 journal, Southwestern Ontario 1).

As mentors shared these experiences with the researchers very much in real time, I felt the conflicts and burden of limited spheres of influence. Through this project, I could accompany students and guide them to limit the impact of linguistic insecurity and discuss linguistic ideologies with them. However, I could not directly address the source of the negative experiences lived by these Francophone students from extreme minority and extremely minoritized regions—a lack of awareness by university personnel (staff and teaching faculty) of the realities of Francophones from these regions and the tremendous efforts these students put forth in choosing to attend uOttawa to 'improve and maintain their French'(Focus groups, 2010–2011), ensuring the continued vitality of diverse Francophone communities of practice in Ontario.

As a tenure track junior faculty member undergoing her tenure review, and as a Francophone from an extremely minoritized region, I knew firsthand the impact of these linguistic ideologies within the university. The first excerpt presented at the beginning of this section is a comment that was made to me in December 2008, during my first semester as a tenure track professor at the University of Ottawa. I was dumbfounded at the comments that had been communicated to me by a staff member. The committee that had reviewed my proposal had assumed that as a graduate of the University of Toronto I was more at ease writing in English, whereas I had the vast majority of my coursework for my MEd and PhD in French. As a confident adult, I could find my voice but found myself feeling moments of professional insecurity in light of my 'precarious' position as an early career researcher in a tenure track position.

I found these same feelings surfacing as I presented initial findings to the larger research team, not knowing the limits wherein I could fully express the analysis of my findings. Students and mentors had revealed to me names of colleagues who had professed the statements reflecting dominant monolingual ideologies. Ethical considerations required me to share nuanced responses with students and mentors, when inside I felt just as outraged as them, if not more so. An awareness of my journey of researcher, through my reflexive and critical lens, helped me identify an opportunity to create a transformative moment of empowerment by sharing my own experiences of transition to uOttawa (albeit transition as professor) with students and mentors. This sense of knowing they were not alone in their experiences, that even a 'Francophone' professor experienced them, contributed to their sense of linguistic security, and their rejection of both the symbolic violence and the linguistic stigma.

OPPORTUNITIES

The built-in reflexive component of this research project presented several opportunities to the research team to transform future students' experience of being a Francophone student from extreme minority regions at uOttawa. Mentors were essential in providing factual accounts to our university staff coresearchers, to help to ensure that policies and practices could be informed by research.

The linguistic crisis experienced in the fall of 2011 by Francophone students in their French foundational language course led to the creation of a new French language course, at the students' request, to help them bridge the gap between their linguistic repertoire and the literacy requirements in French medium-of-instruction programs at the University of Ottawa. Mentors were instrumental in recruiting students for this new course by helping new incoming students make research-informed decisions on course choice for the fall of 2012.

This project provided an opportunity to demonstrate the impact of student voice in evidence-based practice to develop and implement far-reaching institutional policies and practices. Empowering students by providing them opportunities to share their opinions and to see how they are incorporated into the decision-making process is transformative and helped fulfill the critical foundations of the research project.

Bringing together academics, administrators, researchers, students, and staff from various sectors of the university was in itself a unique opportunity to bring further awareness about the significant changes in the university's student body over the past decades. The project provided the opportunity to understand that these changes are more complex than what can be apprised by variables such as mother tongue, language of instruction, or language of use. It provided an opportunity to bring to light the nature of linguistic ideologies prevalent across different populations on campus: students, staff, and faculty, as well as the complexities of multilingual spaces within an official languages framework.

Participating in a collaborative research team with students as coresearchers and with university administrators also provided a unique opportunity to break down traditional silos so common to universities or, for that matter, any institutional setting. Anticipating and planning for reflexive moments in the research as part of the design further enhanced the collaborative nature of the team and the project.

Perhaps the greatest opportunities that came from this critical reflexive ethnographic project at uOttawa are the experiences that the mentors take away. Mentors write:

- Before I was a mentor, I felt more like a number. Being a mentor enables me to contribute something to the University. It makes me feel as if I am part of it. (Mentor 3, Winter 2012)
- I love the students and this is an important job for me because I think we are truly helping them. I also think la francophonie is very important and I feel I can help them be more at ease about who they are and how they speak. (Mentor 1, Winter 2012)
- I have made many contacts in the different Faculties and with services offered on campus. (Mentor 2, Winter 2012)

These excerpts, from mentors' winter 2012 journals, reveal their heightened sense of belonging, their feeling of empowerment, and their increased social capital. As mentors, they are now better equipped to navigate the university, its regulations, and its services not only in the service of others but also to impact positively on their own student experience(s).

CONCLUSION

As I conclude this chapter, I feel compelled to admit that the writing of this chapter has been one of the most difficult writing experiences I have encountered. As I attempted its various drafts, awaiting the final decision on my tenure and promotion, I became acutely aware of the impact of the power relations on my ability to adequately share the challenges and opportunities revealed during this project. I would censure my thoughts before my fingers could transform keystrokes into words. Perhaps, then, this was one of the greatest challenges that I had not anticipated in the planning of the pre-, in-, and postfield experiences of this collaborative project.

I received confirmation of my tenure and promotion a few days before the deadline to submit this chapter. This unanticipated liberation highlighted the constraints of not knowing and of the precariousness of undertaking critical reflexive ethnographic work in multilingual spaces when that space is your workplace. But reflecting on this as I wrote also heightened the challenges that students may feel being coresearchers in research teams where, despite collaborative approaches and best intentions, power relations remain between employer and employee, professor and student, administrator and student.

Chauvier posits 'introspection remains under the authority of the institution' (Chapter 7, this volume: 207). However, thanks to the support and collaboration of my coresearchers, the discussions around the planned reflexive moments of this project enabled us to transform most challenges into learning opportunities not only for participants and researchers but also for administrators and the university as an institution.

A large challenge still remains: raising the awareness of all university staff and personnel of the monolithic linguistic ideologies that still linger on campus, as well as their impact on French language speakers from extreme minority regions and regions where French is highly minoritized. However, small yet important steps are being made as new discursive spaces open through disseminating the findings of this study. Once we have raised the level of consciousness on this issue, new opportunities to transform the university to better meet the needs of all students within this multilingual space will present themselves for action.

Looking back on the results of the research project, I recognized that many methodologies were available to us as we designed the project. Though the results of the data analysis may well have been the same, I doubt that the opportunities that presented themselves because of the critical reflexive nature of the ethnographic component of this research would have been noticed or taken up as they did. In this sense, the use of critical reflexive ethnography for this project allowed us to 'liberate' introspection from the grips of 'institutional authority.'

ACKNOWLEDGMENT

I would like to thank our student mentors, our graduate assistants Karine Turner and Megan Cotnam-Kappel, as well as Alain Malette, Associate Registrar–Recuitment, Jean-Luc Daoust, Manager Academic Support Unit, and Sonia Cadieux, Associate Registrar–Operations for their continued support, enthusiasm, and trust. Without you, this project would not have been possible.

NOTES

1. See the university's archive site for more information: www.archives.uottawa.ca/eng/history.html
2. Article 4, section (c) of the province of Ontario's 1965 University of Ottawa Act states that 'the objects and purposes of the University are, to further bilingualism and biculturalism and to preserve and develop French culture in Ontario.' (www.uottawa.ca/governance/university-act.html). However, in its mission statement of the 2020 Strategic Plan, the University states that 'our university is characterized by its unique history, its commitment to bilingualism, its location both in the heart of the national capital and at the

juncture of French and English Canada, its special commitment to the promotion of French culture in Ontario and to multiculturalism' (www.uottawa.ca/governance/mission.html). It is interesting to note a shift from biculturalism to multiculturalism, yet the insistence on bilingualism (French-English) remains, reflecting the evolution in Canadian policy since 1969 and the adoption of the Official Languages Act.

3. In recent history, there have been instances of strong antagonistic sentiments toward members of the Francophone community (i.e., school crisis in Penetanguishene). Conversations persist about the 'special' status afforded to French in an officially unilingual province where other linguistic groups are present in greater number than Francophones continue or, for that matter, about the costs of official bilingualism in Canada. For example, see comments posted following the Fraser Institute's January 2012 report on the costs of Official Bilingualism: www.torontosun.com/2012/01/15/bilingualism-costs-ontario-big-bucks

4. Symbolic violence is a concept developed by French sociologist Pierre Bourdieu (1982) that describes how certain hegemonic ideologies held by dominant groups that minoritize certain minority groups are seen as true by some members of the minority group, further enforcing the domination and minoritization of the minority. Bourdieu does not imply that the minority contribute to their domination but rather that this perception of hegemonic discourse is a result of their socialization process and the reproduction of inequalities by institutions.

5. We were informed, among others, by the work of Bellinger & Baker (2011), Campbell & Campbell (1997), Colvin & Ashman (2010), Ehrich et al. (2004), Ferrari (2004), Sanchez et al. (2010), Smith (2008), and Terrion & Leonard (2008).

6. We were informed by the work of Astin (1993), Attinasi (1989), Hernandez & Lopez (2004), Kanno & Harklau (2012), LeSure-Leser & King (2005), Montgomery (2010), and Watson et al., (2002).

7. We were informed by the work of Erlich & Lucciardi (1998), Gaudet & Loslier (2009), Parmentier (2011), Pollet & Delforge (2011), and Salmon et al. (2011).

REFERENCES

Astin, A. W. (1993). What matters in college? *Four critical years revisited*. San Francisco: Jossey-Bass.

Attinasi, L. C. J. (1989). Getting in: Mexican Americans' perceptions of university attendance and the implications for freshman year persistence. *Journal of Higher Education*, 60, 247–277.

Aull Davies, C. (2010). *Reflexive ethnography: A guide to researching selves and others*. London: Routledge.

Baumbusch, J. (2011). Conducting critical ethnography in long-term residential care: Experiences of a novice researcher in the field. *Journal of Advanced Nursing*, 67 (1), 184–192.

Bettinger, E. P., & Baker, R. (2011). *The Effects of student coaching in college: An evaluation of a randomized experiment in student mentoring*. NBER Working Paper No. 16881.

Boissonneault, J. (2004). Se dire . . . mais comment et pourquoi? Réflexions sur les marqueurs d'identité en Ontario français, Actes du colloque annuel 2004 du Centre de recherche en civilisation canadienne-française (CRCCF), tenu à l'Université d'Ottawa le 5 mars 2004, 'Mémoire et fragmentation. L'évolution de

la problématique identitaire en Ontario français.' *Francophonies d'Amérique*, 18, 163-169.
Bourdieu, P. (1982). *Ce que parler veut dire: L'économie des échanges linguistiques*. Paris: Fayard.
Bourdieu, P. (1991). *Language and symbolic power*. G. Raymond & M. Adamson (Trans.). Cambridge, MA: Harvard University Press.
Byrd Clark, J. (2008). Representations of multilingualism and language investment in a globalized world. In M. Mantero, P. Chamness Miller, & J. Watzke (Eds.), *Readings in language studies*, Vol. 1: *Language across disciplinary boundaries* (pp. 261-277). New York: International Society for Language Studies.
Byrd Clark, J. (2012a). Heterogeneity and a sociolinguistics of multilingualism: Reconfiguring French language pedagogy. *Language and Linguistics Compass Blackwell Online Journal*, 6 (3), 143-161.
Byrd Clark, J. (2012b). Vous n'êtes pas francophone, vous, vous êtes francophile: Que veut dire être et devenir francophone? In S. Lamoureux & M. Cotnam (Ed.), *Prendre sa place: Parcours et trajectoires identitaires en Ontario français* (pp. 79-84). Ottawa: Éditions David.
Campbell, T. A., & Campbell, D. E. (1997). Faculty/student mentor program: Effects on academic performance and retention. *Research in Higher Education*, 38, 727-742.
Colvin, J. W., & Ashman, M. (2010). Roles, risks, and benefits of peer mentoring relationships in higher education. *Mentoring and Tutoring*, 18, 121-134.
Cotnam, M. (2012). Le choix de la langue d'instruction en milieu minoritaire: Reflet de l'identité linguistique? In S. Lamoureux & M. Cotnam (Ed.), *Prendre sa place: Parcours et trajectoires identitaires en Ontario français* (pp. 115-142). Ottawa: Éditions David.
Dewey, J. (1929). *The Quest for Certainty: A Study of the Relation of Knowledge and Action*. London: George Allen & Unwin.
Ehrich, L. S., Hansford, B., & Tennent, L. (2004). Formal mentoring programs in education and other professions: A review of the literature. *Educational Administration Quarterly*, 40, 518-540.
Erlich, V., & Lucciardi, J. (2004). Le rapport à l'écrit des étudiants d'université. *Spirale*, 33.
Ferrari, J. R. (2004). Mentors in life and at school: Impact on undergraduate protégé perceptions of university mission and values. *Mentoring and Tutoring*, 12, 295-305.
Frenette, M. (2003). *Accès au collège et à l'université: Est-ce que la distance importe?* Ottawa: Statistique Canada.
Gaudet, E., & Loslier, S. (2009). *Recherche sur le succès scolaire des étudiants de langue et de culture différente inscrits dans les établissements collégiaux francophones du Canada*. Ottawa: Réseau des cégeps et des collèges francophones du Canada.
Gérin-Lajoie, D. (2003). *Parcours identitaire de jeunes francophones en milieu minoritaire*. Sudbury, UK: Prise de parole.
Goffman, E. (1975). *Stigmate: Les usages sociaux des handicaps*. Traduit de l'anglais par Alain Kihm. Paris: Les Éditions de Minuit.
Hernandez, J. C., & Lopez, M. A. 2004. Leaking pipeline: Issues impacting Latino/a college student retention. *Journal of College Student Retention*, 6, 37-60.
Holt, N. L. (2003). Representation, legitimation and autoethnography: An autoethnographic writing story. *International Journal of Qualitative Methods*, 2(1), 18-28.
Hornberger, N. (2006). Negotiating methodological richpoints in applied linguistics research: An ethnographer's view. In M. Chalhoub-Deville, C. Chapelle, & P. Duff (Eds.), *Interference and generalizability in applied linguistics: Multiple perspectives* (pp. 221-240). Amsterdam, The Netherlands: John Benjamins.

Kanno, Y. & Harklau, L. (2012). *Linguistic minority students go to college: Preparation, access, and persistence.* New York: Routledge.
Labrie, E. (2012). La construction identitaire dans la francophonie ontarienne: Le cas des franco-majoritaires. In S. Lamoureux & M. Cotnam (Eds.), *Prendre sa place: Parcours et trajectoires identitaires en Ontario français* (pp. 23–44). Ottawa: Éditions David.
Labrie, N., Lamoureux, S., & Wilson, D. (2009). *L'accès des francophones aux etudes postsecondaires en Ontario: Le choix des jeunes.* Rapport final. Toronto: Centre de recherche en education franco-ontarienne de l'Université de Toronto.
Lamoureux, S. (2007). *La transition de l'école secondaire de langue française à l'université en Ontario: Perspectives étudiantes. Thèse de doctorat non publiée (PhD).* Toronto: Ontario Institute for Studies in Education, University of Toronto.
Lamoureux, S. (2010). L'aménagement linguistique en milieu scolaire francophone minoritaire en Ontario et l'accès aux études postsecondaires: interprétations et retombées. *Cahiers de l'ILOB/OLBI Working Papers,* 1, 1–23.
Lamoureux, S. (2011a). D'élève à étudiant: Identité et competences linguistiques et experiences de transition. *Bulletin Vals-Asla,* 94, 153–165.
Lamoureux, S. (2011b). Navigating pre-, in-, and post-fieldwork: Elements for consideration. *Journal of Language, Identity and Education,* 10(3), 206–211.
Lamoureux, S. (2011c). Public policy, language practice and language policy beyond compulsory education: Higher education policy and student experience. *Cahiers de l'ILOB/OLBI Papers,* 3(1), 27.
Lamoureux, S. (2012). Linguistic heterogeneity and non-traditional pathways to postsecondary education in Ontario. Paper 1 in the symposium "We all have our parts to play: The roles of students, peer-mentors and administration in creating pathways to higher education and student success for minority-language students," organized by S. Lamoureux, Society for Research in Higher Education Conference, December 12, 2012, Wales, UK.
Lamoureux, S., & Malette, A. (2012). Linguistic heterogeneity and non-traditional pathways to postsecondary education. Paper presented at AACRAO's Student Enrollment Management Conference, November 5, 2012, Orlando, Florida.
Lamoureux, S., Diaz, V., Malette, A., Daoust, J-L., Mercier, P., Bourdages, J., Turner, K., & Cotnam-Kappel, M. (2013). *Linguistic heterogeneiety and non-traditional pathways to postsecondary education in Ontario.* Toronto, Canada: HEQCO.
LeSure-Lester, G.E., & King, N. (2005). Racial-ethnic differences in social anxiety among college students. *Journal College Student Retention,* 6, 359–367.
Mezirow, J. (2000). *Learning as transformation: Critical perspectives on a theory in progress.* San Francisco: Jossey-Bass.
Montgomery, C. (2010). *Understanding the International student experience.* London/New York: Palgrave Macmillan.
Parmentier, P. (Ed.). (2011). *Recherches et actions en faveur e la réussite en première année universitaire. Vingt ans de collaboration dans la Commission 'Réussite' du Conseil interuniversitaire de la Communauté française de Belgique (CIUF).* Brussells, Belgium: CIUF.
Pennycook, A. (2010). *Language as a local practice.* London: Routledge.
Pollet, M. Ch., & Delforge, M. (2011). Comment developer les competences langagières des étudiants? In P. Parmentier (Ed.), *Recherches et actions en faveur e la réussite en première année universitaire. Vingt ans de collaboration dans la Commission "Réussite" du Conseil interuniversitaire de la Communauté française de Belgique (CIUF)* (pp. 50–54). Brussells, Belgium: CIUF.
Preston, A. J. (2011). Using Autoethnography to explore and critically reflect upon changing identity. *Adult Learner: The Irish Journal of Adult and Community Education 2011,* 110–125. Retrieved December 20, 2013 from www.eric.ed.gov/PDFS/EJ954307.pdf

Salmon, D., Houart, M., & Slosse, P. (2011). Pourquoi mettre en place des dispositifs d'accompagnement et de remédiation, et comment en évaluer l'efficacité? In P. Parmentier (Ed.), *Recherches et actions en faveur e la réussite en première année universitaire. Vingt ans de collaboration dans la Commission 'Réussite' du Conseil interuniversitaire de la Communauté française de Belgique (CIUF)* (pp. 32–38). Brussels, Belgium: CIUF.

Sanchez, B., Esparza, P., Berardi, L., & Pryce, J. (2010). Mentoring in the Context of latino youth's broader village during their transition from high school. *Youth and Society*, 43, 225–252.

Simon, R. I., & Dippo, D. (1986). On critical ethnographic work. *Anthropology and Education Quarterly*, 17(4), 195–202.

Smith, T. (2008). Integrating undergraduate peer mentors into liberal arts courses: A pilot study. *Innovative Higher Education*, 33, 49–63.

Statistics Canada. (2006). *2006 Community Profiles.* 2006 Census. Statistics Canada Catalogue no. 92-591-XWE. Released March 13, 2007 at www12.statcan.ca/census-recensement/2006/dp-pd/prof/92-591/index.cfm?Lang=E

Terrion, J. L., & Leonard, D. (2007). A taxonomy of the characteristics of student peer mentors in higher education: Findings from a literature review. *Mentoring and Tutoring*, 15, 149–164.

Turner, K. (2012). L'enseignement en Ontario français: Au-delà de l'enseignement des connaissances. In S. Lamoureux & M. Cotnam (Eds.), *Prendre sa place: Parcours et trajectoires identitaires en Ontario français* (pp. 51–78). Ottawa: Éditions David.

University of Ottawa. (2012). *Faculty of Education Mission Statement*, 2012. Retrieved September 12, 2013 at http://education.uottawa.ca/thefaculty/mission?lang=en.

Watson, L., Terrell, M. C., Wright, D. J., Bonner, F., Cuyjet, M., Gold, J., Rudy, D., & Person, D. R. (2002). *How minority students experience college: Implications for planning and policy.* Sterling, VA: Stylus.

Zittoun, T., & Perret-Clermont, A-N. (2001). Contributions à une psychologie de la transition. (Communication présentée dans le cadre du Congrès International de la Société suisse pour la recherche en education et de la Société suisse pour la formation des enseignantes et des enseignants. Aarau, October 5, 2001).

6 Reflexivity in Motion in Language and Literacy Learning

David Malinowski and Mark Evan Nelson

INTRODUCTION

Exploring the changing nature of writing in the early days of electronic texts, Jay David Bolter (1990) identified *instability* as a defining aspect of computer-supported literacy practices. In contrast to the formal structures of printed books, whose pages and words were assumed to transparently represent a logical, objective truth (cf. Ong, 1986), the ephemerality and instabilities of digital texts (e.g., multimedia CD-ROMs, web-based hypertexts) made it impossible to hide their architecture, to ignore the dynamic interpenetration of how texts are seen and how they are understood. Bolter explained, 'The text can be transparent or opaque, and it can oscillate between transparency and opacity, between asking the reader to look through the text to the 'world beyond' and asking him or her to look at the text itself as a formal structure' (1990: 167; cf. Lanham, 1993; Lemke, 1998). In this chapter, we examine afresh such theorizing of meaning in multimodal texts as inherently contingent and *in motion*—the kinetically cumulative product of reflexive, alternating attention to both structure and significance—as a corrective to unhelpful conventional conceptions of writing as stable representation of the world *as it is*. We argue that consciously reflexive awareness of semiotic instability and oscillation is vital to constructing knowledge in and about multimodal texts, as well as to understanding our digitally mediated world. We further recommend a preliminary taxonomy of *semiotic oscillations*, each a type of *meaning making in motion*, involving special meaning-making implications and reflexive learning opportunities.

This chapter represents a methodological exploration too. Through numerous project planning discussions, we speculated that insight into reflexivity in multimodal communication might naturally emerge from research that was itself necessarily reflexive. Accordingly, we determined to analyze our own previous research into multimodal meaning making: dismantling, connecting, and textually reconstructing the research itself, our written representations of it, and, significantly, our own positions as *textualizing subjects*. Not unlike the learners we serve, our own ideological commitments were challenged and reformulated in creating this chapter, through confronting the words and images of our own authorial pasts. As follows, we present an integrative thematic secondary analysis of four of our published research papers, all examining cases of multimodal design, after which we critically reflect upon the value and limitations of this approach.

MULTIMODALITY AND SEMIOTIC INSTABILITY

Our task here is not to redefine the 'electronic text' per se; we are concerned with multimodal textuality and textual practices more broadly and with the power of multimodality to facilitate reflexive semiotic awareness[1] in present-day readers and writers. These aims especially align with theory and research in the fields of *social semiotics* (cf. Halliday, 1973, 1978; Hodge & Kress, 1988; Kress, 2010; van Leeuwen, 2005) and *multiliteracies* (cf. Cope & Kalantzis, 2000; Kalantzis & Cope, 2012; New London Group, 1996), each regarding language, and all communication, as the interest-driven selection and systematic deployment of semiotic resources to serve social functions. M. A. K. Halliday, progenitor of both frameworks, explains, 'context plays a part in determining what we say; and what we say plays a part in determining the context. As we learn how to mean, we learn to predict each from the other' (Halliday, 1978: 2–3). This systemic-functional perspective on linguistics has been extended for purposes of analyzing other modes of representation and communication, such as visual art and imagery (Kress & van Leeuwen, 1996/2006; O'Toole, 1995) and music and sound (van Leeuwen, 1999), as well as how different semiotic modes may interact (Kress, 2003, 2010).

In language and literacy pedagogy, over the past two decades this social semiotic view of meaning making has gained recognition and influence, mainly through the promulgation of *multiliteracies*. Introduced in 1996 by the scholarly consortium known as the New London Group (NLG), the multiliteracies framework's core aim is fulfilling social participation for all, accomplished through critically, productively negotiating diversity in its multiple forms: cultural, linguistic, and textual/representational (New London Group, 1996). Since the NLG's first call to reform, several robust pedagogical frameworks have appeared, translating the principles of multiliteracies and multimodality into practicable terms. For instance, Unsworth (2001) provides a comprehensive systemic-functional approach for sensitizing learners to the different 'grammars' involved in constructing meaning in and across modes in various print and digital texts, for example, picture books. Bearne and Wolstencroft's (2007) social-semiotic approach scaffolds students into understanding and performing different written language genres through image analysis and other visual strategies. (See also Anstey & Bull, 2006; Kalantzis & Cope, 2012; Sheridan & Rowsell, 2010).

As helpful as this and related work has been, we suggest that its attachment to grammatical and systemic coherence may actually short-circuit the dynamic creative potentials of multimodal communication that are fundamental to learning. Pedagogical theory, research, and practice around multimodality, in the main, have defined systems of semiotic convergence and divergence, comparing the *semiotic affordances* and *constraints* (meaning-making potentials and limitations, approximately) of particular modes in communicative use (e.g., spoken language, photographic images) to explain intermodal or cross-modal relationships of meaning (cf. Kress, 2003; Rowsell, 2013). Although such explanations facilitate the teaching and learning of multimodal communication, they may also unhappily reproduce a crucial misapprehension about semiosis itself—namely, that each type of mode and, by implication, each image, sound, or other element in a given multimodal text should have a systematically identifiable meaning, a priori. Multimodal meaning is thereby epistemologically framed as stable and static, encoded within words, pictures, and so forth, and in predictable formal relations between these. We believe that a reflexive approach to multimodal learning, one that focuses on readers' and writers' evolving understandings of the transformations, repetitions, ruptures, and other forms of *motion* of meaning across modes—may help to resolve this troubling contradiction.

REFLEXIVITY AS METHODOLOGY AND METHOD

In authoring this chapter, we have taken a dialogic, reflective approach, making a recursive, back-and-forth compositional process the actual stuff of the textual product. We first articulated two principal research questions:

- What observable role(s), if any, can reflexive awareness play in the designing of multimodal meaning, and to what effect(s)?
- Can a reflexive analytic approach facilitate understanding of reflexivity in multimodal meaning design? If so, how?

The methodological path to addressing these questions was an admittedly circuitous one. Applying the lessons of Bourdieu's (1994) epistemic reflexivity, intended as 'a means of underwriting, rather than undermining scientific knowledge' (Maton, 2003: 57), we sought to *objectify our own prior objectifications* by revisiting our published research on multimodal composing and communication.

However, this approach was fraught for three reasons at least. First, asking whether and how to study our own work, thereby increasing awareness of ourselves and our learning over time, made us quite self-conscious. Who were we early-career researchers to presume that a retrospective examination of our few contributions would illuminate anything? Was this epistemic reflexivity or perhaps a baser case of hermeneutic narcissism (Maton, 2003; Bourdieu, 1994)? Second, how would we choose these works? Might any selection of publications betray an analytic bias [cf. Popper's (1957) Oedipus

Effect]? Third, how would we go about analyzing our analyses? Should the papers themselves be coded as textual data? Or should we reexamine the data and analyses of the previous studies themselves, the publications being only textual traces and unavoidably partial representations of the research?

After a month of e-mail and Skype-mediated discussions from our separate geographic and institutional positions [each other's electronically recorded utterances and likenesses transmitted across space and time (zones) between Australia, the United States, and Japan], we saw that these initial 'problems' were not actually barriers but windows onto a new reflexive awareness. Self-consciously questioning our warrant to review our prior research seemed precisely to validate Bourdieu's recommendation of a reflexive stance; our own reflexive process, ideologically foregrounding our assumption that only distinguished scholars may retrace their intellectual trajectories, sparked the recognition that such self-consciousness may contribute importantly to a *consciousness of self*.

We also saw that our selection of papers could never be unbiased or pretheoretical: We undeniably held preformed judgments about multimodal communication and learning that would color our choices. Thus, we saw that we must critically examine both our previous papers and the metanarratives (cf. Lyotard, 1979) we had constructed around them. Ultimately, then, our puzzlement over defining our data collection and unit of analysis reflexively shaped not only our method but also our theorizing of the research problem itself—a productive double-layeredness occasioned by engagement with one's own textual representations, similar in this sense to Chauvier's (Chapter 7, this volume) 'manufacture of the text in the analysis' of both stereotypes of marginalized urban youth and anthropological method. Our unit of analysis was the articles, and it was not. The answers to our questions were not in the printed words *or* what they meant *or* what we knew about the research from which they had come *or* what we had learned since, but in all of these. In effect, the problem and solution reflexively brought each other into focus. Looking both *at* and *through* (Bolter, 1990; Lanham, 1993) our prior work, we imagined, would reflexively position us to understand the work of the designers we had studied, through exposing the structure and artifice of the 'textual designs' we ourselves had created in representing these cases.

The data collection consisted of four articles, a refereed journal piece, a coauthored book chapter by Nelson (2006; Nelson et al., 2012), and single-authored and coauthored book chapters by Malinowski (2009, in press). The selection criteria allowed for two earlier pieces and two recent ones, representing development over time of each author's thinking on and interests in multimodal communication. Our analysis was situated within the qualitative tradition of thematic coding, beginning with a brief start list of two codes: reflexivity and movement.[2] The coding scheme was elaborated in an iterative, stage-wise manner, applying both open and comparative coding strategies (Bogdan & Biklen, 2007).

Preliminarily, to establish intercoder reliability, we each analyzed a recent article by Gunther Kress (2012), chosen for its thematic relevance to our project and generic similarity to our data. We independently analyzed the article for its rhetorical and conceptual representations of movement and reflexivity, then discussed our findings. We took the same tack in analyzing one another's works, with the plan of responding afterward in writing to the other's analyses. This approach was conceived to reexamine our work from a new vantage point, as it was re-presented to us. This resulted in a series of analytic discovery memos and responses, through which our revised understandings of our own and one another's works were made visible (cf. Flower, 1994). These memos are synthesized and elaborated in the sections to follow. Still evident in them, we think, are the conflicting interpretations and tensions that sometimes arose as we collaboratively negotiated our analytic and compositional processes. Although we agreed on the validity of each of the other's interpretations, we ultimately did not come away from this exercise entirely of the same mind. However, the process undeniably expanded and transformed both of our understandings of our own work and of the field at large.

ANALYSIS AND *REFLECTION*

Malinowski Reading Nelson (2006): Inside Synesthesia, Shifting Ideas, and Emergent Creation

In his 2006 article, 'Mode, meaning, and synesthesia in multimedia L2 writing,' Nelson foregrounds the social semiotic concepts of synesthesia and attendant processes of transformation and transduction of meaning ('the purposive reshaping of semiotic resources *within* and *across* modes, respectively': 56; cf. Kress, 2003) in the composition of multimodal texts. These concepts, he argues, hold great potential for understanding the development of authorial voice because the very conditions under which authorship takes place have been under radical transformation in recent decades. Illustrative of this shift toward 'the pictorial' (Mitchell, 1994), the data from Nelson's article derive from undergraduate English language learners' digital stories on language, culture, and identity—verbally narrated texts with image and music that had themselves been refashioned from academic-style written essays. From his analysis of interviews, journals, and the multimedia stories depicting experiences of life between cultures, Nelson posits a number of facilitators of and hindrances to the realization of authorial voice in multimodal text authorship. Students' choice to repeat certain semiotic elements in their digital stories, their attentiveness to the topology (cf. Lemke, 1998) of language, and the task of expressing an idea across more than one communicative mode were found as benefits; the inability to resolve conflicting demands of different genres of expression across communicative modes and purposes and the overaccommodation of an imagined audience appeared to vitiate the student-authors' ability to find their voices and 'engage synesthesia in its truly creative sense' (72).

Already apparent in the article's framing of questions of L2 authorship and voice with the language of social semiotics from Kress in new and multiliteracies are metaphors of movement. Visual, verbal, and other modes of communication are understood to each proffer its own affordances for meaning making, and elements of each in a multimodal text must be 'orchestrated,' 'braided,' or otherwise brought together. The key formulations of transformation and transduction, defined as the reshaping of resources '*within* and *across* modes,' might lead the reader to fall back upon conventional, linear metaphorical understandings of the movement of ideas like rigid objects: The shifting of meaning as a manner of *traversal* (of an idea across an extensive and varied semiotic landscape, for instance) or *exchange* (of messages between speakers, genres, texts, modes).

Yet Nelson's formulation of synesthesia leaves no doubt that ideas do not 'move straight across' modal boundaries; the paradigmatic form of movement characteristic of multimodal meaning making in the article is *emergence*, where multimodal composers' work leads to the 'creation of qualitatively new forms of meaning' (56). This is attested to by the student-authors themselves, as they narrate their own design practices in Nelson's study: The L1 Hmong speaker Carrie and Mandarin-speaking Bonnie both attest that 'additional meaning can accumulate within the same image as it is repeated due to the defining influence of what is said, shown, and so on, 'in between,' to use Carrie's words, different instantiations of the image as it is presented in the digital story' (63). Nelson's three facilitators of authorial voice—Resemiotization through Repetition, Recognition of Language Topology, and Amplification of Authorship—each describe a form of synergistic development of meaning between and beyond the individual semiotic resources that a multimodal author deploys in the composition of texts over a period of time.

Yet, if the *emergence* of multimodal meaning in complex semiotic environments (and not its linear development) is foregrounded in this article, there still remains, in my view, a paradox of agency underlying the notion of synesthesia proposed therein. Revisiting Nelson's definition of synesthesia ('the emergent creation of qualitatively new forms of meaning as a result of "shifting" ideas across semiotic modes'), I ponder just *who creates* in processes of 'emergent creation,' and I wonder if the scare quotes around 'shifting' in fact signal its simultaneous identity as a transitive and intransitive verb. To wit, do ideas in multimodal meaning-making practices shift on their own? Or do students like Nelson's ELL students Emma, Bonnie, and Carrie shift them as they compose? And, to the interests of the present volume, does the ambivalence between these two signal an opportunity for the development of a multimodal author's reflexive awareness?[3]

Nelson's Response

Malinowski's interpretation here prompts me to consider afresh some of my most preliminary thoughts on questions of authorial voice in multimodal expression and the potentials and complexities of 'saying what one means' within and across the semiotic parameters of different modes. Especially generative for me is the metaphor of transitivity to frame vital questions about intention, volition, and agency in relation to the emergence of new forms of meaning and knowledge through multimodal composing processes. Usefully complicating my own efforts to operationally define Kress's (2003) notion of synaesthesia, Malinowski's analysis aptly re-presents new synaesthetically derived ideas and understandings as entities/processes that might be transitively produced/enacted or else, in a manner of speaking, be actors themselves. This foregrounds for me the inherent paradox in equating a facility in multimodal composing with the textual realization of an intention (if such a thing can truly be done). Intentions are as dynamically changeable and malleable, I recognize, as whatever meanings are constructed on the basis of their transduction into textual forms. I now see more clearly in my initial analysis the new meanings actually obtained through the reflexive shifting or toggling or oscillation between both transitive and intransitive creative energies. Interestingly, it seems that our intentions and beliefs do not only shape what we express; they also take shape in the act of expressing them.

Nelson Reading Malinowski (2009): Emplaced Texts and Excitable Authorship

This chapter investigates the design and positioning of shop signs in a commercial district in Oakland, California, wherein restaurants, groceries, and other businesses associated with the Korean American community are common and conspicuous, as is the appearance of the uniquely Korean script, *hangul*. Malinowski specifically asks, 'What is the symbolic and political significance of a particular code's appearance with other codes in bilingual signs?' (107). The author's analysis centrally applies Judith Butler's (1997) concept of excitability, articulated with theoretical tools from the broader linguistic field of pragmatics and work around the notion of multimodality, as interpreted within the framework of social semiotics, which regards a priori all instances and systems of human communication as stemming directly out of social needs and functions. On the empirical bases of interviews with shopkeepers, participant observation, and multimodal textual analysis of the emplaced signs, Malinowski proposes an understanding of meaning within the linguistic landscape (LL) as only ever partly determined or controlled by the sign creator (viz. proprietor-author), pointing up the creative instability and emerging, shifting semiotic potentials—effecting what the author describes as an animate 'agency' of sorts—on the part of the built, inhabited environment.[4]

Common to each of the presented cases of shop-sign authorship is a multilayered and multiplex semiotic formula of expressive intentions, anticipation and accommodation of diverse audiences and their respective expectations, conventional representation, personal inspiration and innovation, lucky and unlucky happenstance, and differential investment in the design process, to name just a few of the many constituent factors. The imagery, language(s), script(s), and composition of each of the signs that Malinowski examined, shop owners themselves admitted, were expected to 'speak,' in part and whole, to different segments of the public in different ways for different reasons, such as to communicate an identifiable alignment with the Korean culture and community, to reach out to a wider non-Korean audience/customer base, or to do both.

Authorship, as evinced by Malinowski's findings, is naturally and unavoidably participatory, conscripting viewers into the process of newly co-constructing subjective meaning in the sign on the basis of who they are and what they bring to an act of interpretation. Significantly, the forms and extents of deliberate, designful thought applied to the acts of labeling the businesses with their signs varied from case to case: Some owners are explained to have carefully considered the representational implications of each choice color, code, word, and the like, while others, for example, simply inherited the names and signs from previous proprietors. Nonetheless, what the signs, in part and whole, might mean to each of their innumerable unknown viewers within ever changing space and time was and is largely beyond the effective control of even the most semiotically alert and deliberate designer.

In view of the present project, this semiotic instability identified in Malinowski's analysis, akin to what Harris (2009) terms a 'radical indeterminacy,' may be newly interpreted as the cumulative, cooperative result—or potential semiotic effect, perhaps—of multiple, variously interrelated types of movement or change: physical, symbolic, psychological, practical or financial, temporal, political, philosophical, and so on. Shop signs may seem materially fixed and constant, durably predictable amid the gadding about of people of themselves and ephemerality of human lives; however, Malinowski's study demonstrates the representational operation of emplaced multimodal texts as more like a *semiotic difference engine* than an invariant formula for meaning. Such texts are aggregators-in-motion of semiotic work, performed deliberately and unknowingly, proximally and distally, in the past, present, and anticipated future. Further illustrating this point, Malinowski's recruitment of Butler's (1997) notion of excitable speech is perhaps even more apt than he may have realized, which is to suggest that the particular sense of excitability belonging to the domain of quantum mechanics, likely unintended by Butler herself, may offer a special metaphorical utility in refining Malinowski's already helpful application of the term to understanding multimodality. A molecule, for example, is brought to an excited state as it is bombarded with energy not present in its ground state. The component atoms of the molecule subsequently move, resonate, and collide in new ways, propelling a stable configuration of known parts on a path of *becoming*, toward being and doing something else. Excitability, then, whether atomic or semiotic, can aid us in theorizing multimodal texts as rich stores of *potential energy*, emergent possibilities for new forms of movement and becoming, as well as of potential meaning.

Malinowski's Response

> Butler's notion of excitability still holds great sway for me, in conceiving of and theorizing the power of people to mean beyond the various intentions they put into their spoken, embodied words and, in turn, the power of those words to signify and to act beyond all expectation. And this agency of language, indeed a kind of potential energy, must be even greater to the degree that we adopt a broader, multimodal notion of language. Whereas Kress (2003) proposes that 'if the meaning of a message is realised, "spread across," several modes, we need to know on what basis this spreading happens, what principles are at work' (35), Butler suggests that one operative principle may be that the 'spreading across' of meaning is itself formative of the communicators. She writes, 'Untethering the speech act from the sovereign subject founds an alternative notion of agency and, ultimately, of responsibility, one that more fully acknowledges the way in which the subject is constituted in language, how what it creates is also what it derives from elsewhere' (Butler, 1997: 15–6). This is, for me, the sometimes confounding but always rewarding lesson to be learned from the study of semiotic landscapes, where, as Scollon and Scollon (2003: 119) note, in order to understand what multimodal signs in the material world mean, 'we must have some evidence from *outside* the signs themselves.' The notion of the linguistic landscape as a 'semiotic difference engine,' as Nelson suggests, is a powerful one indeed.

Malinowski Reading Nelson, Hull, and Young (2012): The Reorganizing Power of 'Irruption'

Six years after publishing his 2006 article investigating the potentials of synesthesia for the realization of authorial voice in multimodal composing, and the better part of a decade after beginning to chronicle the creative processes of the multimodal composer RelixStylz (Hull & Nelson, 2005), Nelson (in Nelson, Hull, & Young, 2012 returns to the compositional story of RelixStylz. The chapter, drawing from interviews with the San Francisco Bay Area–based poet, musician, and artist on his digital story composition processes, turns on the notion of 'effective surprise' (Bruner, 1973): a state of awareness that is produced in creative acts that may be either productive and receptive (or both) or, in Bruner's words, 'the unexpected that strikes one with wonder and astonishment' (220). Inquiring into the 'habits of mind and the semiotic strategies that constitute [multisemiotic, multimodal, and multimedial] literacies' (216), the authors aim to add empirically based, interpretive, and longitudinal perspectives to the often programmatic, top-down characterizations of 'twenty-first-century skills' (e.g., Partnership for 21st Century Skills[5]). In RelixStylz's own epiphanies about the meanings in his own multimodal orchestrations, and in designing numerous digital stories so as to lead his viewers to such epiphanies, the chapter's authors find evidence that, they write, 'artistic practice can be especially productive of these critical moments of emergent understanding and, as such, that creative expression might be seen as a central component of education and literacies for the twenty-first century' (216).

In addition to the *emergence of meaning* as a dominant paradigm of semiotic 'movement' in multimodal authorship [identified in my reading of Nelson (2006)], the reader of Nelson, Hull, and Young's chapter is privy to an additional phenomenon of movement that is sudden, transformative, and, crucially for our own reflexive engagement with reflexivity in *this* chapter, leaving of a trace (a form of evidence). Significant space in the data analysis of Nelson, Hull, and Young's chapter is given to documenting RelixStylz's own experience of effective surprise—not during composition or performance of one of his many digital stories, but during the research interview itself. The authors recreate for the reader a moment in which RelixStylz, asked by his interviewers about the meaning of a sequence of images in one of his digital stories, returns to give new significance to an image they had previously glossed over:

> [I]n the process of discussing the image of headphones on the sidewalk and underground hip-hop, a surprising innovation occurs. RelixStylz apprehends and actualizes the meaning potential in the connection of the image of 'sneakers hanging on a power line' to the discourse and practices—or 'semiotic domain', to borrow Gee's (2003) term—of professional basketball and the associated custom of 'retiring' the jerseys of all-star players by framing them and hanging them in the rafters of the team's home court. (225)

The inclusion of this data, in which RelixStylz 'redesigned' meanings in his multimodal text during the interview itself may, on my reading, open the door to a broadened understanding of reflexive processes in multimodal authorship, via a form of movement that can be termed 'irruption.' As St. Pierre (1997) relates in her investigation of transgressive data in qualitative research, this term signifies an almost violent epistemological breakdown and reconstitution *from within*. Indeed, irruption as an unpredictable and inward-sweeping transformation that operates on a subject's preexisting layers of semiotic, cognitive, and emotional resources seems apt to characterize RelixStylz's transformed understanding; Nelson, Hull, and Young emphasize that the exact time and place of an effective surprise cannot be specified, or even guessed in advance. In fact, this phenomenon operates as much on the multimodal author's 'store of memories and experiences, and what might be called "accrued connections" among these' (230) as it does on the author's intentional and future-oriented operations on a text.

Through the transformations of irruption, then, we see one way in which an author's varied interactions with texts across time can change understandings of both *texts and selves* in relation to those texts. As Nelson, Hull, and Young assert, borrowing the words of Bruner, 'the surprise may only come when we look back and see whence we have come' (221). In this sense, these three authors' chapter serves as more than a contribution to a body of literature on language and literacy learning. It is itself a record of one storyteller's epiphany, a durable tool with the potential to inform his future understandings. In the end, to the interest of the development of multimodal authors' reflexive awareness, it seems we must ask who would RelixStylz be, and who would we all be, without these material and social traces?

Nelson's Response

Once again, Malinowski's deconstruction of this recent chapter is a stimulus to meaningful reflection and a productive connection to the ideas expressed in the 2006 piece discussed here, as well as other intervening work. The question with which he concludes cuts to the core of our present project and to the key concerns of this volume at large. Such phenomena as epiphanies and surprises, by their nature, would seem somehow inscrutable, irreducible, even perhaps magical to a certain way of thinking; I do not recall ever having scheduled, or even having specifically anticipated, an 'aha moment.' Curiously, too, it is the flashes of 'Eureka!' (to invoke A. G. Bell's well-worn phrase) that are most often identified and celebrated as the fountainheads of inspiration and ingenuity. Though we recognize the processual, incremental, and syncretic aspects of how new meanings and understandings emerge, we might also see that the epiphany moment is that in which prior semiotic material achieves its newness, which is to say becomes presently salient and consciously relevant. In this sense, Bruner's notion of 'predictive surprise' may well usefully describe, in part, the engine of semiotic creativity that Kress (2003) termed 'synaesthesia,' as the chapter discussed here suggests. But Malinowski's comments and our larger collaborative project reported on here have put me in mind of the fundamentally kinetic nature of semiotic emergence, a necessary, iterative prediction and revisioning, a zooming out and zooming in, a dynamic interaction between Barthes's (1978) 'anchorage' and 'relay,' that is, a continual cognitive shift between connecting the various components of a multimodal text to context and personal experience, and connecting these components to one another. It seems that our present conceptions of multimodal communication are rooted mainly in one or the other of these processes but perhaps not enough in the dynamic interaction between them.

Nelson Reading Malinowski and Kramsch (2013): Looking for, and as, the Mobile, Multiform Reflexive Gaze

In this recent piece, Malinowski and Kramsch apply Bakhtin's (1981) notion of heteroglossia as an analytic lens through which to view computer-mediated communication (CMC) across boundaries of location, language, and semiotic mode. The authors take particular issue with commonsense assumptions about the capacity of CMC to provide second or foreign language (S/FL) students with direct, unmediated access to a special diversity of potential meanings and authentic 'voices' when learning and using the target language, that is, meanings and voices presumed to be comparatively inaccessible in conventional S/FL classroom settings. Presenting qualitative data analysis from an investigation of videoconferencing interactions between beginning students of French at a California university and their graduate student tutors in France, the authors argue that CMC technologies and practices do significantly mediate and influence interaction in ways that can complicate and even obfuscate communication.

Mediation, as applied here, denotes an intermediacy, a liminal, situated, shifting amalgamation of words, sounds, pixels, feelings, discourses, and the like that conveys interactions across time and distance. Inherently, then, multimodal mediation is multimodal motion—meaning that all aspects of context and elements of communication are dynamically codefined, reflexively determined, also according to the contingencies of space and time [Bakhtin's (1981) chronotope]. By way of example, consider Malinowski and Kramsch's analysis of data from the case of Ann, an American university student learning French. As the authors explain, a salient aspect of Ann's online communication experience was her consciousness and seeming concern over not looking a French male, her tutor Jean, directly in the eyes on the basis of her expectation that such gestures can be perceived as unduly forward, even sexual overtures perhaps, within the French cultural milieu. Curiously, Ann ultimately seems to re-see Jean in less stereotypical terms, apparently achieving a level of comfort with direct eye contact; yet she persists in asserting, *en français*, that she cannot meet his gaze, even as she does precisely that. In their analysis, the authors include and discuss a collage, created by Ann, that visually represents her revelation over finally being able to 'look twice' at French men. The collage depicts the outline of a computer display, inside of which are seven pairs of distinctly male eyes, seemingly clipped from magazine pages. This central complex of images is flanked on all sides by differently colored handwritten phrases in French, translated as 'the eye,' 'the look,' 'forbidden,' 'the revelation,' and 'looking twice'—a parsimonious narrativization of Ann's reported epiphany.

Convinced of the sincerity of Ann's multimodal depiction and recognizing an accordant change in her videoconferencing behavior, the researchers were struck by the obvious contradiction in Ann's continued (verbal) insistence that she could not make eye contact with Jean. On the basis of this 'multimodal oxymoron,' to coin a phrase, Malinowski and Kramsch conclude that 'the medium [of videoconferencing] did not facilitate a deeper dialog about the stereotype itself, in part because of the linguistic and cultural limitations of the two interlocutors, and in part because of the ambiguity of the communicative situation' (19, ms).

Considering the reproduced collage by Ann and the authors' interpretation of it, however, I was struck with the realization that the numerous pairs of male eyes centered in the composition, explained by the researchers as signifying the French male 'look,' are conspicuously not the eyes of French males. In fact, the largest component image by far, and the one positioned atop all of the others, clearly represents the eyes of Matt Damon, the *conspicuously American* actor and director. Could this image, I wonder, be reinterpreted as a kind of reflexive domestication of the French male gaze, a textual transformation of *the foreign* into *the familiar*? From this interpretive vantage, the initial contradiction or seeming paradox is resolved, perhaps refuting the authors' initial finding and also highlighting the vital importance to multimodal communication research of reflexively *re-seeing* for oneself the multilayered and changing relations between interacting subjects, text, cotext, and context. To focus principally on the mediation of the videoconferencing per se may be to overlook other complex, important connections and forms of multimodal mediation.

Malinowski's Response

Nelson's comments here are insightful and provocative, forcing me to *re-see* some of my assumptions about the data from a study that, I think, had perhaps become overly familiar to me. It is no exaggeration to say that, even prior to our interview with Ann, Kramsch and I had subjected her drawing to what Goodwin (1994) terms 'professional vision'—a sort of radical decontextualization that proceeds through coding, highlighting, and the subsequent production of another material representation—that is, the paper we wrote and that Nelson critiques here. Certainly, at the time of writing, neither Kramsch nor I recognized the eyes of Matt Damon or any of the other American models and actors from whose faces they were taken. And, unfortunately, we will never likely know the nationality or other salient traits that Ann might have attributed to the eyes in her drawing.

Reflexivity in Motion in Language and Literacy Learning 151

However, what Kramsch and I had first noticed when we set out to interpret Ann's words and drawing—and what strikes me even now as I pen this response—is the seeming absence in this French language student's verbally recorded expressions of a reflexive self-awareness as an outcome of her learning. To be sure, I recognize the paradox, as Nelson does, in Ann's audio-, video-, and linguistically mediated moment of interchange with Jean: Even as she asserts her inability to engage in the forbidden (*défendu*) act of looking at a French male, she discovers the ability to look at Jean. But, to return to Bolter's language of oscillation in the reading of digital texts, in this exchange I see Ann as taking the opaque for the transparent—reading Jean's seemingly direct gaze on her screen as evidence of the narrowing or even elimination of French-American difference, a 'domestication,' or stoppage, of the movement in intercultural meaning making.

DISCUSSION

As elaborated in the introduction and mentioned in Malinowski's response, we open our discussion with reference to Bolter's (1990; see also Bolter & Grusin, 2000) observation of the salience of a particular kind of movement in the reading of new textual forms. Effective multimodal meaning designers, of all kinds, must attend constantly to the complex, sometimes unpredictable affordances of technologies and other resources for making meaning, even as they strive for their voices to be heard 'as they are.' They work amid moving (semiotic, material, cognitive, biological, etc.) fields and, we have argued here, the sensibilities and sense-making faculties of the authors themselves change as well thereby. In our own past texts, we found several layered, iterative types of movement among people, multimodal textual forms, and worlds of meaning. We explain these as follows:

1. *Emergence in the synesthetic design of meaning.* As highlighted in Malinowski's commentary on Nelson (2006), when Nelson's class of English learners designed multimodal narratives of identity and belonging, attempting to express what they had previously written in the academic essay genre with the unfolding juxtapositions of voice, image, and text, they found new meanings. The power of synesthesia, capitalizing on the transformation of meaning both within and across communicative modes and semiotic resources, appears here and in the other studies we analyzed [especially Nelson et al. (2012) and Malinowski & Kramsch (in press)] not just to amplify authorial intent but to force existing sign relations into new circumstances, with sometimes unknown outcomes. The learners in these studies did, in certain cases, experience amplification and extension of authorial voice through available tools for multimodal composition. But, in

others, they experienced a distancing from their familiar, authorial voices, as expressive intentions contended with the iconic, generic values of available images and sounds.
2. *Excitability and resonance in the life of the text.* Nelson's analysis of Malinowski (2009) closes with the metaphor of multimodal texts (in that case, bilingual shop signs) as molecules, their component atoms 'elevated' to excited states when bombarded with energy. Such texts are 'aggregators-in-motion of semiotic work,' susceptible always to reinterpretation in light of new 'physical, symbolic, psychological, practical or financial, temporal, political, philosophical' conditions. In addition to the transformation of claimed or imputed authorial voices demonstrated through the paradigm of 'emergence,' metaphors of excitability and resonance attest to the potential energy, even agency, of the complex, unstable nature of the multimodal text itself.
3. *Sudden reorganizations in designer epistemologies.* Acknowledging the textual instabilities and semiotic changes that attend to multimodal design (recognizing reading as one kind of creative design), the relation of the intentional author to his or her own textual creations is itinerant indeed. This finding is proposed in Malinowski's reading of Nelson et al. (2012), where the authors' concept of effective surprise (drawing upon Bruner, 1973) is read as epistemological *irruption*, an 'unpredictable and inward-sweeping transformation that, significantly, operates on a subject's pre-existing layers of semiotic, cognitive, and emotional resources.' And yet, as in the case of the visual and performing artist RelixStylz, an author's sudden confrontation with his/her past works and consequent reevaluation of her/his own communicative intent are not just an occasion for creative growth; it evidences ways in which authorship practices extend and change over time, effectively producing the author anew at these multiple, critical junctures.
4. *Openings and closings of reflexive potential over interactive time.* As Nelson points out in his remarks on Malinowski and Kramsch (in press), and as indicated as well in Malinowski's response to these remarks, language and literacy learners' designing of meaning in environments of densely, heterogeneously mediated communication entails numerous opportunities for 're-visioning'—for seeing anew not only other parties in interaction and shared texts and mediums of communication but also seeing *themselves* anew. Students of language utilizing desktop videoconferencing technologies like Skype, and writing and drawing about their interactions as well, seem to have multiple and multilayered opportunities to reflect on themselves *as others* in interaction—their words, voice, and image digitally captured, available for repeated playback and display. However, as the dialog between Nelson and Malinowski intimates, the question of whether these opportunities for reflexive self-awareness are in fact recognized and seized remains, unfortunately, unanswered.

Although each of these metaphorically imagined types of motion between multimodal author, text, and world illuminates various situations, perspectives, and scales of multimodal meaning-making processes, we have suggested in this chapter that the metaphor of oscillation may usefully subsume them all, in that it points to the scale and nature of lived experience of those reading and writing texts. As Bolter wrote in the early 1990s, examining the dominant digital text form of the time:

> The oscillation between looking through and looking at can become so rapid that the two experiences merge: the structure of the hypertext is then always present to the reader as he or she reads. In a hypertext there is no escaping the text as a structure of elements, a network of what semioticians call 'signs'. (167–168)

From the standpoint of language and literacy learners' developing the capacity to perceive and critically reflect upon their own discursive and ideological positionings (on these facets of reflexivity, see Byrd Clark and Dervin's introduction to this volume), we see in Bolter's statement both a reflexive promise and a danger inherent in the ubiquitous digital textualities of today. On one hand, the *presence* of formal structures in the texts written and read by Emma, Bonnie, Ann, RelixStylz, and other multimodal authors is impossible to ignore. Contemporary Internet browsers, digital storytelling software, desktop videoconferencing clients, and, indeed, the multilayered semiotic resources of densely populated city streets all attest to the inescapability of the multiple, intersecting 'structures of elements' forming present-day work, study, and play environments. In addition, to the extent that meaning-making activities foreground incongruities, gaps, or tensions in expressive potential in any one mode or combination of modes, we have seen the potential for reflexive positioning and growth amid the various forms of movement outlined here: Bonnie felt her ability to express her Taiwanese identity, amplified by the emergence of imagistic meanings in the spoken lines of her digital story, even as her recognition of the generic, iconic nature of available images of Taiwan (in juxtaposition to her essay written in her own voice) forced her to accept the possibility of perpetuating stereotypes through an outsider's touristic vision. RelixStylz, when viewing and explaining his own piece years after its creation, may have experienced an 'unpredictable and inward-sweeping transformation' in his understanding of what his composition meant and what he had intended. Like Ann in her videoconferencing exchange with her tutor Jean, RelixStylz, Bonnie, and the other focal authors in these studies had numerous opportunities to confront not only the meanings of their texts through recursive engagements with their visible structures but also to confront *themselves*, written into and through various electronic mediums.

However, with momentary openings in the self-reflexive potential of multimodal composition, reading, and performance, momentary closings threatened to become more permanent ones. In our reanalysis of the cases taken up in our past works, we find that we must ask anew when and how the ability to see structure and meaning in a multimodal text leads to greater awareness of and critical reflection upon self and world—and when it may not. Illustrative, perhaps, of the latter, Bonnie, the same student just referred to, may have recognized the stereotypical nature of the images she chose to represent as Taiwan in her experience. However, she also 'allowed her sense of the expectations of her audience to effectively override what she [knew] to be accurate according to her own experience' (Nelson, 2006: 70) and decided to use the stereotypical images anyway. RelixStylz, the highly self-aware composer and performance artist of Nelson, Hull, and Young's case study (in press), used language in the creative epiphanies he experienced as a 'vehicle for consciously mapping connections between the images and his own experience' (225). Yet, after his attested epiphanies, we are not sure what, if anything, will remain of his spoken words to serve for him as 'durable proof of his epiphany, reminding the "artist" of his creative act' (215), as did the poetic phrase uttered and consciously recorded by the protagonist of James Joyce's *A Portrait of the Artist as a Young Man* (the opening vignette of Nelson, Hull, and Young's chapter). While these language and literacy learners can and do see themselves written into the texts they produce, what remains unclear in many of the instances of multimodal authorship and reading taken up in this chapter are the conditions under which these learners' emergent and sometimes changing understandings of themselves and the world may themselves be textualized and made available for observation and reflection. What is missing in our picture of the oscillatory motion of readerly and writerly attention between surface and significance, between structure and idea in the digital, multimodal texts of today would appear to be a third oscillatory terminus—the human subjects, self and other, being ceaselessly written into the text, themselves as focal objects of attention.

CONCLUSION

In this chapter, we have investigated meaning making and reflexivity in multimodal texts through self-reflexively resituating, analyzing, and drawing new meaning from our own prior writings. Indeed, this dialogue, conducted remotely from three separate countries, over multiple electronic mediums, and amid trying life circumstances, was not without its dangers: As was the case for Lamoureux (Chapter 5, this volume), the writing of this chapter was one of most difficult experiences of professional writing we have undertaken, in that it required the exposure of a deep personal relationship in a textual form that, as is visible in the previous pages, is not always harmonious.

However, if dangers cannot be avoided, they can at least be acknowledged, perhaps even productively embraced. As we have subjected each other's past voices to careful analysis and reinterpretation, we have confronted a danger that, in kind and consequence, might resemble the foundational danger faced by all multimodal authors in language classrooms, in after-school literacy programs, and in informal learning contexts more broadly. To wit, to toggle one's attention between texts past and contexts present, between the formal constraints of the semiotic resources at hand and one's momentary expressive or interpretive interests, is not just to recognize the omnipresent salience of multilayered textual structures in multimodal communication. It is also to be *subject* to multimodal textual processes at various levels, scales, sites, and times. Pennycook's (first person plural) observation that reflexive accounts in research 'constitute the very affairs of which we speak' (Pennycook, 2005: 300) is as true for texts of all sorts (and for 'we's' of all sorts) to the extent that language is understood to be not just written but performed and thus productive of writing subjects (Pennycook, 2005: 301). As authors perform semiotic work across multiple modes, casting and finding their intentions between surface and significance, we see opportunity for them to be in the world, in motion.

NOTES

1. Here and later in the chapter, we understand 'reflexive awareness' as a fundamental aspect of social actors' moment-to-moment posturing vis-à-vis the interpretation and composition of multimodal texts. Such reflexive awareness integrates social semiotic and multiliteracies approaches to 'designing' meaning (as will be reviewed) with an emergent consciousness of self and other that, we argue, is a potential outcome of an actor's simultaneous engagement with textual structure and significance ('looking through' and 'looking at'). In the context of the present volume, this conceptualization of reflexive awareness might be seen as one way of specifying processes of experiential and transformational learning (Jackson, Chapter 1), for example.
2. Movement was chosen for its metaphoric flexibility, so to say. We required a code expansive enough to initially account for motion, change, and/or transformation of any type potentially relevant to reflexivity: semiotic, material, cognitive, subjective, etc. Movement semantically encompassed any possibility we could imagine, and so we elected to start there.
3. Interview questions about the students' use of repeated images and textual forms in their digital stories 'evidenced an emergent awareness on their respective parts of a deeper, more complex, more abstract quality of meaning that developed within the image-word sign in a multimedia composition as it progressed' (62).
4. For a nuanced depiction of the circulation, generation, and contestation of power through the linguistic landscape, see Chun (Chapter 8, this volume).
5. www.p21.org

REFERENCES

Anstey, M. & Bull, G. (2006). *Teaching and learning multiliteracies*. Newark, DE: International Reading Association.
Bakhtin, M. (1981). *The dialogic imagination*. Austin: University of Texas Press.

Barthes, R. (1978). *Image-music-text*. New York: Hill & Wang.
Bearne, E., & Wolstencroft, H. (2007). *Visual approaches to teaching writing*. London: UKLA & Sage.
Bogdan, R. C., & Biklen, S. K. (2007). *Qualitative research for education: An introduction to theories and methods* (5th ed.). Boston: Pearson Education.
Bolter, J. D. (1990). *Writing space: The computer, hypertext, and the history of writing*. London: Routledge.
Bolter, J. D., & Grusin, R. (2000). *Remediation: Understanding new media*. Cambridge, MA: MIT Press.
Bourdieu, P. (1994). *In other words*. Cambridge, UK: Polity Press.
Bruner, J. (1973). *Going beyond the information given*. New York: Norton.
Butler, J. (1997). *Excitable speech: A politics of the performative*. New York: Routledge.
Cope, B. & Kalantzis, M. (2000). *Multiliteracies: Literacy learning and the design of social futures*. London: Routledge.
Flower, L. (1994). Teachers as theory builders. In L. Flower, D. Wallace, L. Norris, & R. Burnett, *Making thinking visible: Writing, collaborative planning, and classroom inquiry* (pp. 3–22). Urbana, IL: NCTE.
Goodwin, C. (1994). Professional vision. *American Anthropologist*, 96(3), 606–633.
Halliday, M. A. K. (1973). *Explorations in the functions of language*. London: Edward Arnold.
Halliday, M. A. K. (1978). *Language as social semiotic: The social interpretation of language and meaning*. London: Edward Arnold.
Harris, R. 2009. *New ethnicities and language use*. London: Palgrave Macmillan.
Hodge, R., & Kress, G. (1988). *Social semiotics*. Ithaca, NY: Cornell University Press.
Hull, G. A. & Nelson, M. E., (2005). Locating the semiotic power of multimodality. *Written Communication,* 22(2), 224–261.
Kalantzis, M., & Cope, B. (2012). *Literacies*. Cambridge, UK: Cambridge University Press.
Kress, G. (2003). *Literacy in the new media age*. London: Routledge.
Kress, G. (2010). *Multimodality: A social semiotic perspective on contemporary communication*. London: Routledge.
Kress, G. (2012). Thinking about the notion of 'cross-cultural' from a social semiotic perspective. *Language and Intercultural Communication*, 12(4), 369–385.
Kress, G., & van Leeuwen, T. (1996/2006). *Reading images: The grammar of visual design*. London: Routledge.
Lanham, R. (1993). *The electronic word: Democracy, technology and the arts*. Chicago: University of Chicago Press.
Lemke, J.L. (1998). Metamedia literacy: Transforming meanings and media. In D. Reinking, M. C. McKenna, L. D. Labbo, & R. D. Kieffer (Eds.), *Handbook of literacy and technology transformations in a post-typographic world* (pp. 312–333). Hoboken, NJ: Taylor & Francis.
Lyotard, J. F. (1979). *The post-modern condition: A report on knowledge*. Minneapolis: University of Minnesota Press.
Malinowski, D. (2009). Authorship in the linguistic landscape: A multimodal-performative view. In E. Shohamy & D. Gorter (Eds.), *Linguistic landscape: Expanding the scenery* (pp. 107–125). New York: Routledge.
Malinowski, D., & Kramsch, C. (2013). The ambiguous world of heteroglossic computer-mediated language learning, pp 155-178. In A. Blackledge & A. Creese (Eds.), *Heteroglossia as practice and pedagogy*. New York: Springer.
Maton, K. (2003). Reflexivity, relationism and research: Pierre Bourdieu and the epistemic conditions of social scientific knowledge. *Space & Culture*, 6(1), 52–65.
Mitchell, W. J. T. (1994). *Picture theory: Essays on verbal and visual representation*. Chicago: University of Chicago Press.

Nelson, M. E. (2006). Mode, meaning, and synaesthesia in multimedia L2 writing. *Language Learning & Technology*, 10(2), 56–76.

Nelson, M. E., Hull, G., & Young, R. (2012). Portrait of the artist as a younger adult: Multimedia literacy and 'effective surprise.' In O. Erstad & J. Sefton-Green (Eds.), *Identity, community, and learning lives in the digital age* (pp. 215–232). Cambridge, UK: Cambridge University Press.

New London Group. (1996). A pedagogy of multiliteracies: Designing social futures. *Harvard Educational Review*, 66, 60–92.

Ong, W. (1986). Writing is a technology that restructures thought. In G. Baumann (Ed.), *The written word: Literacy in transition*. Oxford: Clarendon.

O'Toole, M. (1995). *The language of displayed art*. Leicester, UK: Leicester University Press.

Pennycook, A. (2005). Performing the personal. *Journal of Language, Identity, & Education*, 4(4), 297–304.

Popper, K. (1957). *The poverty of historicism*. London: Routledge & Kegan Paul.

Rowsell, J. (2013). *Working with multimodality: Rethinking literacy in a digital age*. Oxford: Routledge.

Scollon, R. & Scollon, S. (2003). *Discourses in place: Language in the material world*. New York: Routledge.

Sheridan, M., & Rowsell, J. (2010). *Design literacies: Learning and innovation in the digital age*. London: Routledge.

St. Pierre, E. A. (1997). Methodology in the fold and the irruption of transgressive data. *International Journal of Qualitative Studies in Education*, 10(2), 175–189.

Unsworth, L. (2001). *Teaching multiliteracies across the curriculum*. Buckingham, UK/Philadelphia: Open University Press.

van Leeuwen, T. (1999). *Speech, music, sound*. New York: St. Martin's.

van Leeuwen, T. (2005). *Introducing social semiotics*. London: Routledge.

7 Uses of Digital Text in Reflexive Anthropology
The Example of Educational Workshops for Out-of-School/Educationally Excluded Adolescents

Eric Chauvier

My meeting with the adolescents of the Association Vers la Vie pour l'Education des Jeunes (AVVEJ) [Association of Life-long Education for Youth] occurred within the framework of a mission funded by the Departmental Council of Seine-Saint-Denis, in the north of Paris. In partnership with the visual artist Saraswati Gramich, my research project was to write up an interactive digital text focusing on the adolescents of AVVEJ. This mission allowed me to combine experimentally two fundamental aspects of my method: attention to the language of the observed persons and to the language used in the textual format. I want to show that it was possible to produce knowledge by involving the teenagers in the co-construction of the anthropological text. I led them to speak about the text, to read in their own words, to rectify the text, to validate it, and especially to comment on it.

The first stake in this process concerns research action, that is, allowing the adolescents to be captured during their daily lives both within and outside of the institution.

The second stake is related to the edification of a more fundamental reflexive knowledge: By being interested in the peculiar lives of the teenagers, by giving them voice, it is possible to reconsider certain stereotypes used about them.

This digital text now exists, but only after undergoing various adjustments, forcing me to (re)imagine methods for its suitable reproduction/presentation of findings. I will present these methods here by demonstrating how they lead to a new reflexive way of producing knowledge, both *for* and *with* adolescents.

PRESENTATION OF THE INSTITUTION

Abdel Ajenoui, department manager, defines educational workshops as a space where 'there is access to education and knowledge for every teenager under sixteen years old, who has dropped out of formal education.' The teenagers are between 12 and 18 years old. Many are still within the ages for compulsory schooling but have dropped out of secondary school months or even years ago. It should be pointed out that these youth come from towns other than Saint-Denis (e.g., Sarcelles, Aubervilliers, Bobigny, Aulnay-sous-Bois, and Villiers-le-Bel), as a means to remove them from their everyday world and certain negative influences, most often related to drug trafficking. Finally, it should also be noted that in the evening, the adolescents return home to their families.

'We adapt the workshops to each of the teenagers. If one of them is not ready, we go to his home to discuss the situation, take time to spot any mental blocks,' explains Ajenoui. No two courses are the same. 'Some people are in big difficulties. They are "Incasables," (These young people are in great difficulty which no institution manages to be able to address in the long term) with chaotic backgrounds and high-risk behaviour,' Ajenoui adds. The objective of AVVEJ is the return of the teenager to nonpolitical circuits in education or in training. In other words, it is a question of supporting their social (re)insertion. When I led this investigation, 12 teenagers were regularly present at AVVEJ at the time. They had very different levels of education and therefore followed different workshops: Some studied reading and writing. Others prepared a *brevet d'etudes professionnel* (a certificate to prepare a professional baccalaureate). Of about 1000 accompanied teenagers, 75 percent found their way back into school or training,' explains Abdel Ajenoui.

In the workshops, their instruction is adapted to suitable certificate course projects. It is a question of developing individualized plans. '*Du sur-measure*,' says Ajenoui. 'Each must find his rhythm, his personal interests, his tools.' The workshop is opened all week long, but a specifically separate adapted program is also possible. Ajenoui specifies: 'We keep as many places as possible for runaways or "*décrocheurs*."' This uninterrupted accompaniment reassures a lot of the teenagers, who are accustomed to go from one institution to the other because of failure and/or rejection. Ajenoui adds an important point: '[T]he involvement of the parents, with whom we maintain a maximum of relationships throughout the schooling.' The objective is therefore not only to return to school but also to develop a dynamic and peaceful relationship with society and with oneself. Workshops work with a reactive pedagogy, which alternates cognitive contents with awakening techniques, learning of social life, bodily expression, and self-knowledge/reflexivity. Education is computer-aided with a method considered 'learning while you play' by Abdel Ajenoui. Education through mediations likely put the notion of pleasure in the middle of study: poetry slams, handicrafts, graffiti art, theater, storytelling, and horseback riding as well as relaxation. According to Ajenoui, '[T]he fact that it doesn't have to be immediate, or subjected to a program or a group, gives a lot of freedom to the instructors.' There are four teachers at AVVEJ, each supported by a psychologist.

The length of time spent in the institution varies for the teenagers. It depends on the level of studies obtained and especially on the capabilities of the young people to reenter and reintegrate secondary school. Six to 12 months are needed on average for the intervention to be effective.

Finally, Abdel Ajenoui adds, '[T]he workshop is not suitable for everyone. It is necessary to quickly determine that at the beginning so that if it doesn't work out then this is not to be considered as an additional failure, but rather as a reorientation.'

THE DIGITAL TEXT: KEY THEORETICAL ISSUES

Derrida (1967) demonstrated that Lévi-Strauss denied 'primitives' writing so as to better maintain their 'innocence.' I would like to take the opposite angle by providing the observed subjects (whom I in no way liken to primitives) the power to cowrite the anthropologist's text, so that they lose, if not their innocence, then at least the 'group spirit,' or social categorization, to which they are confined—as being labeled delinquents, desocialized, out-of-school, drug traffickers, religious fundamentalists, victims, and the like. The goal is to work with them and lend them a voice by restoring their uniqueness in such a way as to shatter the stereotypes attached to them. However, they are not to be given the last word. In the co-construction process, the anthropologist must establish a regulatory framework for the observed subjects' participation in producing the text. It is in that way that I define reflexivity in anthropology. It implies the manufacture of the text in the analysis and, as a result, the situation of interview between the observer and the observed (the negotiations that allow the creation of the text). The purpose is not to restrict this experience to the wings of anthropology but to produce knowledge from this reflexivity.

The objective of this mission is to engage the adolescents in the processes of correcting or modifying the digital text written by the anthropologist in such a way as to perceive the reality of the institution no longer via a physical form but rather by way of a *mimesis* or, in other words, a textual reality. Immediate (cognitive, sensorial, and memory-based) experience is replaced by a reading-based experience. In concrete terms, the adolescents read themselves in the midst of speaking, via texts reproducing their own words or the words of other adolescents. To echo Paul Ricoeur, reading allows for a metaphorical use of the text. In this manner, an introspective distance is created that is not permitted by real-life experience. This 'experiential gap' (Ricoeur, 1983) guarantees uniquely autonomous speech. When debriefings carried out by the instructors no longer generate verbal reactions by the adolescents regarding their everyday lives, the text will free up this speech by transferring the framework for institutional verbalization to a literary medium. Social interaction no longer seems like a 'stage,' on which each actor can lose face (Goffman, 1974) and is called upon to make such a deep investment; rather, it is carried out in a metaphorical manner allowing for commentary, adjustment, and correction. To pursue Goffman's theatrical metaphor, with the text, the stage is finally clear because the investment is without risk.

The ethnography of communication broadly drew inspiration from educational practices (Gumperz, 1989: 116). It allows us to consider more precisely how to catch the words of the teenagers. Their 'conversational competence' is increased when certain contextual mental blocks are overcome. Interactive commitment (Goffman, 1961) becomes easier because it is defined by the rules of commentaries. These rules introduce two advantages. First, experience is offered to the teenagers as a manner of co-constructing a text in the style of a game. Second, they are invigorating for the teenagers because the text speaks about them.

The effect of this type of method on adolescent readers must be assessed. By reading and reacting to the text, they are no longer simply speakers in an everyday life in which memory is necessarily limited: The succession of situations of daily life prevents me. On the other hand, graphical reasoning (Goody, 1979)—in other words, the written translation of their daily life—lends them the status of archivists, of firsthand witnesses qualified to speak, thanks to the official and unifying nature of the text. This 'archival speech' (Campagne, 2012) could constitute a means of neutralizing the parodic nature of the institution as seen by the adolescents (Goffman, 1968). Goffman demonstrates that totalitarian institutions rely upon a social contract that is perceived by their residents as a parody of life outside the institution. This also explains the limits of speech within the institution. According to Goffman, the 'impression of reality' is insufficiently intense to fully convince the actor (Goffman, 1973: 25). This can be observed during debriefings, in which tired or disruptive adolescents seem to disbelieve what is being said. They therefore prefer to remain silent. Because the tools that would guarantee them such introspection remain under the authority of the institution and its 'stock of words' (to borrow the expression of Ludwig Wittgenstein), the parody is not avoided. If the digital text constitutes a way out or loophole, it is because its use is situated both *within* and *outside* institutional life.

It is, however, necessary to note an obstacle to be overcome concerning certain resistances of the teenagers in relation to texts. Would another population (for authority, company employees and hospital nurses) have reacted more strongly? The question is worth asking, for it assumes that text reception varies according to social class. This hypothesis would seem to be based upon, if one considers the viewpoint of the adolescents, the text's reflecting a process of failure begun back in secondary school.

VARIOUS WAYS OF WRITING A DIGITAL TEXT

Immersed in a situation of participant observation five days a month over a period of eight months, I first wrote down in a notebook my observations regarding the adolescents' everyday life in their educational workshops (horseback riding, theater, storytelling, and visual arts). I wrote down what I heard said, as well as my own reactions, including my own prejudices and

Prendre du recul - Dans l'art du graph, les petits défauts que l'on voit de près deviennent des réussites si l'on recule de quelques pas pour découvrir la vue d'ensemble. Quelques pas de recul ne sont-ils pas le secret de la sagesse ?

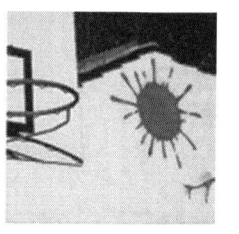

Figure 7.1 Prendre du recul

stereotypes. For instance, I was clumsy by presupposing that the daily lives of 12 adolescents were linked to urban ghettos and drug trafficking. They did not seem to appear as I had initially imagined. Some people were really lookouts for local traffickers, which is what led to their educational exclusion. But I discovered that others were intentionally kept in their home by their parents, who refused to let their children become delinquents. Others also progressively dropped out of secondary school to wander in the city. These so-called invisibles do not actually have links to drug trafficking.

I then wrote up short texts that included a key word (to assist the texts' memorization by the young people) and a brief, open analysis meant to surprise the adolescents and spark their desire to react to the texts. For example:

> Cap. He's always wearing a cap, under his hood. It's a way of showing that he's not doing any better; that his face is unreceptive to dialogue, that his body flees communication. They're also self-imposed shackles, as though he were atoning for some crime he's unaware of or that perhaps doesn't exist.

Then, with the help of Saraswati Gramich, we posted the texts on the website in the form of a wiki, thereby allowing the adolescents to interact with and react to them via writing or illustration (drawings, graffiti art, or photographs). Saraswati Gramich had designed the site, and used photos in an attempt to recreate the atmosphere of the educational workshops.

PROCEDURE 1: SPARKING A REACTION FROM A DISTANCE

Rather quickly, after about a month, we informed the adolescents that they could react at a distance to the texts via any computer with Internet access. We provided them with a login (username) and password in order to easily access the site. We also informed them that Saraswati Gramich and I were the site moderators.

This initial experiment proved a partial failure. Despite our announcement, no adolescent connected to the site. With the benefit of hindsight, this failure was due to our proposing this stage too early, even before the adolescents had become familiar with the interactive uses of digital texts. To the adolescents, the proposal seemed too sudden and theoretical, to the extent that they did not perceive any immediate benefit. It was necessary that they immerse themselves in the mimesis of the texts—in other words, the reality such as it appears in the text—by participating in their creation.

During the scholastic workshops, their attentiveness depends on their simultaneously participating in the proposed cultural activities (storytelling, theater, drawing, poetry slams, etc.). Because the institution's back-to-school strategy relies on this coupling, the simple proposition of reacting to the text is perceived by the adolescents as an incomplete learning process.

Finally, more broadly speaking, the question becomes centered on the youth's representation of this experiment within the institution. One must not forget that they are being encouraged to write, an action that, in their eyes, is a priori synonymous with failure. This observation leads us to adapt our protocol for these specific expectations.

PROCEDURE 2: TRIGGERING A VERBAL REACTION IN FRONT OF THE SCREEN

The failure of the first procedure allowed me to reflect on my own assumptions. I had thought that the teenagers could react to the remote text considering their use of social networks, notably Facebook. Besides, Sara (Saraswati) and I had removed the iconography of Facebook. I realize that the interface I had wanted to implement has no comparison with Facebook's popular interface.

As such, I then offered the adolescents the opportunity to react to my texts directly in front of the computer screen. I let them read the texts, occasionally lending my own comments, and I then encouraged the adolescents to provide either written comments (on the digital text) or oral comments, in which case they allowed me to note and write down what they said. The teenagers did not react significantly to this change. For them, we had an experimental step, and they accepted this idea. On the contrary, I showed them that we had gone off course and that we were willing and ready to adapt to fit their expectations. This decision was intended to show them our goodwill. Moreover, this stage of adaptation of procedures seems inevitable to me.

Although, in theory, writing 'frees us from constraints proper to oral speech' (Bazin & Bensa, 1979: 9), in our context, it can also paralyze by calling upon a so-called stock of culture that intimidates the adolescents who do not master the registers and rules of the proposed texts. In the work of Pierre Bourdieu (1979), this sum of distinctive signs produces domination by the perception of asymmetrical social reports. Here, risk really holds in (contains) the symbolic violence, which I can impose by the cultural capital linked to the text and by my presence as observer.

This is evident in our example:

> Cap. He's always wearing a cap, under his hood. It's a way of showing that he's not doing any better, that his face is unreceptive to dialogue, that his body flees communication. They're also self-imposed shackles, as though he were atoning for some crime he's unaware of or that perhaps doesn't exist.

This text can have an intimidating effect due to its explicitly literary register. The 'face' that is 'unreceptive,' the 'body' that 'flees,' and the 'cap' as a 'shackle' present associations of ideas and images that can dissuade the adolescents from interacting. They were a hint to me that the text could not be improved. The same can be said regarding the final gradation centered on the 'fault,' from its absence from conscience to its almost nonexistence. This playing with nuances can be likened to metaphorical rules already familiar to the adolescents (who must not be underestimated) via the music they listen to or their manners of speaking (notably centered on picturesque jokes). But rules are not everything. The adolescents explain to me that the learned nature of the syntax used ('unreceptive,' 'atoning') and the syntactic associations ('unreceptive face,' 'self-imposed shackles') paralyze them:

> Writing—as compared to oral communication, which illustrates its conformity—necessarily imposes rules of proper speech (grammar) and proper thinking (logic) and a model of pleasant discourse (rhetoric). (Bazin & Bensa, 1979: 13)

Grammar, logic, and rhetoric will here be perceived as divisive elements, revealing the hidden structure of a symbolic domination. The adolescents sense this gap between the anthropologist's text and their own linguistic abilities. The text becomes a measure of their inadequacy and so of their incompetence. By arranging meanings within a two-dimensional space (Bazin & Bensa, 1979: 11), 'graphical reasoning' demarcates a private space that becomes the anthropologist's creation and property, thereby excluding de facto any interaction with the adolescents. Here we see the limits of writing as 'the intellect playing with language' (Bazin & Bensa, 1979: 11; see also Séror, this volume). Another aspect remains essential and must be considered: that of the reading context and the text's reception. This is precisely what is amiss in this first example.

Finally, one must consider the symbolic violence inherent in the very act of observation. Although cultural communities—understood as a series of 'acts of communication' (Goody, 1979: 86)—never cease their 'intercalibrations,' the framework of ethnographic observation almost always exacerbates this tension by establishing 'learned' and 'unlearned' classes (unless the observed subjects' status renders them learned). When such compartmentalization appears, it largely compromises the desired co-construction (see Byrd

Clark & Dervin on hyper-reflexivity, this volume). Indeed, at the end of this first exercise, all (or almost all) of the adolescents said to me:

> Yes, that's good. [embarrassed smile]
>
> Or:
>
> Yes, that's it. [closed expression]

This recognized accuracy of the text triggers nothing more than these words that reflect more the adolescents' intimidation than a desire to participate in the writing activity. In their eyes, the exercise remains elitist. It is anyway in the way she (the adolescent) interpreted it. Another teenager confirms it to me by becoming the spokeperson for the others:

> It is not easy. . . . We don't always have the desire to react. . . . And then it is you who write, not us.

By revealing and throwing the exclusive character of my position back in my face, this teenager showed me implicitly that he is not qualified for writing. It is a polite way of saying to me that we don't have the same competences and that these are governed by a game of social class. For a second, I think again of the inquiry of Loïc Wacquant (2001) into the boxing rings full of African Americans when the African Americans showed him benevolently that, due to his social class, he had no good reason to stay in these boxing rings with the poor black people of the city. For an anthropologist, it is a failure that is difficult to accept.

This failure must be qualified and discussed, particularly if I decide to reformulate the text not only to read it but to render it oral. One advantage is to be found in the interactional framework for reading the text: A reformulation can mitigate the adolescents' expectations before the screen, via structured conversation. A second advantage consists of removing the mystique surrounding graphical reasoning. This rendering oral—or, perhaps one could say, this detextualization—of my words proved better suited to triggering comments by the adolescents.

PROCEDURE 3: WRITING THE TEXT WITH THEM

The first two procedures proved counterproductive due to their insufficient reliance on oral expression in the co-construction of the text. Speech cannot be incited by the text if conversations are not first held early in the writing process to mitigate its private nature. In short, the text must be constructed a posteriori by involving the adolescents in its creation. More specifically, the procedure consists of encouraging adolescent A to speak on themes of concern to him or her, then entering into a structured conversation with this adolescent, and, finally, transcribing the words onto the website. Adolescent B will then read the words of adolescent A and react by giving an opinion. In the end, one rule proves essential: The final digital text must strictly recreate the intermingling of voices that constitute the text.

With regard to this procedure, certain limits can be identified a priori. They concern the 'verbal conscience' of the adolescents in the process of commenting on the text either orally or in writing (Althabe, 1990). Indeed, they tend to choose their words according to their presuppositions concerning my expectations. Within the institution, the adult presence is limited to teaching (during the educational workshops) and evaluation. Even though the project is first explained to them (my exact words: 'Together, we're going to write a book on you'), the adolescents do not a priori perceive my work with them as being anything other than a cultural activity, comparable to the storytelling, theater, or visual arts workshops. This is what they told me. As a result, they will express a point of view in accordance with what they suppose that I expect from them, that is to say, speech appropriate to my presence as an authority figure.

However, this limit must be put into perspective, first because the procedure becomes a matter of habit: The more the textual reconstruction experiences are reiterated, the more the verbal conscience fades, thereby favoring spontaneous speech. In this regard, the confidence and trust that develops between them and me plays an important role. The second reason is specific to most of the adolescents encountered: They are all used to having their biographical information circulate within the institution and among the authorized persons. As a result, most of the adolescents speak spontaneously to me about their lives outside the institution, drugs, violence, the police, their being held in custody, the use of firearms, and other aspects of their lives.

To resume: I ask each adolescent a very simple question: What does AVVEJ represent to you?

In reply to my question, Cécile says to me:

AVVEJ is a point of reference.

These words provide a glimpse of their daily lives outside the institution as lacking points of reference. This is what I write, in a manner reproducing this analysis, but attempting to remain open.

Reading Cécile's analyzed words, Djenna adds:

It's something that I chose.

This comment illustrates, once again by default, life outside the institution as one full of constraints. Once again, what I write is paired with an open assessment: Here, it is a question meant to attract the reader's attention. It is necessary to point out the importance of having knowledge of the historical background of the institutional space as well as of the social backgrounds of the adolescents. For example, a person in charge of the department informs me that the French used at AVVEJ is limited and marked furthermore by syntactical difficulties. 'One of the girls has the vocabulary of a 10-year-old child,' he says to me. This information has an influence irrefutably on my manner of considering conversational competences of the teenagers. I try spontaneously not to use too much refined language. However, I am aware that this situation is progressive and that this stereotype can be deconstructed.

As I ask Chérazed the same question (What does AVVEJ represent to you?), she reads the words of Cécile and Djenna and replies:

It's having something in hand to transform your life.

I write that Chérazed said that AVVEJ is 'having something in hand to transform your life.' I then ask the question:

Does that mean that outside, life doesn't change?

It's the straight and narrow [says Haïtam, after reading the contributions of Cécile, Djenna, and Chérazed. It should be noted that Haïtam usually participates very little in this project].

It's a family [says Saïf, after reading the words of Haïtam, Cécile, Djenna, and Chérazed. Saïf adds that he did not enjoy secondary school, the childishness and incessant jibes].

There isn't that childishness here [he says].

You're guaranteed a certain calm, no stress.

I add, in the form of a question:

Does that mean that outside the institution, fear and anxiety reign?

Anastasia reads the others' words, along with my own comments that usually end with a question. She is intimidated. She never participates in the project, but after reading the others' comments, she finally speaks to me, for the first time:

Yes, that's it.

One must measure the significance of each adolescent's contribution. These few words, though shy, constitute a visible and rare sign of Anastasia's involvement.

Sabrina, who also usually remains silent, reads all these comments and says:

Here, you can speak.

Nonverbal signs must also be taken into account. Sabrina's eyes clearly light up, and a contented smile appears. In light of what Sabrina experiences (or endures), this exercise may seem insignificant, but it constitutes first and foremost a step forward—the possibility to comment on her life outside an institutional framework of verbalization.

A second phase can now be initiated: Djenna reads what Haïtam, Cécile, Djenna, and Chérazed said and wrote in the wake of her own comment. This allows her to delve deeper and speak some more:

> Meeting saved me. Otherwise, I'd be out on the street or fucking around.

Djenna makes a stronger comment the second time, digging deeper into her existence. It will also help trigger reactions by the others regarding a more specific theme: After considering their perception of AVVEJ, we now turn to their perception of risks—risks linked to violence, isolation, drugs, wandering, and other threats. In this manner, a series of interrelated accounts and themes is created, which is constantly structured by the anthropologist but whose content is directly influenced by the adolescents. The opening made by Djenna allows the others to rush in and provide further details. Looking to her example of self-expression, they share more intimate biographical information themselves: If Djenna spoke about herself in this manner, then they can too by a process of conformity or one-upmanship.

'ANTHROPOLOGICAL INQUIRIES'

To return to Procedure 3, I ask Alvin to describe to me where he lives. I offer him syntactical suggestions: his 'estate', his 'neighborhood'. Against all expectations, he decides to write a short text on what he calls his 'estate':

> The estate's dangerous. Sometimes it's cool, sometimes not so cool, but basically, no matter what, it's shit . . . It's almost war . . . Deep down, we all love our estates, our buildings, our blocks, but we all dream of getting out . . . The estate, it's like work, except our only pay is prison.

I imagine that here I have the basis for a reflection on violence, but when I read Alvin's text to the others, nothing goes as I expected. Chérazed does not agree:

> Life in my neighbourhood [also listed as a ZEP, or sensitive urban area] is very different. Life there isn't anything like what Alvin describes. It's much less violent. In my neighbourhood, people talk to each other and get along well.

Saïf fully agrees with Chérazed:

> What Alvin experiences in his neighbourhood is just one side of the story.

Illan goes further:

> I live in the 15th arrondissement, in Paris. Alvin's story doesn't concern me.

Djenna, however, confirms what Alvin said:

> He's right. Me, I'm fed up with living here, with the smell of piss and dope in the stairwells, with all the gunshots! I can no longer even go to the public park, right nearby, because it's become too dangerous. I can no longer even go to the pool, because there's always drug dealing over there. Me, I want to live in the country, with the fresh air and little birds. The countryside bores me to death, but it's better than here! Anywhere's better than here!

At this point, it would seem pertinent not to limit the digital text to serving as an introspective and reflexive tool for the adolescents (as a sort of action-research) but rather to underline their heuristic contributions based on the use of words (here, for instance, the words 'estate' and 'institution'). One hypothesis is that, when usage gaps appear, it becomes possible to initiate what I would call 'anthropological inquiries,' which consist of questioning the pertinence of the categories in use for a given theme.

Alvin's writings demonstrate, for instance, that day-to-day life in identical neighborhoods can be experienced in very different ways. Whereas, for some of the adolescents, 'the law of the ghetto' seems 'a reality,' for others it does not or does only to a very limited extent. One hypothesis is that these nuances play an important role in deconstructing the essentialistic reasonings at work concerning the so-called estate culture. Here, the housing estate is alternately 'a ghetto,' 'a normal life,' 'a life with close relations,' and the like. It cannot be reduced to violence alone; the social life experienced with friends and family is a priori of no less importance than the issues of violence and delinquency.

Although recreating this polyphony of speech (and voices) does not allow anthropologists to be representative, it does offer them the possibility for questioning the validity of theoretical categories currently applied to themes related to the 'estates.' Borrowing terms from sensationalism, repression, prevention, or victimization, these models would seem inappropriate insofar as they produce overly broad categories (groups, populations, and ethnicities) that reduce the debate to a unilateral approach. Anthropological questions arise:

How can we consider the life of these adolescents without resorting to these huge, broad categories?

Does their being categorized a priori on the fringes of society (as desocialized, out of school) oblige us to consider their life through the prism of groups?

Does this situation excuse us from considering adolescents as individuals experiencing unique situations? Must the categories delinquents, youth of Seine-Saint-Denis, little savages, and victims necessarily imply, for instance, to that of mental disorders? Indeed, for most of the adolescents, melancholia is the obvious diagnosis. And yet, in the mass media and in university research laboratories, this categorization is not often applied to them. By a sort of cultural reflex, the majority of these adolescents are subject to so-called invariants of gigantic categories—categories with serious implications and consequences.

Finally, the use of the digital text highlights a key epistemological issue: approaching observed subjects as unique individuals, so as to potentially help them to restore their individual voices in order to reconsider them no longer as cultural objects or areas, but—in a more reflexive manner—in the epistemological terms used in these debates. The result amounts to producing knowledge differently by introducing a need for nuance. With regard to methodology, representativeness is replaced by the art of questioning. Just as philosophy could be seen as the art of asking the right questions, reflexive anthropology could become the art of questioning the validity of the categories used in characterizing various areas of social life. In any case, this would serve as a possible alternative to more objectifying approaches.

ACKNOWLEDGMENTS

I would like to thank the editors, in particular Julie Byrd Clark, for her invaluable comments and edits of my text.

REFERENCES

Althabe, G. (1990). Ethnologie du contemporain et enquête de terrain. *Terrain*, 14, 126–131.

Bazin, J., & Bensa, A. Preface, In Jack Goody, *La raison graphique, pp. 5–20*. Paris: Les Éditions de Minuit.

Bourdieu, P, (1979). *La distinction. Critique sociale du jugement*. Paris: Les Éditions de Minuit.

Campagne, J. (2012). *Tu m'as pas jetée, c'est moi qui suis partie. Enquête sur les disputes de couples*. Lormont, France: Le Bord de l'eau.

Chauvier, E. (2011). *Anthropologie de l'ordinaire. Une conversion du regard*. Toulouse, France: Anacharsis.

Derrida, J. (1967). *De la grammatologie*. Paris: Les Éditions de Minuit.

Goffman, E. (1961). *Asylums: essays on the social situation of mental patients and other inmates*. New York: Anchor Books.

Goffman, E. (1968). *Asiles. Études sur la condition sociale des malades mentaux*. Paris: Les Éditions de Minuit.

Goffman, E. (1973). *La mise en scène de la vie quotidienne, t.1, la présentation de soi*. Paris: Les Éditions de Minuit.
Goffman, E. (1974). *Les rites d'interaction*. Paris: Les Éditions de Minuit.
Goody, J. (1979). *La Raison graphique. La domestication de la pensée sauvage*, Paris: Les Éditions de Minuit.
Gumperz, J. (1989). *Engager la conversation*. Paris: Les Éditions de Minuit.
Ricoeur, P. (1983). Temps et récit, *Tome I: L'intrigue et le récit historique*, Paris: Le Seuil Collection Points. Essais.
Wacquant, L. (2001). *Corps et âmes. Carnets ethnographiques d'un apprenti boxeur*. Marseille, France: Agone, Comeau, et Nadeau.

8 Reflexivity and Critical Language Education at Occupy LA

Christian W. Chun

INTRODUCTION

On September 17, 2011, a mass movement coalesced around the anger felt by many about the deepening social and economic inequalities in the United States. Naming themselves 'Occupy Wall Street' and 'the 99%,' activists decided to occupy a privately owned public space in lower Manhattan to protest the immense wealth disparities between the elites—the 1%—and the rest of society. They demonstrated, conducted general assemblies, and created protest signs naming capitalism as the system working for this 1%. These signs, which were recorded and uploaded via social media, formed a transgressive linguistic landscape in public spaces. This chapter addresses this linguistic landscape (LL) constructed by the Occupy Movement in Los Angeles and the ways in which this landscape's discourses were recontextualized in a filmed workshop I conducted with Occupiers in which we explored language and discourse in the media.

Two weeks after the launch of Occupy Wall Street movement, Occupy LA (OLA) began at Los Angeles City Hall Park. On various blogs and social media sites, there were heated discussions among Occupiers regarding its encampment location. Wishing to parallel Occupy Wall Street's encampment in the financial district, some thought Pershing Square, near where many financial companies have their regional offices, would be an appropriate site inasmuch as many saw the financial industry playing the major role in causing the economic crisis. However, the City Hall Park location prevailed for several reasons. First, due to the Park's expansive North and South Lawns, OLA was able to provide a media center, a library, a food service (for a time), a first-aid area, and workshops. Second, the open area of the South Lawn and the surrounding blocks enabled easier access to the media and its supporting vehicles, which in turn afforded a greater visibility to the Occupiers than the much smaller Pershing Square would have allowed. Finally, the protest held at the City's main municipal building was a public expression of anger at what many perceived as the government's refusal to rein in the increasing corporate power over spheres of everyday life such as health care and education, as well as its lack of support for the disenfranchised, the working poor, so-called illegal immigrants, and the middle class. The OLA movement strove to highlight this systemic crisis with the attempt to enact a working democracy literally on the steps of this institutional space.

City Hall Park is designed to be open to the general public; no gates, fences, or barriers enclose its space. The Park's South Lawn is picturesque with its lawns, water fountain, and multiple trees. The much smaller North Lawn is less impressive; however, this is where the food and water distribution, the media center, the library, and the workshops were initially situated. The Park itself was essentially designed to be viewed and admired, not a physical space that people could actually make use of daily, such as for picnicking on the lawn or exercising. Aside from the occasional rallies or one-day protests held on the South Lawn, this nominal public space has traditionally been devoid of people and everyday activity (other than workers going about their business). Inasmuch as space acts an agentive force in conjunction with human actors in ways that aim to constrain, limit, and dominate our daily practices (Lefebvre, 1991), this symbolic (and literally physical when the police forcibly evicted OLA two months later) conflict between City Hall's institutional space of power and a popular movement practicing direct democracy could not be clearer.

As an agentive space, City Hall's symbolism, both the building and its surrounding Park, relies on spatialized discourses of order, authority, and institutional stability. The symbolic power of this space thus presents a particular institutional notion of democracy that is removed and indeed remote from the everyday practices of most people. This was brought into focus by the Occupiers, who rapidly transformed the Park into a living space complete with makeshift homes in the form of tents and sleeping bags, as well as a food and water supply system (the city provided portable toilets but no showers, and eventually shut down food service, citing health code violations). During the months of October and November until the mayor evicted OLA on November 29 due to alleged health and safety concerns, the encampment grew to nearly 500 tents and boasted a populace that swelled to several thousand people on the weekends. OLA conducted classes, ran the nightly general assembly, performed music, made speeches, created and designed signs, and engaged in the everyday living of communicating, eating, drinking, and sleeping. Lefebvre (1991) argued that 'new social relationships call for a new space, and vice versa' (59). In their attempt to create a more equitable and socially just society, the Occupiers imagined, created, and resemiotized an urban public space designed to reflect institutional power and authority. The resulting resemiotized space, as a material, visual, and meaning-making force in calling forth new social relationships in its bold displays of critique, dissent, and revolt, was a complex layering of what Scollon and Scollon (2003) termed 'discourses in place' (1). These are the nexus sites at and through which particular discourses are circulating in material forms such as the protest signs, social actors' historically lived identities and actions, and the symbolic spatiality of City Hall Park.

My Own Involvement: A Self-Reflexive Account

Many of the Occupiers at the encampment (including those who visited during the evenings and weekends) participated in the marches through downtown LA and attended workshops conducted by those supporting the movement. The workshops were organized by the People's Collective University, which was set up to draw upon the diverse backgrounds and knowledge of its members and supporters. I saw the call for classes on the OLA website and e-mailed the university with a proposal for a one-day class, entitled 'Critical Language in Action.' My stated aim was to explore with the attendees 'an understanding of how language is mobilized in the service of power, and how it shapes, frames, and privileges certain representations about and of the world, which is crucial for any social justice movement such as the Occupy Movement.' My own social justice involvement began over 20 years earlier as an organizer and activist for a national organization calling for anti-intervention in Central America and global nuclear disarmament. The seminal experiences in meeting with and learning from the racially and economically diverse communities across highly stratified Los Angeles strengthened my commitment to work for a more equitable society.

This commitment was also part of the impetus to start teaching ESL in the immigrant communities in Los Angeles. With my students, I began to adopt critical literacy approaches (e.g., Janks, 2010), in which we explored how their classroom texts presented discourses offering different portraits of society that the students were not always willing to accept due to their own conflicting reading and subject positions. These positions would involve not only the students' own differing interpretations of the culture and society in which they found themselves, but also their questioning of the portrayals of immigrants and English language learners that are sometimes presented in their textbooks. Together, we created dialogic spaces in our classroom in which we questioned power and its discourses in both the texts they were reading and their material manifestations in society. A critical reading of the word and the world (Freire & Macedo, 1987) was something that I did not impose on them due to any agenda I might have had. Instead, it was called into being by my students themselves, particularly after the 1992 uprisings in Los Angeles following the Rodney King verdict that directly impacted many of them, including one who lost his livelihood due to his store being looted.[1] Angry and anxious, these students transformed my classroom into a space in which they wanted to know more than just the grammar, vocabulary, and idioms I had been teaching them; they were searching for a language with which to articulate and name the oppressions many of them faced daily.

These experiences of being an activist and a teacher have helped forged my ongoing critical and reflexive practices. These practices, as realized in my classroom, were an integral part of the intercultural and multilingual interactions with my students, in which we often discussed whose cultures and languages count, and why (see also Holmes, Jackson, Najar, & Lamoureux, this volume, for their analyses of these dimensions). Regarding my own societal position in the world, critical reflexivity has involved examining not only my own stance toward institutional and systemic power and my subsequent alignments with oppositional movements, but also my own implication in benefiting to varying degrees from my country's domination and appropriation of the world's major resources at the expense of those source countries. My own critical history dates back to when I first went to college. Coming from a working-class background, I graduated from a high school that was relatively homogeneous in terms of social class and income levels. Despite being the only American of Asian descent in the school, my classmates and I had much more in common than we thought. It wasn't until I was at a private college that I became aware of class markers in addition to racialized ones. There, I met several people who looked like me but who were literally worlds apart in their life experiences. On their spring vacations, instead of staying in the dorm as I did, they would fly off to Switzerland to ski.

Luke (2004) pointed out being critical not only means different things for different people but that it has also been appropriated 'for liberal and neoliberal educational agendas to improve individual achievement and thinking' (21). His definition of the critical is 'to call up for scrutiny, whether through embodied action or discourse practice, the rules of exchange within a social field' (26). Building on this, engaging in critical work necessarily involves addressing and contesting the overdetermined power, knowledge, and discursive formations of social relations, including class, gender, race, sex, and their interconnected combinations. These social relations are overdetermined in that any one factor should never be viewed as the sole determinant in the construction of the social totality, but rather multiple causal factors are acting to varying degrees (Althusser, 1979). These factors might include the economic, the cultural, the social, the political, the ideological, and the historical. It is important to remember that there are always multiple entry points to analyzing formations. For example, those addressing the issues of the economic modes of producing, appropriating, and distributing worker-produced surplus value (profit) are employing just one analytic entry point in interrogating the complex mosaic of overdetermined formations.[2]

An integral aspect of the critical is a reflexivity in the form of a heightened awareness of how things (including oneself) are presented, framed, narrated, and represented in this age of digital social media. Reflexivity is also a heightened critical awareness that situates one's own position vis-à-vis power formations and examines whether one benefits or suffers (or both) from a particular positional relationship to a formation. For example, what does it mean for a research professor who is employed full-time to name, contest, and challenge rules of exchange within social fields, in contrast to the many adjunct instructors struggling to find part-time work who are questioning their own field's rules of exchange? And who gets to decide what the critical is? Is it only researchers and theorists, or do others have a say in deciding what the critical is? This speaks to the complex dialogicalities (Bakhtin,

1984) in a societal culture constituting and constitutive of capitalist-based social relations. How does one define the (critical) self and the (capitalist) other, and what are the clear demarcations, if any, between these two constructs when both are imbricated and intertwined depending on class, gender, racial (and so on) formations? However, these questions raise another issue: If there is no self without the other, then inasmuch as the critical self is always having to define itself in terms of the capitalist other, thus perhaps inadvertently perpetuating an inescapable capitalist-centric discourse (Gibson-Graham, 1996), how does this capitalist other articulate itself in its own relation to the critical self? Does the capitalist other speak through the critical self so that the language of the critical self is adopted to create discourses in aiding its own agenda (Gee et al., 1996)? A critical reflexivity should both examine how constructions of hegemony appropriate these discourses in maintaining 'common-sense' (Gramsci, 1971) societal narratives and representations and strategize the necessary interventions in naming power's discursive guises.

Overview of Chapter

In what follows, I explore these dynamics of the complex dialogical and intersemiotic appropriations between critical selves and capitalist others, with a focus on the reflexivity involved in critical selves countering and naming these discourse appropriations and use of seemingly innocuous words such as 'flexibility' and 'accountability' by corporatized institutions. I employ a reflexive, mediated discourse perspective not only on the 'multimodal ways of engaging with representations of social life' (Byrd Clark & Dervin, this volume) but also on how these cultural representations shape and inform each other.

Data drawn from my photographs of protest signs featured at City Hall Park and a filmed workshop with participants on exploring language in the media is analyzed employing the perspectives of multimodal social semiotics (Kress, 2010), linguistic landscapes (Shohamy & Gorter, 2009), and mediated discourse analysis (Scollon, 2008; Scollon & Scollon, 2003). I first discuss the notion of linguistic landscapes and the accompanying production of politicized space at City Hall Park. This provides the contextual lens through which I then examine two protest signs that were part of the landscape constructed by OLA. Next, I explore how the participants in a workshop drew upon and mediated specific discourses in social circulations featured in these signs. The Critical Language in Action workshop, posted on YouTube, engaged with the participants the ways in which cultural assumptions and motivated agendas involved in neoliberal capitalism have shaped how language is used in current political, economic, and cultural discourses and their ensuing interpenetration into everyday Gramscian 'common-sense' narratives. Examining my own self-reflexivity as a participant, as well as the reflexivity displayed by the workshop participants, I conclude by exploring the implications of these Occupiers and fellow supporters' transforming and resemiotizing an institutional public park into a dialogic space. I address two questions: How were the participants' reflexive moves realized in their taking up the circulation of discourses found at the site of the Occupy encampment and its accompanying larger societal and cultural scale of circulation? Second, in examining my own role as an organizer and participant in the workshop, what is at stake in articulating a critical self that seeks to counter through dialogue the prevailing common sense held by others?

METHODOLOGY

Setting

The research was conducted at the OLA site during October and November 2011. A few weeks after it began, I contacted the people who organized classes and proposed a workshop on addressing media and public discourses from a critical language awareness perspective (e.g., Fairclough, 1992; Freebody, 2008; Janks, 2010). In the proposal, in addition to the description of the workshop and its aim, I provided them with a lesson plan outline. The lesson had three parts: First, I would discuss how language forms construe different meanings (Halliday, 1978) and how this connects to critical literacy. In the lesson handout for the participants, we would go over a selected text from the media (newspaper headlines and lead sentences on the Occupy protests), a short passage from a history text, and an extended quote from a former U.S. Undersecretary of State cited and analyzed by Fairclough (2009). In the second part, the participants would discuss words and phrases prominently featured in economic and corporate discourses that have penetrated popular discourse. These included 'the market,' 'accountability,' 'best practices,' 'flexibility,' and 'transparency,' all of which I selected on the basis of seeing these terms being adopted in North American educational settings at the secondary and university level. The final section called for the participants to characterize or describe in one sentence the aim(s) of the Occupy movement.

The workshop proposal was approved by OLA and set for Saturday, November 19, 2011, at the encampment. It was posted on the OLA website of scheduled classes and on the daily events calendar at the Park. I also posted the event on Facebook and e-mailed friends who I thought might be interested in attending. A friend was interested in filming it and received permission from those who attended. After filming it, he uploaded the video to YouTube under the title, 'Critical Language in Action.' The workshop lasted approximately one hour, and the video recording was edited to a running time of approximately 42 minutes.

Participants

Several attendees initially sat in on the workshop but left before it concluded. Other people, passing by the open-air tent that housed the library assembled by OLA and that served as the school, stopped by to listen before moving on while some stayed. In addition to the filmmaker documenting the workshop, the core participants in the workshop who were there from the beginning until the end totaled nine people: three males and six females. Of these nine people, I knew six of them personally; they are friends of mine who had either received my e-mail invitation or had seen my Facebook posting and who are critical in various ways. I hadn't met the other three people before the workshop, although I recognized two of them from seeing them at the encampment.

Data Collection and Analysis

The data presented is drawn from two sources. The first are the photographs I took of the Occupy demonstrations and its encampment, which included protest signs outside their tents and the various areas such as the general assembly area. I wanted to document as much as I could of OLA through photographs because I felt it was a historical moment in both the United States and the world through its linked movements to the European protests and the Arab Spring. My method in documenting through photography was twofold. The first was to record the daily minutiae of OLA with their artifacts of the tents, musical instruments, books, and sites that they established, including the library and media center. The second approach was photographing the protest signs carried during the demonstrations and marches and those situated at the Park. The signs were imaginative in their use of popular imagery (examples will be presented), color, and messages addressing the inequalities created by the economic system. I used my cell phone camera to take and save the photographs, and then e-mailed them to myself to store on my computer for later viewing and analysis. Some of these photos I uploaded onto Facebook so that I could share them with a larger audience who were not able to visit the Park. The second data source presented here was the YouTube video of my workshop, which captured the participants' discussions and reactions to the texts I provided them with, as well as their addressing the discourses in circulation at the site. I viewed the video repeatedly and took notes of the participants' interactions among their group members and the workshop as a whole. I also transcribed the participants' interactions in order to present selected extracts here. The extracts were selected for the ways in which the participants' critical and reflexive stances are illustrated in their engagements with the texts I provided.

My analysis was informed by a multimodal and mediated discourse analysis approach. Multimodality analysis approaches attend to the multiple ways in which we employ various semiotic resources in the making of meanings and examine the relationships among these modes, such as visual, gestural, aural, and verbal ones in their social contexts (Kress & Van Leeuwen, 2001). In examining why a particular mode may be privileged over others in meaning making, Kress (2010) and others have explored the specific affordances of a semiotic modal choice. They also focus on whose interest and agency are involved in these meaning makings. Agency in this context is the act of drawing upon and choosing from an available repertoire of semiotic resources to (co)-construct particular meanings in specific social contexts, as will be evident in the protest signs and the participants' discussions. Kress and Van Leeuwen (2001) cited two principles of multimodal discourse analysis. The first is to ask where signs come from because 'we constantly "import" signs from other contexts . . . into the context in which we are now making a new sign, in order to signify ideas and values which are associated with that other context by those who import the sign' (10). The second is 'experiential meaning potential,' defined as 'the idea that signifiers have a meaning potential deriving from what it is we do when we produce them, and from our ability to turn action into knowledge' (10). As such, multimodal discourse analysis is compatible and indeed part of a mediated discourse analytic approach (Norris & Jones, 2005).

A main aim of mediated discourse analysis is 'to explicate and understand how the broad discourses of our social life are engaged (or not) in the moment-by-moment social actions of social actors in real time activity' (Scollon, 2001: 140). How the Occupiers engaged with societal and economic discourses is reflected in the mediational tools of their protest signs documented in my photographs. My analysis of these signs addresses how these dominant discourses were taken up and challenged by the Occupiers. Iedema (2003) described the complex ways in which discourses and their meanings are received through various means, such as media and popular discourse, and then are recontextualized by people as 'resemiotization.' This process involves 'how meaning making shifts from context to context, from practice to practice, or from one stage of a practice to the next' (41). In analyzing how OLA people made their own meanings from dominant discourses in circulation such as globalization and capitalism, I focused particularly on how these discourses were recontextualized, or resemiotized 'across a wide variety of times, places, people, media, and objects' (Scollon, 2008: 233). Indeed, in my examination of what Scollon (2008) called 'discourse itineraries' (234) as discourses that are recontextualized into other modalities to make new meanings and thus 'transformed semiotically' (234), I adopted Stroud and Mpendukana's (2009) notion of 'rescaling,' which consists of 'the processes whereby persons, goods, cultural artifacts, imaginations, and languages are circulated and transported between locales and sites of different dignity' (367–368). Employing the methodological approach of rescaling is intended to address the 'circulation and insertion of elements across contexts' involving 'hierarchies and economies of value' (368). Certainly though, there is not a direct reproduction or transferal of 'messages' between the two sets of data, that is, between the protest signs and the participants' meaning makings. The analytic challenge is in tracing the particular discourse itineraries as they circulated throughout the protest signs sharing common themes, the participants' discussions, and the Park itself imbued with these discourses. Thus, I will be focusing on the dialogicality of discourses as they are rescaled along the sites presented here. The discourse itineraries and the processes of resemiotizing do not end with my participants but continue with my own analysis of the protest signs documented in the photographs and the discourses taken up in the workshop I conducted. To that end, my unit of analysis is the discourses, which are not strictly confined to either the protest signs or the YouTube video itself but instead traverse multiple modes as well as sites, both physical and online. My own reflexive engagement with these discourses and the participants' taking up of these discourses are, of course, part of these discourse itineraries across space, time, and artifacts.

Dialogicalities of a Linguistic Landscape at City Hall

Stroud and Mpendukana (2009) argued that 'one way in which *place* is constituted is through the language used in signage and in speakers' public displays, performances and interaction—so called *linguistic landscapes*' (364). Linguistic landscapes (LLs) have mainly been viewed thus far as consisting of public displays authorized by government agencies such as traffic and street signs or of commercialized billboards, advertisements, and storefront signage (Backhaus, 2007; Gorter, 2006; Shohamy & Gorter, 2009; Shohamy, Ben-Rafael, & Barni, 2010). Yet another category of LLs has emerged with individuals placing signs in public spaces; these signs are mainly of a personal nature, such as graffiti (Pennycook, 2009), or 'any sign that is in the 'wrong' place' or 'in some way unauthorized' (Scollon & Scollon, 2003: 146). If these individuals' signs are unauthorized, then the handmade displays by Occupiers are a legitimate form of an LL; one that is not created by government agencies or business interests but that is instead a highly politicized form speaking back to power. In this way, the LL of Occupy can be seen as unauthorized not only in the sense that Scollon and Scollon meant in terms of its not having official permission to be in a particular location but also in the sense of its not having the stamp of approval for its messages challenging an institutional and economic system and its accompanying discourses. This is an LL that can be seen as transgressive beyond the notion of its being unauthorized or in the 'wrong' place.

In contextualizing the politicized space produced by the LL at City Hall Park, it is instructive to take note of Lefebvre (1991)'s observation that inasmuch as 'social space is a social product,' it is produced in ways that both 'serves as a tool of thought and of action' and also as 'a means of control and hence of domination, of power' (26). The conflicting discourses in place (Scollon & Scollon, 2003) at the Park reflected this tension between the authorized and legitimated spaces of institutional power (embodied in the City Hall building and the police headquarters across the street) and the space produced by the Occupiers at the Park that called for thought and action. What Lefebvre (1991) called 'spatial practices' were observable in their attempts to recreate social relations at the encampment in forms of the general assemblies reflecting direct democracy, as well as the communal, collectivist nature of shared food and material necessities. Certainly, these practices resemiotized the spatial meanings intended by City Hall's institutional space.

The Occupiers' spatial practices included importing signs from other contexts and turning this semiotic recontextualizing action into knowledge (Kress & van Leeuwen, 2001). This is evident in the protest sign in Figure 8.1. The popular board game, *Monopoly*, features a character named 'Rich Uncle Pennybags,' who wears a top hat and tails and who sports a prominent mustache. Sometimes mistakenly named 'Moneybags' in popular usage, this character has come to visually signify in popular discourse the figure of a multimillionaire or even billionaire who controls and dominates a large sector of the industry (a near monopoly). In addition, the Pennybags/Moneybags figure is also seen as a stand-in for the very wealthy, the elite, or, to use the discourse of the Occupy movement, the 1%. In this context, the 1% refers to that fraction of society to whom the majority of mass-produced wealth accrues. In this Occupy sign, we can see the dialogic appropriation of this *Monopoly* character. Pennybag's face has been placed on top of cutout figure that is dressed in a suit. A hand-lettered sign has been attached to the trunk of this figure and features a text that reads, 'I've had enough trickle down economics.'

Figure 8.1 A protest sign at City Hall Park.

182 *Christian W. Chun*

The protest sign draws upon a number of intersemiotic dialogic references. It references the board game and its famous icon. The icon is resemiotized as not only the face of Wall Street, capitalism and of the 1% but also of those in the government who are complicit in facilitating the accumulation of profit into the hands of the few. The reference to specific government policies is indexed by the term 'trickle-down economics,' first associated with the economic policies of U.S. President Ronald Reagan's administration during the 1980s. The phrase was meant to convey the idea that if the major corporations, financial institutions, and their associated elites were given generous income tax breaks by the government, the money saved would supposedly help the rest of society by eventually 'trickling' down to them in the form of more jobs and cheaper prices on consumables. This sign thus assumes that the viewer, or addressee, would understand the historical (and indeed recent, as witnessed in the 2012 U.S. presidential election debates) references connected to this term. In addition, the viewer/addressee would need to realize how the material manifestations of this trickle-down economic policy have adversely affected the general populace due to decreased revenues from corporate taxes that impacts government funding for schools, infrastructure, and so on. This is indicated by the first part of the text, 'I've had enough...,' which speaks to the fatigue among a large sector of society who have seen their wages stagnate and decline during the last 30 years of rising corporate profits. The discourse that names capitalism as the system enabling rising inequalities is also indexed in the next sign, shown in Figure 8.2.

This sign also resemiotizes the *Monopoly* character of Pennybags as well as the logo of the game itself by using the identical font and similar

Figure 8.2 A related sign at the Park.

background color to replace the word 'monopoly' with the phrase 'corporate welfare.' The term 'welfare' has also had a long controversial usage in the United States since the Reagan administration. The popular meanings of welfare have now been shifted through Right wing political and media discourse to signify that those who are collecting it are somehow gaming the government. This has been indexed in part by the phrase used by the Right in the past, 'welfare queens,' which is a blatantly racist epithet intended to portray a predominantly inner-city community of mainly African Americans and Latinos who are supposedly living the high life off government handouts while not working for years. In this sign, however, the discourse of 'welfare' has been brilliantly recontextualized to define the bailout money that the banks and major corporations received from the federal government during the financial crisis of 2008–2009 and that severely impacted them as welfare itself. The text underneath the 'Corporate welfare' logo ('All the rewards of Capitalism with none of the risks') speaks to this discontent and, more importantly, names the structural system itself and the major players involved as being the ones collecting unwarranted and undeserved benefits from the government. The historical dialogicalities surrounding this discourse of welfare are evident inasmuch as this protest sign signifies a major shift reflecting the perception held by an increasing number of people that capitalism needs repeated government interventions to stay afloat—or risk collapse. Associating the word 'welfare' with the adjectival function of 'corporate' in this manner is an important disruption to the commonsense hegemonic discourse of welfare in the United States that had prevailed in the past 30 years.

'Critical Language in Action': A YouTube Video

The dialogicalities of the discourses in these two signs are now addressed beyond their 'spatially definable frames' (Stroud & Mpendukana, 2009: 372) by exploring their recontextualizations at the site of the workshop that I organized and conducted at the OLA encampment. Video-recorded and uploaded to YouTube, the workshop was attended by participants who were either active Occupiers or supporters. The majority of the participants were supporters—people who were not more actively involved in the movement in the sense of living at the encampment and participating daily but instead who had attended several rallies and marches. Figure 8.3 presents a screen shot of the video showing several participants receiving the handouts I had prepared for discussion.

I started off the discussion with a warm-up activity by asking the participants to compare with their partners (each group had three members) the two different versions of the *New York Times* report on the arrest of the Occupiers on the Brooklyn Bridge on October 1, 2011. On the handout, I had copied and pasted screen shots of the online edition headlines and accompanying lead sentences (see Figure 8.4).

Figure 8.3 'Critical language in action' video on YouTube.

Figure 8.4 Two versions from the *New York Times*.

Two participants, Moxie and Sam,[3] share their thoughts on the two lead sentences:

Moxie: This one [referring to the second] . . . calls it a showdown . . . and the second one includes the fact they were on the Brooklyn-bound roadway, which makes it sound more provocative on the protesters' part.
Sam: Oh yeah, the B one [meaning the second version] just looks like the protesters were somewhere they shouldn't have =
Moxie: = right =
Sam: = whereas A [the first version] really shows that the protestors were *allowed* to go onto the bridge and the cops maneuvered =
Moxie: = cut them off =
Sam: = to cut them off, so it looks like a setup.

Freebody (2008) argued that 'the starting point for critical literacy education is this: Societies strive toward convergence in the interpretive practices of their members—toward the production of a culture' (107). These commonsense interpretations, articulated and facilitated by the media to help achieve hegemony, are on display in the two lead sentences. As Moxie and Sam note, in the first version the police are accorded a greater agency than the protesters: '[T]he protesters were *allowed* to go onto the bridge,' as Sam says. His reading that 'the cops maneuvered' the protesters is aligned with Moxie's, as she cites the text, 'cut them off.' Sam repeats this phrase and concludes his reading of the first lead sentence that it presents the event as 'a setup.' In the second version, however, which was published a scant 38 minutes later, the number of protesters arrested has grown from 'dozens' to now 'hundreds,' thus seemingly posing a greater threat to the police. Moxie points out that the event is now described as 'a showdown.' Furthermore, the police are now seen as having to respond to the protesters due to 'the fact they were on the Brooklyn-bound roadway, which makes it sound more provocative on the protesters' part,' as she argues. Sam agrees, 'Oh yeah . . . looks like the protesters were somewhere they shouldn't have [been].' Another participant, Joan, referring to the phrases 'tense showdown' and 'marched on the . . . roadway,' observes that 'this seems to be to escalate it in a way to make it seem the protesters are part of the problem.' The act of arresting the demonstrators is now framed differently. The protesters are now presented as a 'more active and aggressive mass' as a seeming 'threat to law enforcement' (Joan, personal communication) that essentially leaves no choice for the police but to arrest them. Framing the protesters as 'part of the problem' for the police can be seen as an attempt to divert the readers' potential focus on the larger issues of what was causing the protesters to march in the first place.

In this next exercise, I had the participants read an extract of a 1999 speech by a U.S. State Department official, which was cited and analyzed by Fairclough (2009). I thought it would be interesting to have the participants conduct their own analysis of the text:

> Globalization is an inevitable element of our lives. We cannot stop it anymore than we can stop the waves from crashing on the shore. The arguments in support of trade liberalization and open markets are strong ones—they have been made by many of you and we must not be afraid to engage those with whom we respectfully disagree . . . In short, the financial crisis has exacerbated fears in developing countries and could fuel a backlash against globalization. Indeed, the optimistic notion only two years ago that the world was adopting dramatic economic liberalization as a model for economic and political development is under challenge . . . The world must neither resort to protectionist measures in a fruitless attempt to stop globalization nor should we ignore its undeniable risks. (Stuart Eizenstat, 1999, as cited by Fairclough, 2009: 325)

The very concept of globalization has been extensively debated (see Chun, 2012), and one representation of this complex phenomenon is predominant in this text. The extent to which the word 'globalization' has become a metonym for 'capitalism' raises the question of what is at stake for using one word over another? A quick search for the two terms on Google books Ngram Viewer shows that the use of 'capitalism' has declined in the past 30 years, while 'globalization' has dramatically risen during the same timeframe so that the two now intersect. In the following exchange, the participants engage with the State Department official's representation of globalization:

Jack:	It's very Old Testament=
Joan:	=Yeah!=
Jack:	=certainly=
Joan:	=totally!=
Jack:	=it's got a, you know, religious tone to it, you know, it brings up emotions rather than ideas.
Joan:	I was, I was thinking that, I was trying to find a way to pull it out of that as opposed to just an essence, but with the inevitability and the waves crashing on the shore, I felt it had uh, a deification about it=
Christian:	=right, right=
Joan:	=you know what I mean, as, as if it's, it's a force greater than . . . a collective decision=
Christian:	=right=

Joan:	=it's so, you know, this, this has been, this has been a . . . given to us [gestures with her hands motioning as if receiving a gift].
Christian:	'given to us', oh I like that, I like that=
Jack:	=Yeah, this is to *form*, not inform.

In recasting this particular narrative as 'very Old Testament' in its 'religious tone' and 'emotions,' Jack calls into question its seemingly rational justification of globalization. By assigning it a quasi religious meaning, suggesting a faith-based appeal in an unstable system that has provoked a backlash, Jack reflexively bypasses a critique of capitalism on its own terms and thus escapes the trap of having to speak through the capitalist other. Here, he creates a dialogic dynamic between a capitalist discourse articulating a rational-based logic and a religious one relying on having faith in this system, indexed by his comment, 'this is to *form*, not inform.' Joan also employs the same strategy as she frames the narrative with her implication that we need to be somehow grateful for the globalizing capitalism that has 'been given to us' and that is presented as a gift, as shown in her expressive gestural mode seen at 25:08 in the video. Her reflexive multimodal repertoire in resemiotizing this globalization narrative has been preserved in this YouTube video, which at last count has totaled more than 2000 views. The number of views suggests that, in taking up this globalization discourse, Joan and the other participants' resemiotized meanings in constructing their own counterdiscourses have possibly achieved a greater scale of circulation than the original speech.

The next exercise involved the participants defining several terms I had given them, which included 'accountability' and 'flexibility.' The participants were asked what they thought these words meant, how they have been used, and the implications of this usage. I selected these particular words because they have become part of neoliberal discourses framing human life 'in terms of a market rationality' in their 'extending and disseminating market values to all institutions and social action' (Brown, 2005: 40). After discussing 'accountability' in the context of corporations in which their accountability is limited to the board of directors and excludes the public, Sam frames it in the current neoliberal discourse of the assault on public education:

> [I]n the classroom, teacher accountability simply means there is a standardized test and your students have to do well with it, or you're no good as a teacher. It doesn't make any difference if the kids can function in society, communicate, get a job, contribute in any way to the future of society, oh no, everything is pared down to these very narrow specific definitions.

I asked the participants how 'flexibility' was used in the workplace. Moxie's reflexivity in challenging the capitalist Other speaking through a pleasant, seemingly reasonable phrase to mask its disciplinary discourse is evident in her ventriloquizing an employer's demands:

> It's basically used to destroy the, the worker protections we have, like having a designated lunch time, or you know, having to work an eight-hour day, you know, you bash workers by saying, 'you need flexibility, we need flexibility, we need you to put in more time . . . you need to be flexible' . . . as usual, they're co-opting a nice-sounding word to mean something that's used to destroy the rights of working people.

The last discussion point called upon the participants to express in one sentence the aims of the movement or to characterize it. One participant who arrived halfway through the workshop said, 'it is an expression of frustration that society isn't working very well and an appeal for solutions.' Another expressed it this way: '[T]he people want to reclaim a voice in the face of corporate takeover.' An Occupier cited the Los Angeles City Council's initial support of OLA: 'The Occupy demonstrations are a rapidly growing movement with the shared goal of urging U.S. citizens to peacefully assemble and occupy public space in order to create a shared dialogue by which to address the problems and generate solutions for economically distressed Americans.' I think it is worth noting here the observation by Lefebvre (1991) that 'power's message is invariably confused—deliberately so; dissimulation is necessarily part of any message from power' (142) for several reasons: First, the Occupiers did assemble peacefully. So why were they evicted a scant two months later after the Occupation was granted permission to 'occupy public space' at the Park? Second, if in fact this was actually public space, the question arises, which public are we talking about? The homeless, who sometimes camp out nearby in makeshift shelters? And finally, 'shared dialogue,' of course, means at least two participants, but who was listening and who was speaking?

Another Occupier characterized the movement as being 'a global movement of diverse and concerned citizens coming together to redress their economic and social grievances,' to which her group partner, recontextualizing the State Department globalization discourse, added '[W]e're a force of nature.' These discourses—'society isn't working well,' a reference to the economic crisis and a questioning of the system itself in light of its breakdown; 'people want to reclaim a voice in the face of corporate takeover'; and 'diverse and concerned citizens coming together to redress their economic and social grievances'—all draw upon the discourses featured in this particular LL. The Occupiers' protest signs and the participants' interconnected critiques resemiotized the Park's space by dialogically expanding the discourses in a place beyond the institutional ones of order and authority.

DISCUSSION AND CONCLUSION

The intersemiotic dynamics emerging from the participants' articulations of critical selves in this workshop context, my own stances and facilitations involved in running this workshop, and both the protest signs' and participants' resemiotizing of dominant discourses stemming from capitalist others (financial institutions, their mouthpieces, government officials, corporate media, and bloggers) attest to the nature of reflexive, co-constructed multimodal meaning makings traversing space, time, and artifacts. The 'spatially definable frames' (Stroud & Mpendukana, 2009) in which these texts and discourses are first read and viewed can best be seen as ephemeral or even collapsing, as we have seen the preceding discourse itineraries unfolding along multiple sites. These mediated discourses in action (Norris & Jones, 2005), or what might also be termed 'discourses in motion,' are evident through their circulations between and among the various modes of official government speeches, media headline stories, protest signs, and the participants' verbal and gestural meaning makings captured and featured in the YouTube video. All these meaning makings continue to have the potential to be kept in motion, as it were, in the sense that these itineraries have been preserved and showcased in this video, repeatedly played or referenced to as many times as possible, reflecting the interdiscursive dialogicalities (Scollon & Scollon, 2003) of self and others along various levels or scales.

In the participants' reflexive moves in taking up the larger societal (and global) circulation of discourses, one such scale is the LL constructed by the Occupiers, which was intended to be shown to both the immediate passersby at the Park and then, almost immediately, to the broader public via corporate and social media channels. Their reflexivity in creating and physically posting these signs, knowing that many of them would later be posted on sites such as Facebook, Tumblr, and YouTube, not only demonstrates critical engagements with society (through their pointed messages such as 'corporate welfare' and 'I've had enough trickle-down economics') but also what appears to be a reflexive awareness of how these reflections would be represented and positioned in certain ways. Dialogic spaces would, of course, be created in the immediate context of the physical site—the encampment—in which these signs first appeared. These spaces naturally included the interactions and engagements among the physically present viewers of the signs and those who had created them. But just as importantly, the Occupiers were fully aware that the further disseminations of these signs and their representations (as well as of their own performative selves in the act of protesting, critiquing, and demonstrating) via social media would generate countless other virtual dialogic spaces as well. The discourses being taken up and the ensuing discussions on these multiple sites beyond the originating site throw into stark relief the prevailing dominant discourses in their shaping and informing of the other. And, importantly, these sites afford the potential for counternarratives and alternative framings of Occupy and its representations to exist, which help challenge and contest the hegemonic view promulgated by most of the mainstream corporate media.

An interrelated scale is the reflexive performativities of the workshop participants that contributed to dialogic spaces. Knowing that they were being filmed for the purposes of historical documentation on Occupy and that the recording would be eventually uploaded to YouTube and seen by an audience far larger than the one in immediate attendance, the participants (several of them having extensive teaching, performing, and filmmaking experience) deftly co-constructed their meaning makings in engaging with the discourses featured in the handout and indirectly those circulating in the surrounding LL. The globalization discourses featured in the State Department official's speech, which was addressed to a select elite audience, were circulated and mediated on a larger scale through the broader and different audience of (academic) readers of the Fairclough (2009) article. In turn, I helped to facilitate the transport of this particular globalization narrative via Fairclough's presentation and analysis of it through the use of my handout and then subsequent uptake by the participants and me. At this point, this has been further rescaled to an even more diverse audience of viewers who have watched the workshop video, which, of course, creates additional dialogic spaces and possible rescaling to other sites and modes.

And what of my own role as an organizer and participant in this workshop? In particular, what is at stake in my (re)presenting and performing a critical, reflexive self and in the representations of the participants in this video? Thinking of how to support Occupy beyond showing solidarity by marching in demonstrations and also seeing the protest signs speaking back to hegemonic discourses, I was inspired with a simple notion to conduct a class beyond my university environment. In this public space, we would perform and interact with one another as co-constructed critical selves in naming and addressing hegemonic others (and also attempt to examine the extent to which these others have been imbricated within our self views and discourses). Once I knew the workshop would be recorded, uploaded, and then viewed by a much wider audience than the one in attendance, I realized that not only my lived histories and experiences up to that moment would be preserved in the YouTube representation of me as the facilitator and participant in this workshop but also those of the participants. However, despite the fact that this video is embedded within this corporatized website and our critical reflexive performativities are thus archived, our represented voices of dissent should not just be seen as being contained and presented within those frames. Instead, our multimodal representations will continue to traverse along other dialogic sites and modes, enabling possibilities of others taking up and mediating hegemonic discourses of globalizing capitalism via their critical, reflexive selves.

NOTES

1. On April 29, 1992, a jury acquitted three White Los Angeles police officers accused of excessive force while arresting King, an African American, on March 2, 1991. The incident was captured on video by a bystander and released to the media. The acquittal triggered widespread burning and looting of private and public property over the course of several days.
2. Formations is a term used by Althusser, which signifies a structural conception of social life, similar to the term habitus or dispositions as proposed by Bourdieu.
3. Participants' names are pseudonyms. Equal signs represent the overlapping of comments.

REFERENCES

Althusser, L. (1979). *For Marx*. London: Verso.
Backhaus, P. (2007). *Linguistic landscapes: A comparative study of urban multilingualism in Tokyo*. Clevedon, UK: Multilingual Matters.
Bakhtin, M. M. (1984). *Problems of Dostoevsky's poetics*. Minneapolis: University of Minnesota Press.
Brown, W. (2005). *Edgework: Critical essays on knowledge and politics*. Princeton, NJ: Princeton University Press.
Chun, C. W. (2012). The multimodalities of globalization: Teaching a YouTube video in an EAP classroom. *Research in the Teaching of English*, 47(2), 145–170.
Fairclough, N. (Ed.). (1992). *Critical language awareness*. London: Longman.
Fairclough, N. (2009). Language and globalization. *Semiotica*, 173, 317–342.
Freebody, P. (2008). Critical literacy education: On living with 'innocent language.' In B. V. Street & N. Hornberger (Vol. Eds.), *Encyclopedia of Language and Education: Vol. 2. Literacy* (2nd ed.) (pp. 107–118). New York: Springer.
Freire, P., & Macedo, D. (1987). *Literacy: Reading the word and the world*. London: Routledge and Kegan Paul.
Gee, J. P., Hull, G., & Lankshear, C. (1996). *The new work order: Behind the language of the new capitalism*. Boulder, CO: Westview Press.
Gibson-Graham, J. K. (1996). *The end of capitalism (as we knew it): A feminist critique of political economy*. Minneapolis: University of Minnesota Press.
Gorter, D. (Ed). (2006). *Linguistic landscape: A new approach to multilingualism*. Clevedon, UK: Multilingual Matters.
Gramsci, A. (1971). *Selections from the Prison Notebooks* (Q. Hoare & G. Nowell-Smith, Trans.). New York: International Publishers.
Halliday, M.A.K. (1978). Language as social semiotic: The social interpretation of language and meaning. London: Edward Arnold.
Iedema, R. (2003). Multimodality, resemiotization: Extending the analysis of discourse as multi-semiotic practice. *Visual Communication*, 2(1), 29–57.
Janks, H. (2010). *Literacy and power*. New York: Routledge.
Kress, G., & van Leeuwen, T. (2001). *Multimodal discourse: The modes and media of contemporary communication*. London: Arnold.
Kress, G. (2010). *Multimodality: A social semiotic approach to contemporary communication*. London: Routledge.
Lefebvre, H. (1991). *The production of space*. Oxford: Blackwell.
Luke, A. (2004). Two takes on the critical. In B. Norton & K. Toohey (Eds.), *Critical pedagogies and language learning* (pp. 21–29). New York: Cambridge University Press.

Norris, S., & Jones, R. H. (Eds.). (2005). *Discourse in action: Introducing mediated discourse analysis*. London: Routledge.

Pennycook, A. (2009). "Linguistic landscapes and the transgressive semiotics of graffiti. In E. Shohamy & D. Gorter (Eds.), *Linguistic landscape: Expanding the scenery* (pp. 302–312). London: Routledge.

Scollon, R. (2001). *Mediated Discourse: The nexus of practice*. London: Routledge.

Scollon, R. (2008). Discourse itineraries: Nine processes of resemiotization. In V. K. Bhatia, J. Flowerdew, & R. H. Jones (Eds.), *Advances in discourse studies* (pp. 233–244). London: Routledge.

Scollon, R., & Scollon, S. W. (2003). *Discourses in place: Language in the material world*. New York: Routledge.

Shohamy, E., & Gorter, D. (Eds.). (2009). *Linguistic landscape: Expanding the scenery*. London: Routledge.

Shohamy, E., Ben-Rafael, E., & Barni, M. (Eds.). (2010). *Linguistic landscape in the city*. Bristol, UK: Multilingual Matters.

Stroud, C., & Mpendukana, S. (2009). Towards a material ethnography of linguistic landscape: Multilingualism, mobility and space in a South African township. *Journal of Sociolinguistics*, 13(3), 363–386.

9 Weaving a Method
Mobility, Multilocality, and the Senses as Foci of Research on Intercultural Language Learning

Ulrike Najar

INTRODUCTION

> Think of building, or of making more generally, as a modality of weaving. As building is to dwelling, so making is to weaving: to highlight the first term of each pair is to see the processes of production consumed by their final products, whose origination is attributed not to the improvisatory creativity of labour that works things out as it goes along, but to the novelty of determinate ends conceived in advance.
> (Ingold, 2011: 10)

This chapter is concerned with research on intercultural language learning, particularly with the understanding of method as an epistemological tool for grasping diversity and incorporating multidimensional and reflective viewpoints into current research practices. Although the impact of transnational and complex global shifts is increasingly recognized in the understanding of reflexive modes of being and becoming intercultural, a critical and investigative focus on the methods we use to represent intercultural multiplicity remains often a desideratum. In this light, the aim of this chapter is twofold: It first examines on a general level the ways we use and understand methods in the area of intercultural language education and, based on this reflection, argues for a rethinking of method around the elements of movement and transformation.

Let me start with a small meditation on the term 'method.' According to the *Oxford English Dictionary Online* (2011), the Latin word 'methodus' dates back to the 15th century and stands for a 'mode of proceeding.' The identical Greek word 'methodus' originally represented a 'pursuit of knowledge' before it was commonly understood as a 'systematic arrangement,' a 'special form of procedure or characteristic set of procedures,' and 'a mode of investigation and inquiry, or of teaching and exposition.' Interestingly, the Greek word 'methodus' reveals another layer of meaning—from a morphological perspective, the term consists of 'meta' ('after,' 'behind,' or 'with') and 'hodos' ('way,' 'path,' or 'travel'). What emerges from this perspective on the term is, in my view, an understanding of

194 *Ulrike Najar*

method as a process of following a journey, or a way, and implies a general sense of movement that is not bound to a single form. What can an approach to method as such tell us about the epistemological notions of method this chapter is interested in as well as about the weaving of method?

The metaphor of weaving indicates the general direction of my argument, namely a critical reflection of the relationship between method and the journeys or ways language learners take during their experiences of *intercultural being and becoming*. Throughout this chapter, I argue that intercultural language learning should be understood as a multimodal practice, of moving in 'context,' across several locations and along multiple trajectories (Pennycook, 2010, 2012). In referring to the context of language learning and later on to the places and spaces of intercultural experience, I adopt a learning-beyond-the-classroom perspective recognizing the important role that informal and everyday learning environments can play for intercultural experience (see Benson & Reinders, 2011). This more or less spatial approach to research on intercultural language learning borrows the terms 'space' and 'place' from spatial theory while pointing toward meaning-making processes in both physical locations (place) and as part of more abstract conditions of learning (space). As Tuan points out, space can become a place 'as we get to know it better and endow it with value' (2001: 6) or when we start to feel familiar in it. This annotation of value to a specific place highlights the importance of focusing on intercultural experience *in situ* and the factors that may transform space into place and *becoming* into *being* intercultural. Once language learners leave the classroom, they are part of the 'intercultural field,' the postmodern, complex, and highly networked context of learning languages (see Phipps & Gonzalez, 2004). The term 'weaving,' in this sense, means aiming for a synchronization of intercultural practices *in situ* with a range of methodological tools.

'Weaving' also implies an awareness of the positioning and subjectivity of the researcher—not the researcher alone in form of an isolated unit but as embedded in, and journeying across, the research *context*. The question will be raised how I, as the researcher, was part of and took part in intercultural practices (collaboratively) and how my own knowledge and understanding of intercultural learning came to life from a reflective and multimodal standpoint. The term 'weaving' will function in this light as both a metaphor and a conceptual tool to approach method as a reflexive and exploratory process, not a given. Although the aim of the chapter is to clarify and unpack these arguments on the basis of a particularly created 'method assemblage' (Law, 2004), some groundwork needs to be done in order to explain the background and aim of the study from which the arguments in this chapter emerged. The arguments in this chapter should then be understood within the frame of this particular study.

Weaving a Method 195

THE RESEARCH CONTEXT

The arguments presented in this chapter are based on a study that took place in Melbourne, Australia, from 2009 to 2012. The study observed the context of intercultural language learning from the perspective of language learners, who were asked to take me, the researcher, out for a walk to their individual places of 'intercultural significance.' The participating language learners were asked to capture the process of the walk by taking photographs of, for them, relevant moments, landmarks or discoveries on the way, and the like. The choice of the location depended on the experience of each language learner and his/her own understanding of relevant moments and places within the intercultural learning processes (see Figure 9.1). Most of the language learners who agreed to take part in the study were local or international students in Melbourne and were recruited in various language classrooms as well as one language learning club of a local university. It is important to note that many of these language learners were what Rizvi (2007) termed 'cosmopolitan learners,' learners who were *able* to travel across the globe and who were generally interested in and open to intercultural experience. All in all, 26 language learners joined the study, and the ages of the participants ranged from 20 to 68 (with a majority of participants being students of languages at a university level). The cultural, linguistic, and social backgrounds of these learners intersected with a wide array of national backgrounds, such as Singapore, the Philippines, Australia, China, India, Germany, Egypt, and Hong Kong.

The questions at the heart of this research were then (1) how do language learners experience intercultural language learning outside the classroom, (2) what roles do place and space play for intercultural language learning processes and for experiencing diversity, and finally (3) how does this spatial perspective have an impact on research about intercultural language

Unser WG-Wohnzimmer: wo ich Deutsch gelernt habe. Gemütlich oder? Das Fenster war wie ein Fernseher—auf der Strasse gab's immer etwas los.
[The living room of our shared flat where I studied German. Cosy, isn't it? The window was like a TV—there was always something happening on the street.]

Figure 9.1 Thomas' walk 1

learning and its methodological frameworks? Although the study was largely designed within an ethnographic approach, it was aimed at the employment of a number of methodological tools that emerged from the research process itself. Choosing ethnography as an umbrella method was based on the understanding of *intercultural learning as an (in its core) ethnographic process* that transforms language learners into ethnographers (Roberts et al., 2001). A method that takes into consideration the ethnographic practices of language learners should in this vein be as close as possible to its research aims and interests.

What follows is an exploration of the methodological journey of this research project and the processes, which created the final particular method assemblage designed for this study. To present this method only in its final form would seem to undermine the importance of the methodological decisions made 'on the way' and the exploratory aspect of the project in general. Therefore, independent autoethnographic reflections about the methodological process have been included in this chapter to highlight some of the major questions that transformed the research and its design. These notes are entitled as 'from the notebook' and intersperse the flow of the sections to take account of the voice of the researcher and to capture some of the pondering moments that, in my view, concern the weaving of a method. This way of sharing my own ways of engaging with reflexivity aims to shed light on the multifaceted, complex and ongoing dialogical processes that are part of the reflexive research process, as Byrd Clark and Dervin pointed out in the Introduction to this volume.

Finally, this chapter is of interest particularly for ethnographers in the area of intercultural education but also addresses researchers with other methodological preferences. The aim is to critically reflect on the general premises that we base our research on when choosing a particular methodological design that is often framed by disciplinary traditions.

EAT YOUR METHODOLOGICAL GREENS

To critically examine the ways we use and understand method in the field of intercultural language education, we need to raise a number of questions. For example, do the methods we choose to research intercultural learning processes have an impact on a common perception of intercultural matter—beyond the realms of academia? If this is the case, in which way can methods reinforce fixed, rigid, and stable understandings of culture and intercultural being and becoming? And could a need to present research findings as clear and definite to multiple audiences contribute to circulating images of cultural *singularity* as norms of knowledge and thinking? In this sense, how does method relate to the use of static or absolute terminology, such as when talking about 'successful' or 'failed' forms of multiculturalism? The argument underpinning all of these questions and guiding this section is that method and our understanding of it impact reality (Law, 2004). A proposition as such asks us to rethink the nature and foundations of method per se.

A rethinking of method is anything but a quick or straightforward process. It very much starts by raising questions about the purpose and focus of methods, and interrogating assumptions of normativity and the understanding of reality. For John Law, rethinking method in this light means to be

> at odds with method as this is usually understood. This, it seems to me, is mostly about guarantees. Sometimes I think of it as a form of hygiene. Do your methods properly. Eat your epistemological greens. Wash your hands after mixing with the real world. Then you will lead the good research life. Your data will be clean. Your findings warrantable. The product you will produce will be pure. It will come with the guarantee of a long shelf-life. (Law, 2007: 595)

The guarantees Law highlights are not just side effects of those careful steps that are organized for the researcher. Rather, they uncover a much deeper sense of method: the human desire for an understanding of reality as universal, the recurring aim to unlock essential truths (as Kramsch addresses in the Commentary in this volume) or to identify rather stable representations of the world *as it is* (as Malinowski and Nelson state in Chapter 6 in this volume; original emphasis). Underneath the call for a rethinking of method and its inherent terminology is, then, in Kramsch's terms, the attempt to *embrace multiplicity and its paradoxes* and to overcome the idea of method as a tool to seek the 'definite, the repeatable, the more or less stable' (Law, 2004: 6). This argument is in line with Malinowski and Nelson's argument in Chapter 6 (this volume)—criticizing conventional conceptions of writing as stable representations of the world.

From the notebook:

> Entry 9: I struggle with the terms. I aim to find out how and where language learners become and/or are intercultural and I feel somehow confused by expressions such as 'research object' or 'research subject'. Already now, they make me feel distanced from the people I am going to meet. Am I not a 'research subject' involved in this study too? After all, I am an international scholar, away from home and experiencing moments of interculturality every day. This will, of course, filter into my research and the analysis. I might use the expression 'language learners' while explaining that a) I am part of this group and b) it is not a homogeneous group with more or less one set of expectations and learning needs. The term rather refers to particular language learners, who were willing to participate in this study and were largely 'cosmopolitan language learners.'

If Law calls for an overcoming of research that is based on stable and fixed parameters, what does this tell us about postmodern reality in which present-day research takes place? Postmodern reality is not stable in its representative sense but is instead characterized by spatial-temporal transformations that shaped the previous decades and range from an increasing intensity of exchange to the stretching of social relations, the speeding up of global flows, and the impact propensity of global interconnectedness (Held et al., 2003: 69). In particular, the concept of transnationalism, a main element of globalization, has shaped our understanding of the reconfiguration of social formations *across* physical borders and the highly networked and dense qualities of these formations (Vertovec, 2009). Whereas 'nation-states have defined the social and economic conditions under which people work, . . . they are no longer the sole arbiter of governing,' as Popkewitz and Rizvi (2010: 18) point out in order to illustrate how social practice is increasingly detached from its places of origin. Processes of intercultural learning do not appear in isolated space but are rather embedded in transnational and complex networks of flows and mobilities (see Byrd Clark, 2012; Dervin, 2011; Pennycook, 2010, 2012). These spatial-temporal transformations, however, are highly contested processes, which let de Sousa Santos (2006) argue that there are as many globalizations as there are perspectives on and understandings of current global changes. In light of this understanding of postmodernity, it is comprehensible when Law describes the current state of the world as a 'mess' while arguing that the world is much more *indefinite*, that is, 'vague, diffuse or unspecific, slippery, emotional, ephemeral, elusive or indistinct' (Law, 2004: 2). In Law's opinion social science research should attempt nothing more than the capture of those elements that are 'complex, diffuse and messy' (Law, 2004: 2).

A number of questions arise at this stage, such as how do the methods we use in the field of multiculturalism capture the complex, the 'multi-,' the 'trans-,' or the 'inter-' of intercultural practice? How do case studies, conversation analyses, discourse analyses, quantitative studies, or ethnographic fieldwork (to name only some of the most common methods in the field of intercultural education) make an effort to address the postmodern shifts toward mobilities, transnational networks, or even the 'messiness' of what is researched? How can our commonly used *conversation-only* research styles address multiple ways of knowing within constantly transforming and mobilized global networks? And, more importantly, what impact do these postmodern processes have on the role of the researcher, the language learner, the research location, and the research process?

In this chapter I argue that method should imply a critique of those understandings of intercultural reality that are based on monolithic and static notions about culture. Method should concentrate too on the element of transformation and on those hard-to-capture indefinite notions of interculturality that are embedded in the prefixes of 'inter-' or 'trans-.' Following the individual ways and journeys of language learners means to consciously be aware of the potential of method to recreate images of stability, definite knowledge, and 'cleanliness.' One way to approach method from a perspective of transformation is then to base research premises not solely on one correspondent research paradigm but rather to translate multiplicity into a relational methodological framework.

ASSEMBLING A RELATIONAL FRAMEWORK

From the notebook:

> Entry 21: The most inspiring methods I've read about so far are 'walking interviews', arts-based methods (both used in the fields of sociology and psychology). The idea of walking with language learners or letting them draw concept maps to concentrate on the relationships between different modes of experience is both exciting and intriguing. Ideally, I would use a number of methods from different academic fields for this project. I know that using ethnography as an 'umbrella method' seems appropriate given my conceptual understanding of language learners as ethnographers. However, in using more than one methodological tool, the multimodality and diversity of intercultural experience might be better acknowledged. Which impact would this have on my overall research design?

To design a method that responds to a postmodern understanding of reality, a relational and more or less 'open' framework for the research design is needed. What this means is that *method emerges from the field* and leaves space for changes and adjustments along the way in order to align the research tools as closely as possible with the aim and particularity of the study. Designing a research method becomes in this sense a form of crafting, a move beyond the pure collection of data, toward a continuous mode of trying, dismissing, adjusting, and readjusting methods and the combination of these in the flow of the process. Crafting a method corresponds here with what Law terms a 'method assemblage' (Law, 2004), a creative dealing with absences and presences:

> [Social] science should also be trying to make and know realities that are vague and indefinite *because much of the world is enacted in that way.* In which case it is in need of a broader understanding of its methods. These, I suggest, may be understood as methods assemblages, that is as enactments of relations that make some things (representations, objects, apprehensions) present 'in-here', whilst making others absent 'out-there'. The 'out-there' comes in two forms: as manifest absence (for instance as what is represented); or, and more problematically, as a hinterland of indefinite, necessary, but hidden Otherness. (Law, 2004: 14; original italics)

From a methodological perspective, finding out about the constellation of 'absences' and 'presences' not only gives insight into how the major themes of a research project emerge, disappear, or transform their shapes and meanings. It also shows how intercultural experience is enacted and constructed based on traditionally used research methods and common thematic directions (for example, researching through the lens of identity, culture, or nationhood). Researching processes of intercultural becoming and being is guided by absences and presences, by enactments of relations between representations of culture and the individual experience of it. Method, in this sense, has to be able to capture these fluxes and instabilities as well as to incorporate them into the research design.

Yet how, specifically, can this be done? Choosing an *exploratory* research design is convenient in this situation because it considers research projects that have 'no clear, single set of outcomes' (Baxter & Jack, 2008: 548) and that point toward an *inductive* approach (which means that the hypothesis emerges from the field, not vice versa). In intercultural learning, meaning emerges from the process of intercultural exchange and happens gradually with steps forward, steps backward, and a lot of lingering in between. It is exactly those transitional and indefinite forms of learning that exploratory research tries to capture while gradually building itself within an open research framework, with the researcher following the paths and ways of the participants. This focus on 'social experiences and lived realities' (Mason, 2006: 12) underlines the search for a *dialogue between methods* that is based on a 'creative tension.' Mason explains:

> Ideally, this involves a creative tension between the different methods and approaches, which depends upon a dialogue between them. It means that instead of ultimately producing one integrated account or explanation of whatever is being researched (integrative logic), or a series of parallel accounts (parallel logics), one images instead 'multi-nodal' and 'dialogic' explanations which are based on the dynamic relation of more than one way of seeing and researching. (Mason, 2006: 10)

Basically, such a dialogue of methods can create an open research frame that takes into consideration the complex and multimodal ways of making meaning and that aims to give space for a method that is able to capture the circulation of diversity beyond single disciplines and academic fields. A mixed method within a method assemblage approach includes, in this sense, multiple disciplinary foci, making it more interdisciplinary. Researching interdisciplinarily recognizes the interconnectivity of ideas and, instead of 'ironing out the distinctive strengths of different approaches,' aims to 'facilitate the developing of multi-dimensional ways of understanding' (Mason, 2006: 10).

What follows is a discussion of an exemplary method assemblage that was designed for the previously described study on language learning *in situ*. It aimed to create a method that was able to capture both context and dynamic and multimodal modes of intercultural practice. Three main methodological principles emerged from this study: (1) the principle of movement (in particular, walking), (2) the principle of 'multilocality,' and (3) the principle of the senses (or the 'sensed').

From the notebook:

> Entry 15: The element of movement in, and across diverse locations, seems crucial for my research. But how do I include locations and movement in my research design? Can ethnographic interviews capture intercultural experiences in place? Is simply conversing or talking about diverse modes of intercultural being and becoming able to capture the multiplicity and multimodality of the process? In the case of participant observation, where exactly will these take place and in what do I participate? It seems somehow paradoxical to talk about intercultural learning as a social practice while sitting in an isolated place conducting the interview.

REPERFORMING JOURNEYS

> By becoming knowledgeable I mean that knowledge is grown along the myriad paths we take as we make our ways through the world in the course of everyday activities, rather than assembled from information obtained from numerous fixed locations. Thus it is by walking along from place to place, and not by building up from local particulars, that we come to know what we do. (Ingold, 2010: 121–122)

The significance of movement and journeying for intercultural learning processes emerged in a conversation I had with one of the language learners, who agreed to take part in this study, Joshua. He told me about his intercultural experiences in Spain in the following way:

J. I basically spent the whole time I was there, it was about nine months, studying, walking around from, you know, between the different faculties. So I definitely felt like the walking around and the exploring was kind of really connecting me to the place a lot, and much more so than when you are in a car or a bus or something, you know, where you just fly past.
U. So it's something like a different way of moving?
J. Yes, definitely that movement around the city and the slow movement, you know, walking, you really get to know the streets and that kind of thing and also going out. There's a really big tapas culture in Granada and it's free, when you buy a drink you get your tapas. That was a big thing, sort-of meeting with people to go out for tapas. And that's again sort-of little bars, and you walk from one to the next one, and that was a big part of getting to know a lot. I mean, I'd say, walking for me was kind of one of the most important ways in sort-of establishing a connection.

Intercultural learning is strongly connected to movement in and through place and space, as is illustrated in Joshua's narrative. Movement in the course of intercultural encounter happens on both a physical level (traveling by plane, car, bus, train, on foot, and so forth) and a social level. It is the relationship between social transformation and 'processes of place-making'—experiences language learners have in certain locations and the correlating negotiations about those experiences (Ingold, 2011; Ross et al., 2009)—which is at the core of intercultural experience. Physically moving through space came, for Joshua, along with aiming to 'establish a connection,' a process that was then shared through stories and narratives. De Certeau explains:

> Every story is a travel story—a spatial practice. For this reason, spatial practices concern everyday tactics, are part of them, from the alphabet of spatial indication ('It's to the right', 'Take a left'), the beginning of a story the rest of which is written by footsteps, to the daily ;'news' ('Guess who I met at the bakery?'), television news report ('Teheran: Khomeini is becoming increasingly isolated . . .'), legends (Cinderella is living in hovels), and stories that are told (memories and fiction of foreign lands or more or less distant times in the past). These narrated adventures, simultaneously producing geographies of actions and drifting into the commonplaces of an order, do not merely constitute a 'supplement' to pedestrian enunciations and rhetorics. They are not satisfied with displacing the latter and transposing them into the field of language. In reality, they organize walks. They make the journey, before or during the time the feet perform it. (1988) 115–116)

In de Certeau's view, narratives form nets that spread out before or during an actual walk. It is in this vein that language learners follow physically the lines of preexisting narrated stories, be they from a textbook, the media, or friends. Narratives are an integral part of intercultural language learning in that they are performed through movement and 'written by footsteps' (de Certeau, 1984: 116). How can method follow both these narrated and walked networks of intercultural experience?

Placing movement in the center of a study requires the use of a particular set of methods that allow the notion of mobility to enter the study design on a practical level without disconnecting the research from the 'outside world.' In creating a method assemblage for the study here presented, I turned toward *mobile methods* that recognize the relevance of mobility in present (global) societies (see, for example, Büscher & Urry, 2009). Ross et al. highlight that:

> the new mobilities paradigm in the social sciences has turned attention to the ways in which mobile research methods can be utilized to understand everyday experiences through embodied, multisensory research experiences. Journeys themselves are focused upon as dynamic,

place-making practices foregrounding movement, interactivity and the multi-sensory, focusing attention on research relationships, contexts and engagements. (2009: 606)

I incorporated into this method assemblage a particular form of mobile methods called *guided walks*. Recently, 'talking whilst walking' (Anderson, 2004), 'go alongs' (Kusenbach, 2003; Carpiano, 2009), 'guided walks' (Ross et al., 2009), 'language on the move' (Lamarre, 2013; Lamarre & Lamarre, 2009) or 'fieldwork on foot' (Lee & Ingold, 2006) have been acknowledged as qualitative methods that give insight 'into the way people and places combine' (Moles, 2008: 1). These forms of walking interviews are understood as an 'ideal technique for exploring issues around people's relationships with space,' while taking 'the research process out of fixed (safe, controlled) environments' and back into more natural spaces (Jones et al., 2008: 2). Jones et al. describe the roots of walking interviews as follows:

> Of course the idea of studying life in motion is nothing new. Anthropological fieldwork and techniques such as participant observation often ask the research to study the subject in motion, rather than taking a participant out of their everyday context to ask them questions about their life. (2008: 2)

From the notebook:

> Entry 40: I conducted my third 'guided walk' with Vasu yesterday. He is originally from India and came to Melbourne to do his Masters. As soon as we got up, the atmosphere seemed to be much more relaxed. Vasu even mentioned that 'this felt better' once we started walking—a transformation from formal to informal modes of researching? I also noticed that the people I walk with start asking personal questions about myself (topics beyond the scope of the research). It seems that being on the move and the stories we share trigger an exchange of roles of the researcher and the participant.

Guided walks are a form of walking interviews that give the participant a central role while letting her or him guide the route. Guided walks involve a participant 'leading the researcher through *locales of significance*' that form 'part of their local geographies' (Ross et al., 2009: 605, emphasis added). The term 'guided' implies that the participants have a chance to 'convey their movement throughout and site themselves in their everyday environments' (Ross et al., 2009: 608). The term is, however, a working term based on the insight that walking in a pair is not a simple action of following but rather an exchange of different ways of orientating, in which a changed perception of place enables the language learner and researcher to create 'new' and emerging spaces. Guided walks are in this sense a 'co-generated research encounter' (Ross et al., 2009:

Figure 9.2 Vasu's guided walk

609) that moves along through the participant's 'favorite spots' or places, and typical events that occur along the way. This place-making activity is a process of mutual negotiation and thinking about space and experience.

From the notebook:

> Entry 42: I keep thinking about Vasu's walk—it was almost a mini-performance of intercultural encounter. While we were walking, we constantly got interrupted by locating ourselves in Melbourne's downtown, which we had to cross. This physical orientation often interjected with our talk about social orientation, with both themes seemingly intertwined. After about twenty minutes of walking, Vasu stopped to take a picture from the former Parliament house [Figure 9.2], an impressive Victorian building which is now used for weddings and public events.

Our conversation went on as follows:

U. Are they still having the Parliament here?
V. No, it is in Canberra.
U. Ah, OK!
V. It was the national Parliament before they moved it.
U. I remember that the houses in India look a bit the same, right? This monumental . . .

V. It's all the Victorian British influence.
U. So did you find things similar here in Melbourne?
V. No, no, not at all. It is very different.
U. How?
V. The architecture. Everything. It's more closed and conservative, competitive in India. Most of us go out.

Place was not only 'around us'—it was very much a trigger for particular themes, which emerged from the places we moved in. One disadvantage of our moving interview yesterday was, sadly, the strong wind. It caused many side noises on my recording, which meant that some parts of the interview remained only in fragmented form.

Guided walks aim for being *nondirectional* and *nonhierarchical*, with the role of the researcher as that of an orientating nature. Jones et al. (2008: 2) exemplify this when pointing toward the changed power relations between interviewer and interviewee and the 'significant effect on the kinds of data that are generated.' Although mobile interviewing is still at an 'experimental stage,' it is widely acknowledged that it has great potential as a new creative methodology because it can 'move the collection of the interview data in productive and sometimes entirely unexpected directions' (Jones et al., 2008: 7), as Vasu's example has shown.

MULTILOCALITY: RETHINKING THE FIELD SITES OF INTERCULTURAL EXPERIENCE

> In order to follow such an object that travels across multiple field sites, an ethnographic mode other than that, which is orientated towards the traditional, single-site is needed. (Pierides, 2010: 181)

From the notebook:

> I met Veronica today, an Australian language learner who just recently returned from a long-term stay in France and whom I met through an advertisement at the student center of the university. As I wasn't able to go with her on an actual walk since she came back two months ago (and going to France would have been logistically difficult), I asked her to send me pictures from the 'walks' she did in Lyon and Paris, together with small captions to indicate the relationship of the shown places with moments of 'intercultural significance'. I will call these versions of the walks 'virtual walks' but I need to read more about the idea of a 'field site'. Aren't there as many field sites of intercultural learning as language learners are out there?

206 *Ulrike Najar*

Transforming the research process into a reflexive, multimodal, and coexperienced process implies the thinking about the 'field' of research, traditionally understood as a more or less clearly defined locality or a set of localities, in which research can be undertaken and intercultural learning observed. Within the scope of this research project, I was in need of a methodological concept that was able to follow language learners across multiple sites because this is exactly where intercultural learning can be both traced and methodologically located. Allowing the researcher to follow the circulation of persons, meanings, and metaphors within their 'multilocality' meant to shed light on the journeys that language learners take or are able to take while being and becoming intercultural. I recall one part of the conversation I had with Veronica:

> I get very attached to places. I think for me, with Lyon, it was easy because the city is very well set up, like architecturally it is designed so you can really understand. I don't know how to explain this. Like you can see a long way and you can see the way everything is set up. I went to Paris four or five times, but I never felt like I was connected to the city because I felt I couldn't see it all at once. It was too big for me to understand, like to make a mental kind of picture of [it]. I always felt like Paris was an unfriendly place because I couldn't really grasp its geography very well. . . . I just get the feeling that with Lyon I understood more each area and what people were doing there. I understood the character of each area better because I could kind of work out how they are all connected. In Paris, I couldn't really understand how people were using . . . like people were everywhere but I didn't know what everyone was doing, you know?

Veronica illustrates the relation between the modes of movement and the processes of place and meaning making. Beginning to see connections between place, people, and practices was, in Veronica's experience, based on being able to physically *orientate* and connect to the environment she was moving in.

A particular methodological direction reflecting these thoughts is multisited ethnography that takes place across and within multiple sites. The emergence of transnational space, the increased global mobility, and the deterritorialization of social realities urged ethnographers to rethink and reevaluate their methods and concepts of place and space. Thus, multisited ethnography, as well as its understanding of the field site as more than one clearly defined locality, is the product of these aforementioned processes (see Amit, 2000; Hall, 2009). In the context of this particular study, multisited ethnography embraced the fact that intercultural learning and 'coherent cultural processes may take place across great distances, linking up disparate entities. They may also take place on the move' (Burrell, 2009: 183). Research on intercultural learning in this sense has to acknowledge and even follow these routes and experiences on the move and within multiple sites. Method too performs as a 'place-making activity' (Pink, 2008), in which the researcher follows the different strands and lines of the participants who experience the process of connecting to place, diverse meanings, and practices in their own ways. While recognizing the fluidity, diversity, and interconnectivity of those trajectories, intercultural experience is again observed within a multidirectional research frame that moved beyond the concept of a traditional single-site of research.

ON THE SEARCH FOR THE EPHEMERAL

We have seen that to orientate oneself in space means to relate to space and to connect to it while grasping how it relates to previously learned, remembered, and experienced forms of knowledge. The walks I shared seemed to question absolute knowledge through its multidirectional but also very individual modes of multimodal learning. In the following discussion, I will introduce the terms 'senses' and 'sensing' in an attempt to round off this chapter with a central argument that emerged from the method assemblage and from the walks themselves: Intercultural experience in the particular research project was less about what was learned than how it was learned. The shared practice of walking and of reperforming and sharing stories often centered on using the senses to orientate, allowing transitional and often indefinite modes of intercultural learning to appear. Intercultural learning was here indeed a process of *orientating* in which absolute knowledge was questioned within reflexive modes of learning.

Recalling the conversation I had with Vasu, I remember our misunderstanding of the word 'orientating.' Vasu missed his 'social circle' in Melbourne, and when I asked him if he found it easy to orientate in town, he firstly thought that I asked about orientating as a personal and social modus:

U. Did you find it easy to get an orientation in town?
V. Oh I missed the orientation here in town. Oh you mean orientate in place or orientate in life?
U. I meant in place.
V. I'm used to travel by myself a lot. I'm walking.
U. And orientation for life?
V. Oh, it's OK. I really stick to myself. Spanish was another reason to meet some more people.

The conversation with Vasu shows again how walking as a physical mode was interlinked with the evocation of particular themes during the interview. More importantly, it illustrates the different meanings that the term 'orientating' incorporates. Veronica pointed out that 'understanding' Lyon meant to engage with the way it is 'set up' and 'to grasp its geography' over a longer period of time while 'watching how things change.' Kirsten, a Chinese language learner who spent time in Austria to learn Austrian German, mentioned the 'huge difference' between being a tourist and being a learner staying for a longer period of time. She describes the 'touristy' ways of engaging with new places as follows: 'You feel like they are just skimming the surface, looking on buildings. . . . But you won't appreciate it after a while. And you don't really get an insight into anything.' What remains after the first impressions of unfamiliar environments was then described as a wish for 'connecting' and trying to 'look under the surface' of a place. Interestingly, learning experiences as such cannot always be easily expressed with words—or researched on the basis of spoken or written language only. However, Bagnoli reminds us that:

> in most qualitative research interviews are a standard method of data collection. The use of interviews relies on language as the privileged medium for the creation and communication of knowledge. However, our daily experience is made of a multiplicity of dimensions, which include the visual and the sensory, and which are worthy of investigation but cannot always be easily expressed in words, since not all knowledge is reducible to language. (Bagnoli, 2009: 547)

As stated previously, the aim of this method assemblage was to create a creative tension and dialogue between the chosen methods and approaches that were based on the 'dynamic relation of more than one way of seeing and researching' (Mason, 2006: 10). Going beyond the idea of the interview as 'just about talking' was then to bring space and place back on board and to understand an interview as a 'place-event,' a coming together of different perspectives in one place at a specific time (Pink, 2008). Learning about *how* intercultural learning took place let *a focus on the senses* emerge. The senses structure our experience of space and place (Rodaway, 1994). Even more, they are mediators of relationships 'between self and society, mind and body, idea and object' (Bull, 2007: 5–6, cited in Mason & Davies, 2009: 589). The related term, 'sensing,' then incorporates the notion of 'grasping' (*Oxford English Dictionary Online*, 2011). Grasping or sensing intercultural experience is by nature an intangible endeavor and *is located at the junction of imagining, experiencing, and remembering* (Pink, 2009). All modes are closely intertwined, and imagined forms of the sensory fall together with remembered forms of sensory experience. How, then, can both the sensed and the senses be engaged methodologically?

Multisensory ethnography concentrates on 'the senses from the starting point of the self-reflexive and experiencing body, . . . the ethnographer's own sensorial experiences as a means of apprehending and comprehending other people's experiences, ways of knowing and sensory categories, meanings and practices' (Pink, 2009: 46). Within the realm of multisensory ethnography, the ethnographer is understood as an emplaced researcher who aims to break down hierarchies of conventional interviewing structures while sharing (inter-)cultural practices in situ. Multisensory ethnography is then open to multiple ways of knowing *and* being while aiming to grasp vague notions of experience. Researchers should in this vein ask themselves:

> how methods emphasize the interplay between tangible and intangible sensory experience, including elements of the sensory that were visible, audible, touchable, etc. in the present as well as those which people conjured in their sensory imaginations and ethereal or mystical ways of resembling. . . . '[S]ensory intangibility' is vital to how we see resemblances and to the practice of sensory methodology. (Mason & Davies, 2009: 587)

Focusing on this 'sensory intangibility' follows the aim of finding out about the transitional stages of intercultural learning while focusing on the individual ways of imagining, experiencing, and remembering elements of culture in relation to place, feelings of belonging, and practices of diversity. What the walks visualized is that there are multiple and *multimodal ways of knowing* that are tightly connected to emotions such as Jackson has shown in her case study in Chapter 1(this volume). They also reminded us that transforming the research into a multisensory reflexive process means to ask how our understandings came into being, particularly under the light of the senses. This form of reflexive research should help to move beyond more or less stable categories of data based on similar stable and static research processes. In this light, guided walks represent a possibility to address those dimensions of intercultural language learning that are of a 'sensed-sensing energy with multiple centers' (Thrift, 2007: 17).

WEAVING A METHOD

> My hope is that we can learn to live in a way that is less dependent on the automatic. To live more in and through slow method, or vulnerable method, or quiet method. Multiple method. Modest method. Uncertain method. Diverse method. Such are the senses of method that I hope to see grow in and beyond social science. (Law, 2004: 11)

I started this chapter with the proposition that methods impact reality and that, if used in static and researcher-centered ways, they can in fact recreate understandings of culture as singular, as absolute and universally 'true.' I used the expression of 'weaving' to think metaphorically about the relational character between method, research object, and postmodern theory. Elaborating on the constantly transforming nature of intercultural learning processes, I also incorporated the elements of movement and the context of learning into the research process itself, thereby identifying three research foci: the senses, multiple locations, and mobility. A focus on these elements ties in with the argument that the methods I used to research processes of intercultural learning *could not be disconnected from language learners' practices*. The guided walks of this study were designed within an open and exploratory research process that let many parts of the method assemblage emerge from the field. This shift culminated in a highly reflexive and multimodal methodological practice that constantly aimed to exchange the roles of researcher and participant. A methodological practice as such impacted the negotiation of directions and the incorporation of multiple centers into the research design and indicated that a focus on *how* language learners learn interculturally was of the same importance as *where* the intercultural experience took place.

Finally, I argued that a main desideratum within current research practices centers around the elements of transformation and movement. Studies on intercultural learning tend to disconnect the participants from their everyday learning experiences, doing so on the basis of a number of constraints, such as time, location, or particular research and participant needs. However, if we consider intercultural language learning as a mobile and highly dynamic practice within more or less instable networks, a need to translate these arguments into method arises. Method has an extraordinary potential to perform as an epistemological tool for grasping diversity and acknowledging the interwoven character of place, meaning, and learning *in situ*. In this chapter I have illustrated how this can be done with the help of a method assemblage that invited mobility, multiple locations, and the senses into a multidimensional and reflexive research design.

REFERENCES

Amit, V. (2000). Introduction: Constructing the field. In V. Amit (Ed.), *Constructing the field. ethnographic fieldwork in the contemporary world* (pp. 1–19). London: Routledge.

Anderson, J. (2004). Talking whilst walking: A geographical archaeology of knowledge. *Area*, 36(3), 254–261.

Bagnoli, A. (2009). Beyond the standard interview: The use of graphic elicitation and arts-based methods. *Qualitative Research*, 9(5), 547–570.

Baxter, P., & Jack, S. (2008). Qualitative case study methodology: Study design and implementation for novice researchers. *The Qualitative Report*, 13(4), 544–559.

Benson, P. & Reinders, H. (Eds). (2011). Beyond the language classroom. The theory and practice of informal language learning and teaching. Basingstoke: Palgrave Macmillan.

Bull, M. (2007). *Sound moves: iPod culture and urban experience*. London: Routledge.

Büscher, M., & Urry, J. (2009). Mobile methods and the empirical. *European Journal of Social Theory*, 12(1), 99–116.

Burrell, J. (2009). The field site as a network: A strategy for locating ethnographic research. *Field Methods*, 21(2), 181–199.

Byrd Clark, J. (2012). Heterogeneity and a sociolinguistics of multilingualism: Reconfiguring French language pedagogy. *Language and Linguistics Compass Blackwell Online Journal*, 6(3), 1–19.

Carpiano, R. M. (2009). Come take a walk with me: The "go-along" interview as a novel method for studying the implications of place for health and well-being. *Health & Place*, 15(1), 263–272.
de Certeau, M. (1988). *The practice of everyday life* (S. Rendall, Trans.). Los Angeles: University of California Press.
de Sousa Santos, B. (2006). Globalizations. *Theory, Culture & Society*, 23(2–3), 393–399.
Dervin, F. (2011). A plea for change in research on intercultural discourses: A 'liquid' approach to the study of the acculturation of Chinese students. *Journal of Multicultural Discourses*, 6(1), 37–52.
Hall, T. (2009). Footwork: Moving and knowing in local space(s). *Qualitative Research*, 9, 571–585.
Held, D., McGrew, A., Goldblatt, D., & Perratton, J. (2003). Rethinking globalization. In D. Held & A. McGrew (Eds.), *The global transformations reader. An introduction to the globalization debate* (2nd ed.) (pp. 67–74). Cambridge: Polity.
Ingold, T. (2010). Footprints through the weather-world: Walking, breathing, knowing. *Journal of the Royal Anthropological Institute*, 16, 121–139.
Ingold, T. (2011). *Being alive. Essays on movement, knowledge and description*. London: Routledge.
Jones, P., Bunce, G., Evans, J., Gibbs, H., & Hein, J. R. (2008). Exploring space and place with walking interviews. *Journal of Research Practice*, 4(2), 1–8.
Kusenbach, M. (2003). Street phenomenology: The go-along as ethnographic research tool. *Ethnography*, 4(3), 455–485.
Lamarre, P. (2013). Catching 'Montreal on the move' and challenging the discourse of unilingualism in Québec. *Anthropologica*, 55(1), 41.
Lamarre, P. & Lamarre, S. (2009). Montréal «on the move»: Pour une approche ethnographique non-statique des pratiques langagières des jeunes multilingues, T. Bulot (dir.) *Formes & normes sociolinguistiques. Ségrégations et discriminations urbaines* (pp. 105–134). Paris, France: L'Harmattan.
Law, J. (2004). *After method: Mess in social science research*. London: Routledge.
Law, J. (2007). Making a mess with method. In W. Outhwaite & S. P. Turner (Eds.), *The SAGE handbook of social science methodology* (pp. 595–606). London: SAGE.
Lee, J., & Ingold, T. (2006). Fieldwork on foot: Perceiving, routing, socializing. In S. Coleman & P. J. Collins (Eds.), *Locating the field: Space, place and context in anthropology* (pp. 67–86). Oxford: Berg.
Mason, J. (2006). *Six strategies for mixing methods and linking data in social science research*. NCRM Working Paper. Manchester and Leeds, UK: ESRC National Centre for Research Methods.
Mason, J., & Davies, K. (2009). Coming to our senses? A critical approach to sensory methodology. *Qualitative Research*, 9, 587–603.
Moles, K. (2008). A walk in thirdspace: Place, methods and walking. *Sociological Research Online*, 13(4), 1–10. Retrieved December 26, 2013 from www.socresonline.org.uk/13/4/2.html
Oxford English dictionary online. (2011). Oxford: Oxford University Press. Retrieved September 26, 2011 from www.oed.com/view/Entry/117560
Pennycook, A. (2010). *Language as a local practice*. London: Routledge.
Pennycook, A. (2012). *Language and mobility: Unexpected places*. Clevedon, UK: Multilingual Matters.
Pierides, D. (2010). Multi-sited ethnography and the field of educational research. *Critical Studies in Education*, 51(2), 179–195.
Pink, S. (2008). Mobilizing visual ethnography: Making routes, making place and making images. *Forum: Qualitative Social Research*, 9(3), 1–14. Retrieved December 26, 2013 from www.qualitative-research.net/index.php/fqs/article/view/1166
Pink, S. (2009). *Doing sensory ethnography*. London: SAGE.

Phipps, A., & Gonzalez, M. (2004). *Modern languages: Learning and teaching in an intercultural field.* London: SAGE.
Popkewitz, T. S., & Rizvi, F. (2010). *Globalization and the study of education: An introduction.* Hoboken, NJ: Wiley.
Roberts, C., Byram, M., Barro, A., Jordan, S., & Street, B. (2001). *Language learners as ethnographers.* Clevedon, UK: Multilingual Matters.
Rodaway, P. (1994). *Sensuous geographies: Body, sense, and place.* London: Routledge.
Ross, N. J., Renold, E., Holland, S., & Hillman, A. (2009). Moving stories: Using mobile methods to explore the everyday lives of young people in public Care. *Qualitative Research*, 9(5).
Rizvi, F. (2007). *Teaching global interconnectivity.* Paper presented at the 21st Century Curriculum: Taking Bearings Conference, Sydney.
Thrift, N. (2007). *Non-representational theory: Space, politics, affect.* London: Routledge.
Tuan, Y.-F. (2001). *Space and place: The perspective of experience.* Minneapolis: University of Minnesota Press.
Vertovec, S. (2009). *Transnationalism.* London: Routledge.

10 Everyday Practices, Everyday Pedagogies
A Dialogue on Critical Transformations in a Multilingual Hong Kong School

Miguel Pérez-Milans and Carlos Soto

1 'WHAT DO YOU MEAN BY "CRITICAL"?' RESEARCH AND SOCIAL TRANSFORMATION IN EDUCATION

It is 11 a.m. on a Friday morning in April 2012 when we meet—a researcher (Dr. M[1]) conducting a critical sociolinguistic ethnography in MAT Secondary School (MATSS[2]), a government-aided school in Hong Kong; and a teacher (Mr. C), who works in this school, teaching English and liberal studies to a group of so-called 'ethnic minority' (EM) students through the lens of critical pedagogy—at the Faculty of Education at the University of Hong Kong. It is almost four months since the fieldwork carried out in the school ended[3], and we are interviewing each other through open conversation to reflect on our experiences in the process of data collection from our distinct positions. Forty-six minutes into the conversation, the interview unfolds as follows (see the transcription conventions in the Appendix to this chapter):

> Mr. C   what do you think your- your critical / or A critical sociolinguistic ethnography can offer me in terms of / my practice / uh / as a- as a teacher in the classroom but then also as a researcher?
> Dr. M   {laughter} wow / uh / uuh // well I—I remember the first day / the first day / when I was observing you in the class / after the class / we were going back home / and we were in the MTR {underground} / and you were making questions about / mmh / *but what do you mean by critical?*
> Mr. C   [{laughter}]
> Dr. M   [laughter] and then [I was trying]
> Mr. C   [I think we are still negotiating that!] [{laughter}]
> Dr. M   [yeah]

As Chun (Chapter 8, this volume) points out, critical reflexivity includes heightened awareness of representation, positioning, and power and involves interrogating the construction of 'critical.' Apparent in this extract is that the negotiation of what counts as criticality was key in the building of our own relationship and rapport. Mr. C was concerned about the possibility of Dr. M benefiting from ethnographic research that might describe but ultimately leave oppressive structures and relationships in place. But to move beyond monolithic understandings of power where the only goal is pointing out how wider ideologies are reproduced and/or contested in the school context, we both agreed on setting up a more productive dialogue focused on the exploration of how identities, tensions, and moments of transformation are produced and negotiated in the moment-to-moment of the classroom's everyday activity. Indeed, we believe that our own difficulties in getting to this meeting point are to be found in the way critical approaches have been developed across different disciplines.

Critique has been the object of numerous discussions, books, and research articles in social sciences since the mid-20th century. In reaction to positivist accounts that had previously conceptualized everyday life and social structures as two different and separate realms, this new ontological position brought with it the understanding of social reality as being discursively constructed, reproduced, naturalized, and sometimes revised in social interaction, in the course of large-scale historical, political, and socioeconomic configurations (see Giddens, 1984). In doing so, critique has paved the way to illuminating how social inequality works at the local level, allowing at the same time the development of transformational projects oriented to empower certain social groups who have been historically oppressed. However, these two aspects, intrinsically linked to critique, everyday life, and social structures, have often been taken up as separate or even incompatible, leading to polarized goals focusing either on knowledge-building or political activism.

This has been particularly the case in the educational field, which has often been conceptualized by reference to metaphors such as 'window' or 'social laboratory' in critical literature, each of these being metaphors driven in many cases by a different research agenda, namely knowledge-building research or action research. Among these research traditions historically approaching the social space of the school from slightly different angles, we see that critical pedagogy (Akbari, 2008; Camangian, 2008; Duncan-Andrade & Morrell, 2008; Freire, 1970; Lin, 2004; Wink, 2000) and critical sociolinguistics (Heller & Martin-Jones, 2001; Block & Cameron, 2002; Lin & Martin, 2005; Martin-Jones, 2007; Kubota & Lin, 2009, Martín-Rojo, 2010, Pérez-Milans, 2013) are useful examples, whereby the former has paid attention to the designing of liberating pedagogies that provide people with tools to critically understand and transform wider social structures, and the latter has devoted most of its efforts in developing a more suitable theory to explain how social inequality in modern institutions is culturally produced, shaped, and naturalized under changing economic conditions.

In contrast to these major disciplinary and historical trends, we aim to provide in this chapter an alternative account, on the basis of an ongoing dialogue between us. We believe this dialogue across the boundaries of disciplinary

Everyday Practices, Everyday Pedagogies 215

traditions (ethnographic sociolinguistics and pedagogy) and institutional identities (university researcher and researched school teacher) sets up a terrain for theory development and localized social transformation in critical approaches to the field of education. As we shall see in the following sections, our self-reflexive conversation enriched our respective research and teaching perspectives and goals, allowing us to engage in what Najar (Chapter 9, this volume) refers to as a 'weaving' of method, at the same time providing a base for long-term collaboration, network building, and other forms of action.

We have organized our chapter into five sections. Section 2 begins with a discussion of our specific research agendas and clarifies the nature of our dialogue and how ethnic minority education in the Hong Kong context fits within it. Then we take turns in Sections 3 and 4 reflecting upon observed practices in one of Mr. C's classes. On the one hand, Section 3 will tell the story of the institutional process of transformation faced by MATSS through Dr. M's perspective, with a focus on how this process shaped the interactional and discursive processes by which Mr. C and his students negotiated meaning and interpersonal relationships through their daily practices inside their classroom and through digital interactions on Facebook.

On the other hand, Section 4 will provide Mr. C's account of his own lived experience, allowing Dr. M to place his analysis in a wider social and pedagogical context that points out a critical moment of transformation at the institutional level of the studied school as well as at the pedagogical order of Mr. C's classroom. Finally, Section 5 will discuss opportunities, tensions, and dilemmas derived from a dialogue such as this, with particular attention to the value of continuity in these forms of collaboration. We envision the involvement of more sites, voices, and resources from here on, especially if our isolated actions as researchers, teachers, and students are to develop into a project as a means of social change.

2 TWO RESEARCH APPROACHES, ONE INSTITUTIONAL SITE: SCHOOLS, ETHNIC MINORITY YOUNGSTERS, AND SOCIAL CHANGE IN HONG KONG

On December 7, 2012, the *South China Morning Post* Hong Kong newspaper published in its Neighbourhood Sounds series a news report titled 'Jordan, Home to a Battling Nepali Community.' Although specifically about the presence of the Nepali community in one of the most famous Hong Kong neighborhoods, this report shows a great deal of the contemporary picture on the EM youngsters portrayed and circulated by public opinion in the Hong Kong context. Accompanied by a photo in which a Nepalese beauty shop owner gives a community worker a quick trim, the report states that 'drug pushers get the ethnic minority teenagers to sell drugs in local schools, because if they're caught, they won't be sent to prison for life,' followed by a further comment on their position within the Hong Kong educational system in which it is said that 'less than one per cent of EM students get into tertiary education, so they lose heart and just want to make money.'

Indeed, this portrayal does not differ from that provided by university researchers, who argue that, although Hong Kong public schools (including government, aided scheme, and direct subsidy scheme schools) serve over 9000 primary and secondary school EM students, those students face a 'lower Chinese standard, limited choices of schools, difficulty of adaptation to school life, and narrow way-out' for further education (Wong, 2009: 1). For some commentators, these conditions perpetuate the exclusion of EM in Hong Kong, both in and out of the system of public education, and intensify 'race and ethnicity' as 'key dimensions of social stratification and inequality in contemporary Hong Kong society (Ku et al., 2005: 1).

However, and although there seems to be some consensus on this panoramic view on the social position of these youngsters in Hong Kong society, in general and in the educational setting in particular, there is less evidence of the everyday situated practices of these social actors. As a consequence of official figures pointing out educational failure for these youth, more resources and researchers are now approaching this issue by trying to explain causes and developing interventions. Nevertheless, most of the ongoing research centers on academic factors and creating 'more suitable' Chinese language education programs for these students (see, for instance, Gao, 2011; Tsung et al., 2009; Jin et al., 2009; Shum & Lau, 2009); that is, a lack of access to Chinese language skills, beyond sufficient exploration of their social experiences, is considered to be the main reason of this widespread failure among EM students.

Against this backdrop, we hoped to shed more light on these issues. Although from different disciplinary traditions, we were both interested in looking closely at these youngsters' everyday lived practices. Indeed, it was along the way in the process of collaboration that we found each other's perspectives particularly useful in that regard, and the fact that we did not see that initially is especially significant to us because it reflects the distrust historically constructed between educators and university researchers in the field of education. On the one hand, Dr. M's focus on the study of the moment-to-moment of situated interactions in the classroom setting offered Mr. C's critical pedagogy project a platform for the localized analysis/transformation of the wider social processes of structurization as played out in the institutional space of the school.

On the other hand, Mr. C's determination to challenge conventions of activity arrangement and evaluation in the everyday of the school in which he worked in order to provide his EM students with learning opportunities, enabling them to reflect critically on their conditions of social oppression, constituted in Dr. M's eyes a key localized moment in which links between the wider economic structures, the social organization of a given (school) community, and the discursive practices through which that community reconstitutes itself as such all get destabilized. At this point, it might be worth taking each of these two angles in turns. We turn now to Section 3 for Dr. M's story.

3 DR. M AND THE STUDY OF INTERPERSONAL COLLUSION

As in the case of any other regular Monday afternoon in the International Section, Mr. C and the 16 students of one of the class groups in Form 2 are already in the classroom at 2.20 p.m. Everything seems to follow the conventional patterns for Mr. C's classes, with a noticeable exception for this day. Against his pedagogical convictions, Mr. C has brought into the classroom a fill-in-the-gaps photocopy about feelings that the students are expected to complete. The school is at this moment working on the preparation of standardized English tests that all students from the Local and International Sections must take in order to allow a comparison of results across the two sections. These standardized practices are common in the organization of educational practices and assessment procedures in the school, particularly in the Local Section, but Mr. C is strongly opposed to those that, according to him, detract from student learning, empowerment, or 'authentic' assessment of learning. However, after arguments with the head of the English language panel in the school regarding previous assessments, Mr. C has agreed to proceed with the test in its existing form in order to avoid further conflict.

Extract 1. 'Sir, keep on talking.'

1	Mr. C	FRUSTRATED &
2	Ajmal	& {in a bored-like fashion} aah
3	Hasan	[{laugh}]
4	Mr. C	[uuh] / A PERSON FEELS [FRUSTRATED] =
5	¿?	[(())]
6	Mr. C	= WHEEN / THEY WANT TO DO [SOMETHING] /
7	Zareef	[{laugh}]
8	Mr. C	BUT THEY CANNOT DO IT (2″) ok // SO LET'S SAY I [WANT YOU] =
9	Ajmal	[{cough}]
10	Mr. C	= to [(())] /
11	Ajmal	[{makes a sound with his hands}]
12	Mr. C	[AND I CAN'T DO IT↑] /
13	[{laughter}]	
14	Mr. C	I will feel frustrated↓] //
15	{laughs and cough}	
16	Mr. C	LET'S SAY I WANT (()) TO BE QUIET &
17	Zareef	{to his peers} & ((OI ! WASIF)) MEN!
18		*hey! Wasif*
19	Mr. C	AND THEY KEEP TALKING↑ &
20	¿ Hasan?	& nothing
21	Mr. C	[(())]
22	Zareef	[(())]
23	Ajmal	[{coughs}]

24		{sounds of Mr. C writing on the blackboard}
25	¿?	disgusted &
26	Zareef	& what? // sir / keep on talking
27	¿?	surprised
28	Ajmal	{laugh}
29	¿Zareef?	{whistles}
30	Ajmal	{laugh}
31	¿?	(())
32	Mr. C	(1″) ok / [EMBARRASSED]
33	Husna	[ARRE] / CHOOR NA YAR
34		*oh please / leave him pal*
35	Mr. C	[yeah]
36	Ajmal	{to Husna} [poor (())] &
37	Mr. C	& YOU GUYS KNOW EMBARRASED &
38	Ajmal	& {to Husna} kya hei
39		*what is it*
40	Zareef	[{laugh}]
41	Hasan	[YEES!]
42	Zareef	{to Husna} you should report [(())]
43	Mr. C	[(())]
44	¿Zareef?	disgusted
45		{sound of a pen falling down near Zareef's seat}
46	Mr. C	DISGUSTED↑
47		(3″){sound of a pen falling down near Zareef's seat }
48	Mr. C	disgusted↑
49	Zareef	I am the one↑
50	Ajmal	{laugh}
51	Hasan	sir / something really [yuck↑]
52	Ajmal	[paalli]
53		*peanuts* {nickname??}
54	Mr. C	A PERSON FEELS / DISGUSTED / WHEEN / uh &
55	Hasan	& they say something yuck↑ / (((hum↑)°)) &
56	Mr. C	& uuh / like /
57	Husna	uusko choor gaya [{laughs}]
58		*he left him*
59	Ajmal	[woo khud bool gaya] / {laugh}
60		*he forgot himself*
61	Mr. C	{in Spanish} cómo se llama↑
62		*how is it called?*
63	Zareef	SIR / {covering his nose with his fingers} YOU ((DO)) LIKE THIS / AND / [(())]
64	Ajmal	[{laughter}]
65	¿?	[(())]
66	Mr. C	[YOU GUYS KNOW / IN CANTONESE]=

Everyday Practices, Everyday Pedagogies 219

67	Hasan	[(())]
68	Mr. C	=wattat?
69	Hasan	no &
70	Zareef	& WATTAT / YEAH YEAH &
71	Mr. C	& wattat / WATTAT IS / DISGUSTING // like uuh
72	Ajmal	{whispering}
73	Ajmal & Zareef	[{laughs and whispering}]
74	Mr. C	[IF YOU SEEE / A DEAD DOG ON THE STREET] / you would say / *oh hou wattat!*
75		/ in English you would say *I feel soo disgusting* &
76	¿Zareef?	& [(())]
77	Ajmal	[{laughter}] &
78	¿?	& (()) &
79	Mr. C	oor / SMELL [SOMETHING]
80	Ajmal	[{laughter}]
81	Mr. C	BAD / {in Cantonese} HOU CHOU / [(((you feel the same...))]
82	Ajmal	{covering his nose with his hand} [SIR / I CAN SMELL NOW!]
83	{laughter}	
84	Zareef	[SIR / (())] =
85	Hasan	[(()) bhatbu↑]
86		* bad smell*
87	Zareef	=SO MUCH WORKING (())
88	Ajmal	[{laughter}]
89		
90	[{coughing}]	
91	Ajmal	SIR / [I CAN SMELL ((NOW))]
92	Mr. C	[{talking to students on the first rows} ((this is-)) &
93	& {coughing} &	
94	Mr. C	& you feel [disgusted]
95	Zareef	[((disgusted))]
96	Mr. C	((makes you feel)) sick &
97	Zareef	& yeah
98	¿?	(((frightened)))°
99	Mr. C	ok / [(((next one))]
100	Zareef	[FRIGHTENED]
101	Mr. C	frightened↓ // means scared // that one ((is)) / easy to remember / [scared]
102	Ajmal	{stretching his muscles} [AAHH!]
103	(3″) {sounds of someone walking, probably Mr. C}	
104	¿?	you know what / ganna lagga ni hai
105		*have to play song *
106	{laughter}	

107	Mr. C	Zareef / I want you to write [(())] =
108	Zareef	[(())]
109	Mr. C	=((now I don't want you)) to talk anymore
110	¿?	[(())]
111	Mr. C	[otherwise you ((would have to . . .))]
112		{there is a parallel conversation in the background which is hardly audible on the recording}

(Classroom interaction in 2D. Recording code: 05122011_2Db_extract)

In the case of the International Section in the studied school, the dialogue with Mr. C was key for the appropriate interpretation of the observed practices in his classes, not only as a participant providing his own retrospective commentary on every activity I observed/audio-recorded/transcribed but most importantly as a window to a long-term pedagogical project that permits one to make sense of the social forms of local positionings displayed by the observed participants during my short two-month period of data collection. Indeed, the understanding of this larger project is central for avoiding a superficial analysis of what participants do in Extract 1, which might be easily described just in terms of a conflict between a group of students and their teacher. Before commenting on this wider pedagogical project, a detailed analysis of this interaction may provide a foundational basis for further interpretations.

The idealized models canonically used for describing instructional moves and officially expected patterns of collaboration in classroom discourse are difficult to apply in this interaction [see Sinclair & Coulthard's (1975) model based on the so-called initiation-response-feedback talk pattern]. Mr. C's interactional attempts to coordinate the student's actions around knowledge-checking exchanges, which focused on the meaning of 'frustrated' (lines 1–32), 'embarrassed' (lines 32–45), 'disgusted' (lines 46–100), and 'frightened' (lines 99–111), encounter the complexities of the (always) dense social relations being built up in the course of everyday activities. Thus, a single question-answer-feedback structure of participation, which in ideal educational contexts would not require more than three interactional turns for each of the focused vocabulary items, takes dozens of lines in the transcription. A close look at the moment-to-moment of the interaction reveals numerous forms of ambiguous collaboration discursively produced by all participants, even by those who seem to engage in disruptive practices that explicitly challenge Mr. C's attempts to complete the activity.

Among these students, Zareef's forms of participation are particularly relevant in that they show the extent to which he is able to cope with the tension of engaging in peer-mocking practices while willing to collaborate with the teacher simultaneously. In other words, he displays different (not necessarily coherent) social positions which allow him to show compliance with goals that could be seen as contradictory from the perspective of an outsider (i.e., pushing the instructional activity to the limits of what is considered appropriate in the classroom context but making room for minimal collaboration with Mr. C so as to get the activity progressed). Such ambiguous forms of social positioning are reconstructed by Zareef through various communicative resources, in the course of the work of each of the focused vocabulary items.

In the opening of the sequence in which Mr. C is trying to explain the word 'disgusted,' Ajmal and Hasan engage in ostentatious sounds and body gestures that overlap with Mr. C's talk, all followed by reciprocal laughter and coughing signaling the common understanding of these practices as potentially transgressive or disruptive from the perspective of these students (see lines 1–15). This frame of interpretation seems also to apply to Mr. C's understanding of the situation, as he immediately reacts by complaining about the fact that other students are talking while he is explaining (line 8), therefore making explicit a legitimate participation framework where students are expected to keep silent unless asked to participate.

At this point of the interaction, Zareef aligns with Ajmal and Hasan by engaging in laughter (line 7). Nevertheless, he disaligns with his peers later on, right after Mr. C has explicitly disapproved their actions, by requesting them to be quiet (line 17) and by asking Mr. C to keep on talking (line 26), although subsequent reactions of laughing and whistling by him and his peers seem to construct Zareef's requests as insincere acts of collaboration with Mr. C (lines 28–30). This ambiguous position is confirmed a few interactional turns after, in the course of the work with the word 'embarrassed.' Once Mr. C initiates the transition to this item by labeling it (line 32), Husna, a 16-year-old female student with Pakistani background, addresses these students in Urdu in attitude of reprimand by asking them to stop teasing Mr. C (line 33), which leads to Ajmal's and Zareef's reactions mocking Husna (lines 36, 38, 42).

Zareef's reaction to Husna's call of attention is nonetheless followed by his labeling of the following item in the vocabulary list, 'disgusted,' therefore anticipating Mr. C's opening of the new pedagogical sequence (line 44). This is a common interactional resource used by students in the classroom context to show interest in the activity and willingness to collaborate with the teacher in getting the task progressed, although in the course of this sequence of action it seems just to reinforce Zareef's ambivalent positioning as he immediately afterward engages in parallel peer interaction, leading to more laughter (see his response to Mr. C's question with another question and the subsequent reaction by Ajmal in lines 48–50). Indeed, such an ambiguous positioning continues in the course of Mr. C's attempts to explain the meaning of 'disgusted' (lines 54–97), when Zareef provides very graphic explanations (line 63) and positive interactional feedback (lines 66–70) in response to the teacher's difficulties to find the appropriate explanation of the word—reflected in Mr. C's numerous self-interruptions (lines 54–56), fillers (lines 54–56, 71) and code switches to Cantonese (lines 68, 71, 74) and Spanish (line 61) in the search for equivalents.

In an interactional context in which some of his peers start laughing and making comments about Mr. C's difficulties to explain the word (see Ajmal's comment in line 59), Zareef's forms of participation could be also taken as instances of overenthusiasm, which contribute to mocking the teacher (see his loud and latched reply to Mr. C's use of the Cantonese term 'wattat' in line 70, just before engaging in more laughing with Ajmal in line 73, or his attempts to move the activity on to the new vocabulary item, 'frightened', in lines 97–101, via latched feedback ('& yeah'), followed by the loud labeling of the word in overlapping with Mr. C. In fact, this seems to be the teacher's frame of interpretation, in light of his later reaction in which he calls for Zareef's attention and asks him 'not to talk any more' (lines 107–109). Nevertheless, it remains open as to the extent to which these forms of participation constitute an interactional practice of 'changing hats' through which the student is coping with the tension of building up solidarity both with those peers who often disrupt the classroom activity (i.e., Ajmal) and with the teacher.

A close examination of moments like these provides a platform for further ethnographic enquiry, beyond the premature interpretations often found in critical research. Although critique in discourse studies has historically looked at the links between local discursive practices and the wider socioeconomic processes of change—with the subsequent expanding of our knowledge on how wider social structures are enacted in everyday life—it has, however, led in some cases to reductionist (modernist) views of power (Rampton, 2006); no matter what set of data is being analyzed, it is taken for granted that one or some participants need to be identified as the holders of powerful positions exercising domination over others. This has been the case at the school; in much of the critical research, teachers are usually described as representatives of the institution, projecting the state's stable forms of symbolic domination on the students' subjectivities, leaving these students no other choice than to accept or resist it.

As a critical sociolinguist looking at the social space of the school for more than 15 years, I have found myself struggling with this reductionist perspective from time to time. I have not been always successful in overcoming it, though. I believe ethnography has much to provide in this regard because it allows the situating of practices within the frame of the participants' lived experiences, therefore avoiding the brutal analytical impositions that have often been attributed to critical discourse analysis practitioners (Blommaert & Bulcaen, 2000). In fact, the social significance of this fragment of interaction relies on its temporal position within the course of the academic year. As mentioned, the framing of this very local practice within the wider pedagogical project in which it took place was possible only through an ongoing dialogue with Mr. C that continued after the data collection period, which included face-to-face conversations, e-mails, and multimodal exchanges through Internet multimedia formats like Evernote and access to their class Facebook group where teacher–student and peer interactions took place beyond the physical boundaries of the school. So this understanding emerged because the ethnography was jointly constructed fieldwork (Holmes, Chapter 4, this volume) that allowed both researcher and the participating teacher to 'reflexively shape' and be 'shaped by the research process.'

These practices and spaces allowed me to see the International Section as a social space in which Mr. C and his students were doing more than engaging in instructional activity; despite their different individual perspectives, goals, life trajectories, and interests, all of them enacted and negotiated in everyday life with the same degree of tension and uncertainty, as shown in Extract 1, they all were collectively involved in a much deeper process of counter-cultural transformation, which was made possible by recent changes experienced in their school.

Due to MATSS's difficulties in reaching the government's required minimum student intake, the school's administrators decided to shift their traditional focus from a sole interest in Chinese working-class families living in the area toward targeting ethnic minority students whose parents had migrated to the school's surroundings after Hong Kong's return to China in 1997. This shift opened MATSS's doors to teachers like Mr C, who had previous experience in the education of ethnic minority students and was able to teach in English through a critical approach. However, due to the school's discursive redefinition of its linguistic and pedagogic policies—from an only-Chinese medium to the incorporation of an International Section driven by a tailor-made curriculum with strong emphasis on English as the medium of instruction and non-test-taking oriented philosophical approaches—it also lead to subsequent dilemmas and paradoxes that derived from the coexistence of these and more traditional approaches in the school's daily life.

The fact that the Local and the International Sections followed different pedagogical approaches reinforced the tensions between teachers across them because they all had to collaborate in order to design standardized tests for each subject and grade in the school. As a result of all these changes and tensions, Mr. C ended up finding increasingly difficult to accommodate, with a high degree of freedom, the Hong Kong local school curriculum in the International Section, as officially announced by the school in its publicity. The polarization between the two sections ended up also reinforcing the lack of cooperation between the youngsters across the two sections, which in turn resulted in experiences of isolation on the part of the ethnic minority students, as explained in the course of an interview by Yamu, a 13-year-old female student with Nepali background from the International Section who stated, about most of her local Chinese peers, that 'they don't like minorities / becausse / uuh // they will think that the teachers have divided / them.'

All in all, the ethnographic exploration of the site provides a wider socio-emotional, institutional, and pedagogical frame for the interpretation of the previously analyzed interaction; it allows for an understanding of those ambiguous forms of interactional collaboration displayed by Zareef and Mr. C in Extract 1 as instances of interpersonal 'collusion' (McDermott & Tylbor, 1986). In other words, these instances enact forms of collaboration across the boundaries of stable institutional roles (teachers and students) under conditions in which they all try to overcome institutional difficulties and dilemmas, beyond simplified accounts reporting domination on the part of either the teachers or students.

I will now pass the floor to Mr. C, who will provide a more nuanced picture of how this pedagogical project looked in the everyday life of his classes.

4 MR. C AND THE STUDY OF MOMENTS OF TRANSFORMATION IN MULTIMODAL PRACTICE

Like Chun (Chapter 8, this volume), I have been committed as an educator to dialogue as a tool for questioning and negotiating discourses of power within spaces created with students. But after moving to Hong Kong from the United States in 2009, engaging in multimodal dialogue and working in a multilingual environment where English was both a 'second' or 'foreign' language was forcing me to think and act in new ways. There was a complex web of processes my students and I were negotiating, and it took the participation of Dr. M in my classes to help me see transformation and turning points more clearly within a microethnographic perspective, essentially turning moments in my critical pedagogy from 'invisible' to 'visible' (Martin, 1999), allowing me to see transformation as a localized everyday experience.

* * *

> Transformative tensions emerge if the study is situated inside the subjectivity of the students in such a way to detach students from that very subjectivity into more advanced reflections. (Shor & Freire, 1987: 19)

Understanding another's subjectivity is challenging, maybe more as the multilingual and multicultural dimensions of a setting intensify. In my classes, students employ a wide range of registers, cultural references, and other linguistic repertoires that may not be intelligible to teachers or observers. So if we are to enter into critical dialogue with students, to make and remake reality, then how do we read their meaning-making practices in order to situate our learning? As a teacher, how do I recognize the 'transformative tensions' that emerge? Answering these questions is crucial if we are to 'open up access to genres, especially those controlled by mainstream groups' (Martin, 1999: 124) and move students from disengagement with academics to proficiency in creating the types of texts necessary for school success. Overcoming this internal struggle requires attention to everyday classroom and social life. Dr. M suggests listening to everyday patterns of interaction and reading beyond the surface. So instead of merely hearing classroom disturbances in Extract 1, we reposition student behavior as part of a negotiated collusion in a space fraught with tensions.

Opportunities for dialogue and learning also arise when we acknowledge students' everyday learning and social lives online. In the rest of this section, I describe an interaction that begins not in the physical classroom but within a class Facebook group and culminates with the publishing on Facebook of visual texts crafted by students. Along the way, students and teachers co-construct a pedagogical interaction that crosses fields of study, online sites, physical spaces, and authorship. From a more practical pedagogical point of view, the interaction introduces participants to new forms of vocabulary and expression while reinforcing existing knowledge in the fields of English, science, art, and popular culture. From the perspective of a critical pedagogy, the interaction offers a window into how dialogue might move in a multimodal setting.

But first we should stop to reflect on the meaning of dialogue, a cornerstone of most critical pedagogies. Burbules (2000) challenges us to 'shift in our understanding of dialogue from a prescriptive model' to one more bounded by context:

> Attending to the social dynamics and contexts of classroom discourse heightens the awareness of the complexities and difficulties of changing specific elements within larger communities of practice. These communities may be the primary shapers of teaching and learning processes, but not always in ways that serve intended or ideal educational objectives; other purposes, such as identity formation or negotiating relations of group solidarity, may predominate. The power of such social processes may restrict lines of inquiry, distort dialogical interactions, and silence perspectives in ways that conflict with the explicit purposes of education . . . Rethinking dialogue along these lines holds promise for developing theoretical accounts of dialogue that are richer, more complex, and better attuned to the material circumstances of pedagogical practice. Dialogue, from this standpoint, cannot be viewed simply as a form of question and answer, but as a relation constituted in a web of relations among multiple forms of communication, human practices, and mediating objects or texts. (pgs. 35–36)

Rethinking dialogue (who is involved, when, where, why, and how it takes place) can lead us as teachers to greater possibilities beyond the prescriptive notions of dialogue and classroom practice. Collaboratively reflecting on the contexts and processes of dialogue with Dr. M helped me to extend my pedagogy beyond the classroom and to situate learning for students within the context of their online worlds, while exposing 'blind spots' (Byrd Clark & Dervin, Introduction, this volume) in my own reflexivity.

An example is a pedagogical sequence that is surfaced through dialogue involving Sita, a 14-year-old student who often described herself as 'bored,' as can be seen in Extract 2.

Extract 2. 'I just want to go outside and see the world/how life is and stuff.'

Mr. C	um / tell me a little bit just about your life
Sita	well / I'm just an ordinary student from Hong Kong and my life in here is quite fine // but for me / I'm always bored because I want to do many things / but I can't because there are problems for me because—there are problems for me in many ways but I don't know (. . .) because it's hard for my mother and for me too // because I'm from a single parent and it's quite hard for me // my mom really wants me to be educated / she really forced me to study and I kind of don't like it because sometimes I think that she doesn't understand what education mean because she always wants me to study books like that I don't like reading books // I just want to go outside and see the world / how life is and stuff
Mr. C	um / so um / what do you think education should be about (. . .) what do you think education should be?
Sita	um / education is also like studying in school but it's more better to learn outside from school (. . .) because we study from books but we don't experience them // to know that what other things that we study we should experience— we should experience it outside the world

(Interview with Sita. Recording code: 060712)

In this extract, Sita points to a theme in her life, boredom. Many educators would dismiss this as a common teen sentiment, but I interpreted it as the absence of possibility for creative engagement with the world. In other words, Sita may see her life as bound by the circumstances of her family and the limiting notions of what it means to be educated, and these circumstances (as well as the school) do not offer opportunities for meaningful experience, for creative play, or for her own dialogue with the world. As a teacher, I try to create these opportunities within the school's physical space, and sometimes dialogue and learning extend into online spaces. This was the case near the end of the academic year as a series of interactions on Facebook culminated with cultural/textual production by a group of students including Sita (see Table 10.1).

One Friday at 9:40 p.m., I began series of posts to our class Facebook page with a link to photographs on the website yowayowacamera.com, where a Japanese photographer posted daily 'levitation' photographs, mostly

Table 10.1 'I love Japan!'

All times on June 22, 2012, in p.m.	
9:40	**Carlos Soto** I think some of you might like this photographer; let me know, I haven't made up my mind yet. よわよわカメラウーマン日記 yowayowacamera.com Lives in Tokyo with two cats. Photographs mainly levitating self-portraits (and cats not levitating). *Yowayowa* is a Japanese term meaning . . .
10:20	**Sita** I love jApan!
10:21	**Sita** Wow. She's like she flying whenever she goes.
10:22	**Sita** Does she have a super power??
10:24	**Sita** I LOVE This photographer YowaYowa! She's a amazing!
10:27	**Sita** MEEEEEE I"M VERY INTERESTED >< OMG
10:33	**Amita** WOW, I WANT TO TAKE PICTURES LIKE HER!!! AMAZING LADY!!!! HOW COULD SHE DO THAT??!!!! I LOVE IT!!!! I AM REALLY INTERESTED ON IT!!
10:36	**Sita** NOW I HAVE SOMEONE WHO I ADMIRE!! "よわよわ"
10:46	**Carlos Soto** She uses a good camera that can take photos at a high speed. she explains on the website. These are "levitation" photos; floating in the air with some super power
10:48	**Sita** Wow!!
10:51	**Sita** What is mean by levitate?
10:52	**Carlos Soto** in the photos, she is "levitating"; staying above the ground

self-portraits depicting her seemingly floating in air in a variety of urban and rural landscapes. They conveyed to me a sense of freedom, invisibility, and otherworldliness, as if she is dislocated somewhere beyond present-time material existence. I had discovered the artist on the blogging site Tumblr, and, when I posted the link, I 'tagged' Sita along with two other students I knew liked to play with cameras.

Sita responded 40 minutes after my initial post, at first to affirm her love of Japan and then to share her interpretation of the photographs, including her recognition of the theme of invisibility. Following this, students entered and exited, showing excitement, seeking clarification of unfamiliar words, and claiming authorship. For example, at 10:43 p.m., Sita posted another levitation photograph, adding 'Now I'm curious! DOES SHE REALLY HAVE A SUPERPOWER???? Owo.' Over the next hour and a half, I continued the interaction with Sita and Amita, another student, trying to encourage them to try this kind of photography. In reflecting on this interaction, Dr. M noted, in an e-mail exchange with me, that:

> this figure is an example of the way you try to bring a new frame of action/interpretation: from acknowledging the photographer's pictures of levitation to involving them into the production of their own pictures. You do this by a first contribution, which brings the space of HK and the fact that other people do it. This first contribution is followed by contributions from Sita and Amita who, although excited (I see also the use of 'likes' here, and I wonder who liked what and when), do not address yet the issue of their own capability to do it, which is followed by a new contribution by you in which you explicitly state 'you can do it', this time leading to contributions oriented towards how they can do it and an to an explicit instance in which you mention the word 'experiment' which is often pedagogically loaded in educational contexts (you wanted them to experiment by themselves!). (E-mail communication between Mr. C and Dr. M, December 18, 2012)

By turning his ethnographic lens onto me and including me in his process, Dr. M allowed me to re-see my own position within the online interaction and made me aware of the subtle semiotic shifts that invited action.

Later on, at 11:04 p.m., Sita started a parallel discussion on another Facebook page moderated by Mr. TS, a Nepali math and science teacher (see Table 10.2). There, she asked him, 'can we people levitate?' and she, Amita, Mr. TS, and Sam, a classmate, discussed levitation in relation to scientific concepts and experimentation.

Over the next few days, the dialogue on levitation continued on the pages, moderated by Mr. TS and myself. The dialogue turned from online talk to engagement with the physical world when Sita, Amita, and a third Nepali girl from the class, Susan, took their own levitation photographs around Hong Kong and posted the photos on Amita's personal Facebook page. Subsequently, we examined the photos in our class as part of our study of Howard Gardner's theory of multiple intelligences.

Reflecting with Dr. M, I was forced to ask myself, 'What am I doing here? How am I doing it? Does this constitute meaningful transformation? Am I being critical?' In the preceding interactions, I tried as a teacher to 'be critical' and to build 'dialogue' in relation to the factors mediating the interactions, including our school and social context, the sites on which we interacted, and the texts we produced, as well as my perceived subjectivities of my students. My perception of Sita's subjectivity included her experiences within a struggling family, her school (which separated

Table 10.2 'Mr. TS can we people levitate??'

All times on June 22, 2012, in p.m. and June 23 in a.m.	
11:04 p.m.	Sita
	Mr. TS can we people levitate??
11:19 p.m.	Mr. TS To levitate is possible if Earth's gravitational pull do not pull us anymore. However, looking at this Japanese photographer, all we need to do is click the shot while jumping in the air . . . QUICKLY!
11:41 p.m.	Sam :D
11:41 p.m.	Sam Moon! :D
12:09 a.m.	Sita ahh yeah we can levitate on the moon! hha-
12:50 a.m.	Amita By GRAVITY :D haha
12:50 a.m.	Amita or by wings..!! =.=
12:52 a.m.	Sita Amita someday let's go to the moon and take our portraits of ourselves > < by levitating!
12:54 a.m.	Amita ahahah,
12:54 a.m.	Sita xDD

learning from experience), and a life in Hong Kong perceived by her as boring. Within this activity, Sita and her classmates used new vocabulary, synthesized art with science learning, and invested in identities as producers of visual texts. Whether this will extend itself into more sophisticated social critique and social action, I can only guess, but it increases my investment into forms of dialogue that go beyond question and answer in a physical space.

To engage Sita in dialogue and move her toward remaking her world meant thinking and acting in a multitextual, cross-disciplinary way, and generating temporal, geographic, and participatory displacement as the dialogue shifted across time and online and physical locations, while participants and authors entered and left the dialogue at various points. Because I was aware of her interests and life circumstances, I interpreted her musings about boredom as expressions of the limiting boundaries of her everyday life. In Zareef's class, seeing the students' everyday resistance as a desire for participation likewise led to change. Thus, meaning making and reflexivity happened in 'motion' (Malinowski & Nelson, Chapter 6, this volume), not through a static process. In both cases, my ongoing dialogue with Dr. M allowed me to gain greater insights into the moment-by-moment development of dialogue and action.

I will now turn to the last section of this chapter, where Dr. M and I discuss what this dialogue highlights for us.

5 BEYOND THE POLITICS OF THE ACADEMIA: CONTINUITY IN MULTISITED, MULTIVOICED, AND MULTIRESOURCED COLLABORATION

The data analyzed here reveals how Mr. C and his students get constructed as value (commodity) in a school system where competition between schools for access to public resources makes English language, internationalism, and pedagogic progressivism an added value for a band-3 school located in working-class areas with high rates of EM population. Although this process of transformation could be taken as a positive feature in that it allows them to access the public system in a context in which EM students have been historically underrepresented in the Hong Kong school population, the research experience in Mr. C's school illustrates the subsequent tensions and dilemmas derived from the actual difficulties to accommodate English language, internationalism, and pedagogic progressivism in the local order of the school, beyond marketing campaigns and official propaganda.

It is precisely in this complex social and changing space where pedagogical projects like the one conducted by Mr. C have a role to play in that they take advantage of the opportunities opened up by these shifting institutional conditions and offer a new space for interactional and emotional collusion where teachers and students can engage more fruitfully in the building of more empowering identities, practices, and communities.

In addition to this broad note, we also conceptualize this chapter as a discursive process of dialogue and self-reflection that has enabled us to engage in further conversation regarding (1) what we have learnt from this research collaboration and (2) to what extent this experience could go beyond grand academic narratives that only advance our professional careers and actually lead to some impact on other people's lives. Mr. C put this way in the course of one of our e-mail exchanges:

> [T]he greater value in this kind of dialogues comes (for researcher, teacher, students) when continuity is maintained. So for example, I was able to understand more about the interaction around the *levitation* photos because we continued to discuss them for the sake of this chapter.... I also tried to maintain continuity between our dialogue and your interaction with my students by soliciting you to post your feedback on our Facebook group page. Your feedback in turn became a classroom activity. I turned your reply into a text that we dissected in class. I wanted students to understand your academic discourse by helping to break it down into chunks that students could digest more easily. Then students had to write a response to you. I'm not exaggerating when I say that one student (Susmita) spent an hour an a half carefully crafting and editing her 102 word response to you. Currently, our on-going dialogue is helping to develop the 'academic literacy' (Gibbons, 2009) of my students. In a broader view, I think that dialogue is enhanced by

a broad set of voices and resources. We are in complex environments, in complex times. Bringing more voices into the dialogue seems to help! (E-mail communication between Mr. C and Dr. M, January 1, 2013)

This chapter has been also an opportunity for us to expand our interaction, bringing it at the same time to other spaces involving Mr. C's students. However, this dialogue extended far beyond the physical space of the school. Students and Mr. C were invited by Dr. M to give a guest lecture in one of the university courses on literacy across the curriculum that Dr. M teaches to Hong Kong educators (present and future) at the University of Hong Kong.

The experience in Mr. C's classroom (both the physical space and the online space), as well as the subsequent dialogue regarding the writing of this chapter, provided Dr. M with insightful perspectives on issues having to do with language education, critical pedagogy, and multimodal literacy. Thus, the arrangement of a joint activity involving Mr. C, his students, and Dr. M at the University of Hong Kong constituted an excellent opportunity for other educators in the Hong Kong context to learn from the experience deriving from our research collaboration, at the same time setting up the conditions to maintain continuity of action for Mr. C's students to navigate across different institutional spaces—in line with Mr. C's concerns about creating stable links between his school and the university level in order for higher education to be part of his students' life from this crucial stage in their academic lives.

For Mr. C, the experience of becoming a researched teacher and the subsequent dialogue around this chapter facilitated the building of academic literacies and university links for his students, while helping him to clarify an understanding of his own teaching practices as well as his notions of what it means to be critical. But as he and his students continue to struggle and negotiate with daily tensions, all their everyday experiences point to the need for an institutional educational space that is more responsive to the pedagogies they seem to favor. We hope this dialogue and what we have learned from it will support our ambitions of creating educational spaces that support transforming researchers, teachers, students, and communities.

APPENDIX: Symbols Used in the Transcripts

Laura:	participant
CR	(CAPITAL LETTERS) loud talking
ee	vowel lengthening
Ss	consonant lengthening
/	short pause (0.5 seconds)
//	long pause (0.5–1.5 seconds)
(n'')	n seconds pause
[ ]	turn overlapping with similarly marked turn
=	continuation of utterance after overlapping
(())	nonunderstandable fragment

{ } researcher's comments
↑ rising intonation
↓ falling intonation
- self interruption
& latched utterances
* * English translation of words uttered in other languages

NOTES

1. Names for the researchers correspond to those forms officially used in the studied school.
2. Pseudonyms have been chosen for schools at random. The initials typically refer to an industrial or charitable sponsoring body.
3. The research on which this chapter draws has been fully undertaken under the funding of the Programa Nacional de Movilidad de Recursos Humanos del Plan Nacional de I + D + I (2008–2011) of the Spanish Ministry of Education (EX2009-0959), with the invaluable collaboration of Centre for Language, Discourse & Communication (King's College London) and the Faculty of Education in The University of Hong Kong through the supervision of Ben Rampton and Angel Lin. Complementary support has also been received from the Programa de cooperación con Asia de la Universidad Autónoma de Madrid y el Banco Santander (2011–2012) through the project Chinese and English as Languages of the Wider World: a Sociolinguistic Study on Second Language Education and Youth's Interests in London, Madrid, and Hong Kong, as well as by King's China Institute.

REFERENCES

Akbari, R. (2008). Transforming lives: Introducing critical pedagogy into ELT classrooms. *ELT Journal*, 62(3), 276–283.
Block, D., & Cameron, D. (2002). Introduction. In D. Block & D. Cameron (Eds.), *Globalization and language teaching* (pp. 1–10). London: Routledge.
Blommaert, J., & Bulcaen, C. (2000). Critical discourse analysis. *Annual Review of Anthropology*, 29, 447–466.
Burbules, N. C. (2000). The limits of dialogue as a critical pedagogy. In P. P. Trifona (Ed.), *Revolutionary pedagogies: Cultural politics, instituting education, and the discourse of theory*. New York: Routledge.
Camangian, P. (2008). Untempered tongues: Teaching performance poetry for social justice. *English Teaching: Practice and Critique*, 7(2), 35–55.
Duncan-Andrade, J., & Morrell, E. (2008). *The art of critical pedagogy: Possibilities for moving from theory to practice in urban schools*. New York: Peter Lang.
Freire, P. (1970). *Pedagogy of the oppressed*. New York: Herder & Herder.
Gao, F. (2011). Linguistic capital: Continuity and change in educational language polices for South Asians in Hong Kong primary schools. *Current Issues in Language Planning*, 12(2), 251–263.
Gibbons, P. (2009). *English learners, academic literacy, and thinking: Learning in the challenge zone*. Portsmouth, UK: Heinemann.
Giddens, A. (1984). *The constitution of society*. Berkeley: University of California Press.

Heller, M., & Martin-Jones, M. (Eds.). (2001). *Voices of authority. Education and linguistic difference*. Wesport, CT/London: Ablex.

Jin, B., Shum, M. S. K., & Teng, H. F. (2009). Issues on computer assisted on teaching of Chinese practical writing. *Yantai University Journal*, 2009.

Kubota, R., & Lin, A. (Eds.). (2009). *Race, culture, and identity in second language education: Exploring critically engaged practice*. New York: Routledge.

Lin, A. M. Y. (2004). Introducing a critical pedagogical curriculum: A feminist, reflexive account. In B. Norton & K. Toohey (Eds.), *Critical pedagogies and language learning* (pp. 271–290). Cambridge: Cambridge University Press.

Lin, A., & Martin, P. (Eds.). (2005). *Decolonisation, globalisation. language-in-education policy and practice*. Clevedon, UK/Buffalo, NY/Toronto, Canada: Multilingual Matters.

Martin, J. R. (1999). Mentoring semogenesis: 'genre-based' literacy pedagogy. In F. Christie (Ed.), *Pedagogy and the shaping of consciousness: Linguistic and social processes* (pp. 123–155). London: Cassell.

Martin-Jones, M. (2007). Bilingualism, education and the regulation of access to language resources. In M. Heller (Ed.), *Bilingualism: A social approach* (pp. 161–182). London: Palgrave.

Martín-Rojo, L. (2010). *Constructing inequality in multilingual classrooms*. Berlin: Mouton.

McDermott, R., & Tylbor, H. (1986). On the necessity of collusion in conversation. In S. Fisher & A. Dundas-Todd (Eds.), *Discourse and institutional authority: Medicine, education and law* (pp. 123–139). New York: Ablex.

Pérez-Milans, M. (2013). *Urban schools and English language education in late modern China: A critical sociolinguistic ethnography*. London/New York: Routledge.

Rampton, B. (2006). *Language in late modernity. Interaction in an urban school*. Cambridge: Cambridge University Press.

Shor, I., & Freire, P. (1987). *A pedagogy for liberation: Dialogues on transforming education*. Westport, CT: Bergin and Garvey.

Shum, M. S. K., & Lau, K. L. (2009). How international mindedness education could be implemented in international baccalaureate diploma programme Chinese classroom in Hong Kong context. *Education Development in Chinese Society*, Macao University.

Sinclair, J., & Coulthard, M. (1975). *Towards an analysis of discourse*. Oxford: Oxford University Press.

Tsung, L., Shum, M.S.K., Ki, W.W., & Lam, M. (2009). *Accessing Chinese: For ethnic minority learners in Hong Kong*, Units 1–3. Hong Kong: Centre for Advancement of Chinese Language Education and Research, University of Hong Kong.

Wink, J. (2000). *Critical Pedagogy: Notes from the real world* (2nd ed.). New York: Addison-Wesley Longman.

Wong, F. (2009). *The views of Hong Kong Unison towards education for non-Chinese speaking students*. Hong Kong. Retrieved September 20, 2009 from www.legco.gov.hk/yr08-09/english/panels/ed/papers/ed0112cb2-579-9-e.pdf

Conclusion
Reflexivity in Research and Practice: Moving On?

Fred Dervin and Julie S. Byrd Clark

> I came to theory because I was hurting—the pain within me was so intense that I could not go on living. I came to theory desperate, wanting to comprehend—to grasp what was happening around and within me. Most importantly, I wanted to make the hurt go away. I saw in theory then a location for healing. (Hooks, 1994: 59)

This volume proposes (*a minima*) three ways of developing the idea of reflexivity in research and practice in relation to the notions of interculturality and multilingualism:

1. Examining the reflexivity of the other (research participants/language users) and helping them to develop reflexivity or become aware of its components
2. Discussing and problematizing the reflexivity of self (the researcher/practitioner)
3. Considering the junctions between self and other (the researcher/practitioner and research participants/language users) and how they (can) influence each other

As a conclusion to this volume, we would like to make a case for research and practice based on the third point involving all the actors—and helping them to create a potential 'location for healing,' as suggested by Hooks in the preceding quotation. In our opinion, this third option appears to be a more proactive and political way of 'doing' reflexivity. Reflexivity should not just be something that is taking place inside the individual; it should lead to concrete, multifaceted actions. At the same time, these actions should lead people to a deeper engagement with reflexivity. Reflecting on reflexivity thus requires, first and foremost, interrogating the role of researchers in the 21st century. We agree with the French anthropologist Laplantine that research should lead to permanent criticality, confusion, perplexity, and complexity (Laplantine, 2013: 30). This means that researchers should move away from God-like positions (pseudo-objectivity), take responsibility for their actions, and question and criticize systematically what they say and do. Only reflexivity can lead to these processes!

But why should researchers be more reflexive? Researchers have an obligation to respect the complexity of individuals—especially those who are seen and constructed as powerless individuals. This is not easy because researchers are also social beings who have to 'do' othering like any other person. Through reflexivity, researchers are duty-bound to promote research participants' *diverse diversities* (Dervin, 2012; Dervin & Keihäs, 2013)—and not just their so-called façade diversity through, for example, a unique language or cultural identity.

The first step requires critically reviewing categories. The main tool of the trade in research is discourse. Certain risky words and social categories constitute these discourses *nolens volens*. For Byrd Clark (2008, 2012), 'Perpetuating the use of monolithic categorizations (L1, L2, ESL, FSL) does not appear to take into account any type of reflexivity on the hierarchical and problematic nature of the imposition of social categories or the recognition of transnational, diverse, plural identities. In other words, it does not reflect the researcher's awareness of his/her own investments in the employment of such categories' (2012: 149). For Gillespie et al., 'an unreflective use of social categories by social scientists results in the same risks as those evidenced in lay thinking' (2012: 399). These categories often reflect the researchers' perspectivism. In his *Introduction to Metaphysics*, the philosopher Henri Bergson asserted that 'the different concepts that we form of the properties of a thing inscribe round it so many circles, each much too large and none of them fitting it exactly' (1903/1999: 19). He also suggested, 'Beyond the ideas which are chilled and congealed in language, . . . we must seek the warmth and mobility of life' (2002: 359). Researchers—and even increasingly decision makers—keep reminding the general public of the importance of multiple/hybrid identities, but are these really taken seriously? Researchers and practitioners alike need to be careful and think hard before engaging with the other. Which words to use? How to respond to certain categories? What influence do they have on the other by asking certain questions? On the other hand, the same should apply vice versa: If a researcher is mistreated or a name is called in her field, something should be done about it.

Perspectivism is a universal sin that does not just apply to researchers. One of our doctoral students was recently bullied by boys in a school who kept calling her 'stalker.' This is why social categories and labels need to be constantly problematized and actors' roles explicated. One significant component of reflexivity should thus entail 'self-conscious introspection guided by a desire to better understand both self and others through examining one's actions and perceptions in reference to and dialogue with those of others' (Anderson, 2011: 305).

Let us now venture a comparison to Lee Hirsch's documentary on bullying in the United States (*Bully*, 2011). The documentary follows several school students who are targets of bullying. Alex, from Sioux City, Iowa, is one of the kids whose life is made miserable by bullies, especially on the school bus. Some of the scenes are difficult to watch and unbearable when defenseless Alex is physically and verbally abused in front of the camera. We started wondering how long it would take for the film crew to start reporting Alex's traumatic bullying on the school bus to the parents and school staff—which they did halfway through the documentary. Of course, to make a 'convincing' point, we understand that the documentary director had to include such verbal and physical abuse.

Should a researcher and practitioner also keep quiet for a while before reacting when she notices that something is wrong with the field, the participants, and/or herself? Shouldn't ethical reflections in research and practice be accompanied by constant, coherent, and consistent reflexivity? We believe that reflexivity should take place before, during, and after research. One of us had a discussion with a Finnish research team on a similar issue some weeks ago. While going through the do's and don'ts of a new ethnography that was going to be conducted in two schools, we asked how the researchers who were going to collect data should behave if they notice that a member of staff had racist, xenophobic, sexist reactions in front of some of the kids. Should they intervene? Should they talk to the teacher or leadership after the incident? Or with the kid and his parents? One of our colleagues argued that we should be careful not to irritate staff because we might lose the 'field.' Finnish schools are so busy with hundreds of studies from all over the world because of its current fame as a 'miraculous performer' in education that it is increasingly difficult to get permission to do research in some of them. But should researchers' and practitioners' presence, empathy, and sentiment of justice be ignored because of the field's power? For Davies, 'reflexivity expresses researchers' awareness of their necessary connection to the research situation and hence their effects upon it' (1999: 7). Should the researcher's effects be ignored?

This leads us to the central issue of power. According to Foucault, power is not a static phenomenon: Those who dominate do not possess power exclusively because power can shift (even just for a few minutes). Foucault writes: 'Power must, I think, be analysed as something that circulates, or rather as something that functions only when it is part of a chain. . . . Power is exercised through networks, and individuals do not simply circulate in those networks; they are in a position to both submit to and exercise this power' (2003: 29). Wrongly, one often asserts that the researcher has power. Certainly she sometimes does, but in some situations, because of her accent, gender, religion, sexual orientation, social class, or other obvious identity markers, the researcher can be othered and positioned in her fieldwork as having a lower status. It is thus important for researchers to be aware of power differentials and to reflect before, during, and after entering the field on how power 'circulates' (to borrow Foucault's term) in order to prepare themselves and to protect others.

Another essential component of reflexivity in research and practice is that of giving back to the field. Another comparison will help to explain. Composed between 1914 and 1918 by the Hungarian composer and pianist Béla Bartók (1881–1945), *Fifteen Hungarian Peasant Songs* is a collection of folk melodies. Bartók traveled through Hungary and Romania to record, notate, and collect these melodies—a bit like an anthropologist who was trying to save the memories of a soon-to-be extinct tribe. Bartók's obsession with preserving these voices was sparked by his overhearing Transylvanian folk songs during his teenage years. He was saving these songs for the future, for other people to enjoy. In a similar vein, closer to our times, the Chinese composer Tan Dun (谭盾, 1957–), better known for his score for the film *Crouching Tiger, Hidden Dragon*, embarked in 2002 on a journey in Southwest China, where he filmed a series of field recordings of three Chinese ethnic groups' music. The result is a piece called *The Map* (a concerto for cello, video, and orchestra), during which, for example, a cellist engages with a videotaped Miao/Hmong singer in a *Feige* ('flying song'). Unlike Bartók, who never played his music for those who inspired him, Tan Dun insisted on giving back to the people who had contributed to his 55-minute piece by bringing a full-sized orchestra to the historical site of Fenghuang Ancient Town in Xiangxi Prefecture in 2003, where he performed for the indigenous villagers who had shared their music with him.

We see many similarities between these two different forms of relations between the composer and his sources of inspiration and the theme of this book. Bartók symbolizes in a sense the way we used to do research many decades ago in unreflective, objectivizing, and distant ways, whereas Tan Dun's approach is closer to what this volume puts forward as *practice* for doing reflexivity in research today. Research should contribute to empower the other (and self!) by practicing advocacy and giving back to the field. At the same time, researchers should constantly ask who is the other and who is the self—and how do we co-construct and represent our identities as well as the field? During the study (or at the end of it), a researcher can provide help to the problems she has noticed. Some researchers have, for example, taught a local language to research participants who were immigrants.

Our last point relates to an important issue: Being reflexive does not mean abandoning criticality. Many researchers are currently trying to give back to their research participants by merely transmitting their voices rather than (co-)analyzing them. As has been asserted many times in this volume, research has changed immensely over the last four decades, and paradigms such as constructivism, poststructuralism, and postmodernism have led researchers to question the voices that they hear and co-construct in research. Many researchers now want to avoid mere 'ventriloquation' (Valsiner, 2002)—or repeating in uncritical ways what participations have co-constructed with them—and to consider instead the contradictory or conflicting voices of their participants (contradictions, 'lies,' power-led discourses, co-constructed utterances, etc.) in order to represent research results that capture more negotiated, balanced, candid, and realistic involvements. Research participants (and ourselves) are members of many different social groups, and thus 'the individual will internalize the voices of many different, even conflicting, communities.' (Gillespie et al., 2007: 38). Dealing with voices in research means considering this ensemble of voices rather than the sole voice of the participant, which is never actually hers because it is a co-constructed voice with third-party speakers and the researcher. Reflexivity means asking aloud or for ourselves this set of questions: Who is really talking and making a statement? From what position(s) is an individual speaking? On whose behalf? Whose voice cannot be heard? In what language(s) are people 'doing' voice, and what impact does it have on what they say and their interlocutors? As we stated earlier in our Introduction chapter, reflexivity could help us to move away from 'surface voices' to deeper grounds by providing us the openness, imaginative resourcefulness, and flexibility that one needs for attempting to get at the complexities, becoming other, and engaging with self–other relations in order to give a fairer, more meaningful image of who and what we are researching. Reflexivity, in this sense and as shown in this volume, could also provide one the opportunity to engage with, the vulnerabilities and blind spots of both the researcher and participants' power and representational systems.

Finally, reflexivity can help us reach 'simplexity' (Berthoz, 2009). Simplexity represents the tensions and oppositions between the simple and the complex that characterize the human. Complexity is a process that the researcher and/or practitioner cannot fully reach—for obvious reasons. Yet we believe that through practicing reflexivity, the researcher can reach some elements of complexity by means of simplexity (see Dervin and Risager's introduction chapter, *Researching Identity and Interculturality*, 2014). As such, the researcher needs to simplify the complexity she/he is presented with while making sure that this 'simplex process' does justice, in a sense, to his/her diverse diversities but also to his/her participants'. This is a big challenge for the future of research but a highly motivating one.

REFERENCES

Anderson, L. (2011). Analytic autoethnography. In P. Atkinson & S. Delamont (Eds.), *Sage qualitative research methods*, Vol. IV (pp. 297–318). New York: Sage.

Bergson, H. (1903/1999). *An introduction to metaphysics*. New York: Hackett.

Bergson, H. (2002). *Key writings*. London: Continuum.

Berthoz, A. (2009). *La simplexité*. Paris: Odile Jacobs.

Bully. (2011). Retrieved October 25, 2013, from http://en.wikipedia.org/wiki/Bully_%282011_film%29.

Byrd Clark, J. (2008). So, why do you want to teach French? Representations of multilingualism and language investment through a reflexive critical sociolinguistic ethnography. *Education and Ethnography*, 3(1), 1–16.

Byrd Clark, J. (2012). Heterogeneity and a sociolinguistics of multilingualism: Reconfiguring French language pedagogy. *Language and Linguistics Compass Blackwell Online Journal*, 6(3),143–161. (Invited/commissioned submission)

Davies, C. A. (1999). *Reflexive ethnography: A guide to researching selves and others*. London: Routledge.

Dervin, F. (2012). *Impostures interculturelles*. Paris: L'Harmattan.

Dervin, F., & L. Keihäs, (2013). *Johdanto uuteen kulttuurienväliseen viestintään ja kasvatukseen*. jyvaskylä. Helsinki: FERA.
Dervin, F., & Risager, K. (2014). *Researching identity and interculturality*. New York: Routledge.
Foucault, M. (2003). *Society must be defended. Lectures at the Collège de France. 1975-1976*. New York: Picador.
Gillespie, A., Cornish, F., Aveling, E.-L., & Zittoun, T. (2007). Conflicting community commitments: A dialogical analysis of a British woman's World War II diaries. *Journal of Community Psychology*, 36(1), 35-52.
Gillespie, A., Howarth, C., & Cornish, F. (2012). Four problems for researchers using social categories. *Culture and Psychology*, 18(3), 391-402.
Hooks, B. (1994). *Teaching to transgress: Education as the practice of freedom*. New York: Routledge.
Laplantine, F. (2013). *Quand le moi devient autre: Connaître, partager, transformer*. Paris: CNRS.
Valsiner, J. (2002). Forms of dialogical relations and semiotic autoregulation within the self. *Theory & Psychology*, 12(2), 251-265.

Commentary

Claire Kramsch

As the editors of this timely volume point out, the poststructuralist, postmodernist turn in the social sciences has put reflexivity at the front and center of research on multilingual/intercultural communication and its pedagogical practice. The editors use an expanded concept of reflexivity that includes (1) critical reflection on the link between theory and practice, (2) sociocultural awareness and self-reflection of researchers on their own research practices, and (3) reflection on the very representation of reflexivity in researchers' and practitioners' narratives of the self and constructions of identity, or hyper-reflexivity. This expanded concept presents exciting opportunities and interesting challenges to both research methodology and pedagogic practice in language and intercultural education.

RESEARCH METHODOLOGY

With regard to reflexivity in research methodology, given the complexity of today's language uses in global cultural contexts, it makes sense to go beyond structuralist, modernist approaches in the study of linguistic practices and to embrace their multiplicity and their paradoxes rather than trying to unlock their essential truths. Thus, it is fitting to adopt research methodologies that encompass, as the editors explain in their Introduction, critical discourse analysis, the dialogic interpretation of events, and the self-reflexivity of the researchers themselves as social actors in the research process.

Pierre Bourdieu himself, who can hardly be called postmodern (in the sense of Derrida, Foucault, or Butler), did call for a 'reflexive sociology' (Bourdieu, 1990) in which researchers put themselves on the line, so to speak, in their role as 'objectivized participant.' Bourdieu was quite explicit in distinguishing participant objectivation from participant observation. The participant observer immerses himself in a foreign social universe so as to observe while taking part, trying to be both subject and object of the observation and critically reflecting both on the object of research and on himself as the researcher (roughly what Byrd Clark and Dervin call, respectively, 'awareness' and 'critical reflection'). By contrast, participant objectivation objectifies the researcher herself and the social and institutional conditions of possibility of her own research (roughly what Byrd Clark and Dervin call 'hyper-reflexivity'). Bourdieu describes this process in an article published after his death in the *Journal of the Royal Anthropological Institute* titled 'Participant Objectivation.'

> Scientific reflexivity stands opposed to the narcissistic reflexivity of postmodern anthropology, as well as to the egological reflexivity of phenomenology in that it endeavours to increase scientificity by turning the most objectivist tools of social science not only onto the private person of the enquirer but also, and more decisively, onto the anthropological field itself and onto the scholastic dispositions and biases it fosters and rewards in its members. 'Participant objectivation' [*l'objectivation participante*], as the objectivation of the subject and operations of objectivation, and of the latter's conditions of possibility, produces real cognitive effects as it enables the social analyst to grasp and master the prereflexive social and academic experiences of the social world that he tends to project unconsciously onto ordinary social agents. (Bourdieu, 2003: 281)

Bourdieu himself, drawing parallels between his fieldwork in Kabylia and his home village in the Béarn, wrote a very moving *Esquisse pour une autoanalyse* [Outline for an Autoanalysis] (2004), in which he showed 'how idiosyncratic personal experiences methodically subjected to sociological control constitute irreplaceable analytic resources, and that mobilizing one's social past through self-socio-analysis can and does produce epistemic as well as existential benefits' (2003: 281).

The papers in this exciting collection all make the unique voices of their authors heard through their personal experiences, their reasons for their choice of representations, their scientific qualms and professional doubts. These voices draw the readers in and are of immense benefit in terms of legitimacy and reliability of scientific inquiry.

On the other hand, if taken seriously, reflexivity—particularly hyper-reflexivity—presents great challenges for the researcher, as Bourdieu was the first to know. For it is not just a question of rejecting the divide and revealing the power relations between researcher and researched. Nor is it only a question of making explicit the doxa of actors in the field (Bourdieu, 1977: 164). Participant objectivation calls for making explicit what biographical, professional, and political power relations made such research possible in the first place. It is not just how big the research grant was that enabled the project, but how the power structure of academia made this project possible while making others impossible, that is, unacceptable. How can one adopt a critical attitude toward one's own practice as a scientist and its political conditions of possibility at the same time as one seeks to gain recognition and legitimacy within the very scientific community one claims to belong to? How to find the right balance between scientific reflexivity and professional savviness? The very publication by a prestigious publisher like Routledge of a collection of papers that attempt to do just that offers a beginning of an answer to these difficult questions.

PEDAGOGIC PRACTICE

With regard to reflexivity in pedagogic practice, the language teaching profession has been caught between the desire to have learners emulate the natural, unreflected verbal behavior of native speakers, that is, their intuitive feel for the game, their practical sense (Bourdieu, 1977: 113), and the obligation to explain and have learners explain the rules of language and of language use (Hymes, 2001: 60) that native speakers don't necessarily reflect upon. The first responds to the demands of a communicative language teaching pedagogy that strives for naturalness, automaticity, and authenticity in the use of language for communicative purposes, that is, a use of language that approximates as closely as possible the nonpedagogical uses of language in the 'real,' that is, nonacademic world. The second responds to the demands of academic learning that is based on knowledge of rules and conventions and the ability to reflect upon them. In Stephen Krashen's (1988) terms, the first favors implicit language acquisition, the second favors explicit language learning. Explicit learning involves reflexivity, but that reflexivity is usually applied to the analysis of grammatical and lexical structures, spoken and written texts, and, in the last 20 years, to the interpretation of materials now accessible on the Internet. The Internet is making such a reflexivity both more attractive to the learners and more challenging for the teacher, who now has to make explicit much of people's implicit practical sense but also the variability and the paradoxes of language use in real time.

But there is another sense in which a more differentiated view of reflexivity has become necessary in language classes. In the multilingual encounters in our global times, it is crucial to develop the symbolic competence necessary to know when to use which language with whom, when to code-switch, what effect one's way of speaking might have on one's interlocutors, and how to frame and reframe topics (see Kramsch, 2006, 2008, 2009). This requires more than being able to account for a subjunctive form or a pragmatic rejoinder. Getting at the complexities of intercultural exchanges and becoming 'other' to oneself require a critical reflection on historical and social relationships of power and authority. They have become a crucial part of language education in intercultural encounters (Sharifian & Jamarani, 2013; Kramsch, 2013). Finally, learners' self-reflexivity has been hailed as a way of validating language learners' experience, giving them pride and enhancing their self-esteem through narratives of the self (e.g., Hanauer, 2013). Hyper-reflexivity in the classroom requires a heightened awareness of how facts, people, and events are represented in various modalities in the media and in everyday life.

In this sense, hyper-reflexivity in pedagogic practice can present challenges. The confessional mode is a familiar narrative mode that illuminates the past or the present but is not necessarily oriented to what Shirley Brice Heath calls 'future scenarios of possibility' (Heath & Kramsch, 2004: 88). It can easily become self-indulgent narcissism or dialogue with the self. Teachers can easily be cast in the role of confidant, discourse analyst, or creative writing expert, for which they have no training. How to find disciplinary safeguards against gratuitous self-disclosure? Reflexivity ultimately is a valuable practice, but one for which teacher trainers themselves have to be trained, or else they might use narratives of the self only to practice grammar and vocabulary.

The wealth of candid personal experiences shared in this volume by empathetic and creative teachers/researchers illustrate the multiple facets of reflexivity in language learning and teaching, both as a research and as pedagogic practice. The authors all share the conviction that today's language learning enterprise is no longer a question of transmitting acquired knowledge from one teacher to a group of learners but a joint voyage in which teacher and learners together explore new representations of self and new possibilities for action based on a new naming of people and events in a new language. In the complex multilingual world in which these learners will be called to operate, such a reflexive component is essential for language learning to be a transformative experience and to lead to meaningful intercultural understanding.

REFERENCES

Bourdieu, P. (1977). *Outline of a theory of practice.* Cambridge: Cambridge University Press.

Bourdieu, P. (1990). *In other words. Essays towards a reflexive sociology.* Stanford, CA: Stanford University Press.

Bourdieu, P. 2003. Participant objectivation (Trans. Loic Wacquant). *Journal of the Royal Anthropological Institute,* 9, 281–294.

Hanauer, D. (Ed.). (2013). L2 Writing and personal history: Meaningful literacy in the language classroom. Special issue. *L2 Journal,* 4(3).

Heath, S. B., & Kramsch, C. (2004). Individuals, institutions and the uses of literacy. *Journal of Applied Linguistics,* 1(1), 75–91.

Hymes, D. (2001). On communicative competence. In A. Duranti (Ed.), *Linguistic anthropology. A reader* (pp. 53–73). Oxford: Blackwell.

Kramsch, C. (2006). From communicative competence to symbolic competence. *Modern Language Journal,* 90(2), 249–252.

Kramsch, C. (2008). Ecological perspectives on foreign language education. *Language Teaching,* 41(3), 389–408.

Kramsch, C. (2009). Teaching the multilingual subject. In *The multilingual subject* (pp. 188–211.) Oxford: Oxford University Press.

Kramsch, C. (2013). History and memory in the development of intercultural competence. In F. Sharifian & M. Jamarani (Eds.), *Language and intercultural communication in the new era* (pp. 23–38). London: Routledge.

Krashen, S. D. (1988). *Second language acquisition and second language learning.* Englewood Cliffs, NJ: Prentice Hall.

Sharifian, F. & Jamarani, M. (2013). Language and intercultural communication. From the old era to the new one. In *Language and intercultural communication in the new era* (pp. 1–19). London: Routledge.

Contributors

Julie S. Byrd Clark is an Associate Professor of Applied Linguistics and French language pedagogy at the Faculty of Education at Western University, Canada. She specializes in critical applied linguistics, social and ethnographic approaches to bi-/multilingualism and identity, language and intercultural education, discourse analysis, and processes of social identity construction. Byrd Clark is the author of *Multilingualism, Citizenship, and Identity: Voices of Youth and Symbolic Investments in an Urban, Globalized World* (London: Continuum, 2009) and has published extensively on the study of multilingualism and identity, language pedagogy, and language policy and planning. She has recently served as guest editor for *The International Journal of Multilingualism* and the journal of *Canadian and International Education*.

Fred Dervin is Professor of Multicultural Education at the University of Helsinki (Finland). He specializes in language and intercultural education, the sociology of multiculturalism, and linguistics for intercultural communication and education. Dervin has published extensively on identity, the 'intercultural,' and mobility/migration. His latest books are *Politics of Interculturality* (coedited with Anne Lavanchy and Anahy Gajardo, Newcastle: Cambridge Scholars Press, 2011) and *Impostures Interculturelles* (Paris: L'Harmattan, 2012). http://blogs.helsinki.fi/dervin/

Eric Chauvier is an anthropologist at the à l'université Victor Segalen Bordeaux 2 (University of Bordeaux), France. His research focuses particularly on social action in the institution and semiurban areas. In his unique approach, he combines both interactionism and the ethnography of communication so as to fully exploit the complex resources of ordinary language in a heuristic perspective.

Christian W. Chun is Assistant Professor in the Department of English at the City University of Hong Kong. His research addresses the discourses of capitalism, globalization, neoliberalism, and consumerism in their circulations, mediations, and relocations in various sites such as the English for Academic Purposes classroom, online blogs and social media, and public spaces. His research has been published in several leading peer-reviewed journals (*Language Assessment Quarterly, Journal of Adolescent and Adult Literacy, Journal of English for Academic Purposes,* and *Research in the Teaching of English*).

Alex Frame (PhD) is Senior Lecturer in English and Communication Science at the University of Burgundy in Dijon. He has been teaching intercultural communication for the last seven years, from undergraduate to postgraduate level. His research in intercultural communication centers on the dialogical sense-making processes used by individuals to apprehend and comprehend multicultural encounters.

Prue Holmes is Senior Lecturer in International and Intercultural Education in the Department of Education and MA Programme Director. She teaches postgraduate modules in international and intercultural education and intercultural communication. Prue's teaching experience includes intercultural communication at the University of Waikato, New Zealand, and English as a foreign language and English language teacher education in Italy, China, and Hong Kong.

Jane Jackson is Professor in the English Department at the Chinese University of Hong Kong. Her current research interests include language and intercultural communication, identity transformation, and L2 education abroad. With the support of competitive research grants, she is investigating the language and (inter)cultural learning and identity expansion of education-abroad students from Hong Kong and Beijing. In addition to numerous book chapters and articles in peer-reviewed journals, her monographs include *Language, Identity, and Study Abroad: Sociocultural Perspectives* (Equinox, 2008) and *Intercultural Journeys: From Study to Residence Abroad* (Palgrave MacMillan, 2010). She recently edited *The Routledge Handbook of Language and Intercultural Communication* (2012) and is now working on *Introducing Language and Intercultural Communication* (Routledge).

Sylvie A. Lamoureux is Associate Professor at the University of Ottawa's Official Languages and Bilingualism Institute (OLBI). Her research, based in critical reflexive ethnography, explores the impact of language policy and language ideology in postsecondary institutions in linguistic minority contexts, notably on the student experience. She has recently codirected special issues of the *Journal of Language, Identity and Education*, *les Cahiers de l'ILOB/OLBI Papers*, and the *Canadian Journal of Education*.

David Malinowski is a Language Technology and Research Specialist at the Yale Center for Language Study of Yale University. Prior to this, David was a postdoctoral scholar at the Berkeley Language Center at the University of California, Berkeley. He also holds a PhD in education in language, literacy, and culture from Berkeley. His research interests include technology in language learning and teaching, space and embodiment in new media studies, and multimodal communication practices in multilingual urban settings.

Ulrike Najar is a Lecturer in Language Education at the University of Melbourne, Australia. Her research interests are actor-network theory, embodiment, and spatial theory. She recently completed her PhD at the University of Glasgow, which dealt with a reconceptualization of context in the field of intercultural language education ('Walking Through the Intercultural Field'). Originally a German language teacher, she has taught mainly in Arabic and African countries and, as such, is interested in the complexity and diversity of intercultural lifeworlds and their representation in second language acquisition theories and research.

Mark Evan Nelson is Associate Professor and Director of Research in the English Language Institute, Kanda University of International Studies, in Chiba, Japan. Upon receiving his PhD in education in language, literacy, and culture from the University of California, Berkeley, Mark has also held academic positions in teacher education at Deakin University (Victoria, Australia) and the National Institute of Education, Singapore. His research interests are in applied linguistics, new literacies, multimodal communication and textual analysis, and new media composing among children, youth, and adults.

Miguel Pérez-Milans is Assistant Professor at the English Language Education Division in the Faculty of Education, The University of Hong Kong. His research interests include social mobility, ethnicity, multilingualism, and language education. He has conducted critical sociolinguistic ethnography in Spain, London, and China and is the author of *Urban Schools and English Language Education in Late Modern China* (Routledge, 2013).

Jérémie Séror is an Associate Professor at the Official Languages and Bilingualism Institute (OLBI)/University of Ottawa, Ottawa, Ontario, Canada. His researchfocuses on the socially constructed nature of academic literacies and multilingual students' educational and social achievement. These interests are motivated by the desire to improve the educational circumstances of multilingual students and their instructors. Jérémie has over 15 years of working as both a French and English language teacher in public schools, overseas, and in university settings.

Carlos Soto is a secondary school teacher and a doctoral student in the Faculty of Education at The University of Hong Kong. He has worked as an educator in the United States and Hong Kong.

Index

access 7, 36, 73, 76, 120–1, 127–8
activists 172
Adams, M. 9, 203
adolescent 33, 158, 159–65, 169–70
agency 4, 11, 31, 34, 53, 85–6, 115–17, 143–6, 179; linguistic 101
Andreotti, V. 9, 14, 37
anthropologists 18–20, 168–70; anthropology 13, 15, 65, 160, 243; linguistic anthropology 29
applied linguistics 1, 5, 9, 10; critical 14, 15, 28; interdisiciplinarity 35, 36, 76, 200; postmodern approaches 10, 11, 28; reflexive turn 1, 24
assemblage: methodological 33, 194, 196, 199–200, 202–3, 208
Aull Davies, C. 12, 13, 17, 29, 123
authority 20, 104, 133, 161, 167, 173, 242
authorship 142–5, 147, 152, 154, 225, 227
auto-ethnography 119, 238
awareness 4, 12, 16–18, 20–2, 36, 175, 213, 240; critical language 28, 177; feedback 75; reflexive 44–5, 83, 189, 235–6; self-awareness 18, 46–7, 54, 58, 111, 116, 131, 151; semiotic 138–9; weaving 194

Becker, H. 23
being/becoming, process 11, 15, 16
Bennett, J. M 43, 44, 45
Bensa, A. 23, 29, 163–4
Bergson, H. 13, 235
bilingualism 11, 49, 133–4; bilingual 49, 119, 121, 144–5
Blackledge, A., & Creese, A. 11, 28–9

blind spots 2, 4, 12, 15, 25–6, 35, 117, 225, 238
Block, D. 7, 15, 23, 43, 45, 214
Blommaert, J. 22, 85, 222
Boas, F. 18, 203
Bourdieu, P. 4, 6, 11, 19, 23, 29, 48, 93, 103, 140–1, 163, 240–2
Butler, J. 21, 144–6, 240
Byram, M. 10, 18, 27, 44, 45
Byrd Clark, J. 11, 23, 28, 44–5, 48, 77, 121, 170, 176, 196–8, 235, 240–1

Canagarajah, S. 7, 11, 16, 18, 25, 27, 76, 102
capitalism 11, 13, 15, 172, 176, 186–7; discourse 182–3, 190; hegemony 190
case study 43, 47–8, 59–61, 65, 154, 209
Certeau, M. de 29, 202
Chauvier, E. 13, 19, 29, 133, 141
class/classroom, 65–7, 75, 101, 106, 128, 149, 164, 173–4, 213–17; online 44, 50–2, 59
class prejudice 18, 19, 23
codes 7, 49, 67, 93–4, 141, 144–5, 173; code switching 10, 222, 242; meshing 7, 11, 23, 26; metrolingualism 29, 36; mixing 10, 50; translanguaging 7, 10, 29, 36
Collier, M.-J. 101, 112
commodity/ies 33, 230
communication 2–6, 14, 66, 83, 106–9, 126, 144, 152, 164; computer mediated (CMC) 149, 152; ethnography 161; intercultural 100, 103–05, 113–16;

interpersonal 82–6, 95; modes 3, 45, 139, 143–6, 151–5, 175, 178–80, 198–201; multimodal 11, 92, 96, 138–41, 149, 150, 155; practices 11, 77, 138, 225
communication accommodation theory 82, 94–6, 143
communities 77, 120–1, 130, 174, 230–1; cultural 164; linguistic 122; of practice 65, 121–2, 225
competence: communication 94, 97; communicative 45; intercultural 14–15, 29–30, 45, 48, 94; multilingual 240
complexities 2–3, 13, 23, 144, 149–50, 152, 173–5, 225, 238, 242; constructing difference 25–6, 34; dialogical processes 2, 175–6, 196, 224; global shifts 193; networks 198, 230–1; positionings 5, 12; postmodern 194; representations 3, 16, 179, 186, 200; social and linguistic practices 10, 28; trajectories 7, 18, 23, 68, 141, 194, 207, 223
complicities 12, 24
content 66, 70, 72–6
Cotnam, M. 121, 126, 128, 133
creative/creativity 4, 7, 34, 146–7, 152, 205, 242–3; tensions 200, 208; writing 4, 242
Creese, A., & Blackledge, A. 28–9, 36
critical ethnography 32, 34, 119, 122–4, 133, 213
criticality 12–15, 22, 25, 36, 103, 213, 234, 237; critical awareness 28, 175; critical reflection 2–4, 12–16, 27, 36, 45, 54, 59–60, 154, 194, 240–2; critical research 15, 213, 222

Davies, C. A. 12–13, 29, 236
Day, S. 20, 25
Derrida, J. 160, 240
Dervin, F. 9–10, 15, 23, 28, 44
design 126, 132, 151–2, 196, 199–200; intentionality 31, 86, 103; multimodal 32, 139, 140–1, 144–5, 151; text-making practices 143; voice 144–6, 149, 151
Dewey, J. 43, 48, 124
difference: cultural, 45, 54, 90, 94–5, 98; processes of social categorization 75, 83, 93, 95; semiotic 145–6; social construction 2, 6, 15–16, 26, 34
digital: social media 47, 49, 175, 215; stories 142–43, 146–7, 155; technologies 1, 28; texts 4, 138, 151, 153–4, 158, 160–3
dilemmas 129, 215, 223–4, 230
discomfort 20–2
discourse analysis 14, 28, 65, 125, 176–9, 222, 240
dogma/dogmatism 3, 22
Duranti, A. 15, 29

economic inequality/ies 172, 188; 'trickle down' economics 181–2; 189
education: intercultural 2, 14, 15, 17, 24–5, 29, 96; international 57; language 18, 194–6, 216, 231; linguistic minority 14; multilingual 2, 17
embodiment 26; embody 12
engagement 2–4, 5, 34, 141, 155; 189, 203; creative 226; reflexive 5, 21, 23–5, 147, 153, 178, 180, 234
Erikson, E. H. 29, 44
ethics 32, 61, 101, 108, 116, 131; ethical 25, 93, 100, 102–3, 111–16, 236
ethnography 12, 22–3, 161, 196, 199, 206, 222–3; multi-sensory 208–9

facework 88, 93; Goffman 85, 92, 97; saving face 21
failure 21, 24–5, 74, 159–63, 165, 216
Fairclough, N. 15, 28, 77, 177, 186, 190
feedback: 30–1, 64–8, 73, 112, 114, 220–2; practices 64–7, 74–6
Fine, M., Weis, L., Weseen, S., & Wong, L. 103–4, 107
first-person narratives 47
Foucault, M. 2, 25, 236
Frame, A. 31, 81, 86, 88–9, 91, 105
Francophone 119, 121–4; minority/ies, 32, 44, 86, 94–5, 125–6, 213–15, 223; representations 129–30, 134
Frankfurt School 13–14, 27, 36
Freebody, P. 177, 185
Freire, P., & Macedo, D. 174, 214, 224

Gallagher, S. 9, 25, 27
Garfinkel, H. 13, 97

Giddens, A. 11, 13, 97, 214
Gillespie, A. 9, 13, 235, 237
globalization 11, 28, 179, 186–90, 198
Goffman, E. 21, 85, 113, 127, 161
Goody, J. 161, 164
Gorter, D. 176, 180
Gramsci, A. 15, 176
Gudykunst, W. 82, 92
guided walks 203–5, 209–10
Gumperz, J. 22, 84, 94, 97, 161

Hall, J. K. 44–5, 103, 296
Hall, S. 8, 9, 25, 27
Halliday, M. A. K. 139, 177
Hawkins, M. & Norton, B. 14–15, 28
hegemony/processes 15, 23, 82, 176, 185: hegemonic discourse 5, 134, 183, 190; identities 94; power 26, 82; social order 15
Heller, M. 11, 14–15, 17, 21, 23, 27, 214
heterogeneity 20, 25, 38, 62, 135, 210; linguistic 120, 136
hierarchies 75, 179, 209; hierarchical categories 10, 12, 34, 90–1, 110, 205, 235; hierarchies of credibility 23; hierarchy 91, 95
Holliday, A. 9, 14
Holmes, P. 26, 31, 174, 223
Hooks, B. 234
Horkheimer, M. 13–14
Hornberger, N. 11, 14, 128
Hounsell, D. 64, 76
Hull, G. A. & Nelson, M. E. 146–8, 154
Hymes, D. 94, 242
hyper-reflexivity 12, 21, 23, 24–6, 33, 165, 240–2
hypermedia 49

identity 7, 9, 28, 86, 91–2, 142–3, 200; construction 240; ethnic 105, 117, 153; foreign 87, 94; formation 86, 175–6, 225; linguistic 120, 122–4, 127; markers 9, 121, 236; misalignments 43, 56, 58–60; narratives of identity 151; national 87, 117; negotiation 21, 55; performed/performance 129; professional 90; reconstruction 59; researched 55, 127; researcher 18, 87, 101, 116; self-expansion 55, 58; social identities 15, 90, 235; solidarity 225; statements 66; strategies 31, 94, 105; symbolic 96; Theory/ies 16, 44, 91, 97; traits 87–9, 91–3
ideologies 5, 16, 18, 65, 75–6, 214; attachments 3, 7, 18, 25, 29, 141; hegemonic 134; ideological positionings 8, 15, 32, 34, 138, 153; monolingual/monolithic 127, 129–31, 133; representations 5, 12, 65
illusions 13, 27; Bourdieu 19, 23
inequality, social 214
Ingold, T. 193, 201–3, 205
intercultural 27, 29, 34–5, 43, 57, 90, 100; competence 45–6, 82, 92; research 22, 100–2, 108, 115; sensitivity 49
interculturality 25, 28, 30, 47, 59, 97
intersectionality 23, 36, 92
intersubjectivity/ies 28, 102; intersubjective 84–5

Jackson, J. 30, 43–6, 49, 155
Jaffe, A. 15, 23
Janks, H. 174, 177
Job 69, 82, 132, 182, 187
Jovchelovitch, S. 13

Kapoor, I. 23–5, 27
kids 187, 235, 236
Kramsch, C. 11, 15, 28–9, 44–5, 149–52, 197, 242
Kress, G. 139–40, 142–4, 146, 148, 176, 178
Kress, G., & van Leeuwen, T. 139, 179, 181

Labrie, N., & Lamoureux, S. 31–3, 82, 154, 174
Lamoureux, S. 120–2, 127–8
language 1, 4, 7, 10, 208, 235–8, 240; alternative approaches/programs 78, 88, 190, 214; contexts 3; English 217, 230; learning 10, 193, 194–6, 200, 243; multilingualism 234; policies 14, 15, 32, 119, 134; second or foreign 10, 224, 232; social practice 28; system 10, 28–9; teaching 29, 34, 242–3; unconventional approaches 140, 146–7, 152, 203; use(s) 4, 6, 11, 29, 242

Lanham, R. 138, 141
Law, J. 194, 197–9, 209
lifeworld 102, 105–6, 117
Lin, A. M. Y. 21, 214, 232
linguistic insecurity 125, 129–30
linguistic landscape 144–6, 155, 172, 176, 180
linguistic practices 3, 7, 10, 240
linguistic repertoire 7, 28, 131, 224
literacy 64, 138, 148; academic/university 76, 127, 230–1; after-school 155; critical 24, 174, 177, 185; event 31, 64, 76; literacies 34; multimodal 231; practices 64–5, 127, 129, 138; processes 67
Luke, A. 76, 175
Lyotard, J. F. 141

Malinowski, B. 18, 103, 31–2, 113–14
Malinowski, D. 31–2, 141–4, 146, 148–9, 151
Malinowski, D., & Kramsch, C. 152
Martin, J. 91, 214, 224
Mason, J., & Davies, K. 208, 209
Mead, M. 18, 83, 97
meaning-making 138, 151, 173; practices 143, 224; processes 48, 153, 194
mediation 149–50, 159–79
methodology 170, 177; dilemmas 21, 24, 25, 35; method/epistemology/tool 193–4, 196, 197–200; 'methodological firmness' 22; methods 140–1, 158–9; multimodality 199, 201; reflexive practice 12, 15, 22, 25, 29; weaving 209
Mezirow, J. 44–5, 129
mindfulness 92, 95–6
Minh-ha, Trinh T. 20–1
minority/ies 120–3, 125, 213–15, 223; visible 44; groups/relations 86, 94, 95
mobility 23, 28, 112, 193, 202, 209–10, 235
Mondada, L. 17, 27
monopoly 181–3
Moscovici, S. 13
movement 143–5, 151; across modes 151, 153, 155; mass movement 172–5, 177, 188, transformation 193–4; within communicative modes 147

multidimensionality 3; dimensions of reflexivity 12, 25; multidimensional 4, 10, 107, 193, 210; transformative 35
multilingual 3–4, 7, 8–10, 213, 224, 240, 242; Canadian 120–1, 124, 128, 131–3; code meshing 10; multilingualism 1–2, 8, 10–12, 28, 234; research 102, 107, 112, 115–17; writers 64, 66, 68, 75
multiliteracies 143, 155; New London Group 139
multilocality 200
multimodality 3, 30, 31–3, 34, 82, 92, 178; semiosis 139, 144, 146

narrative inquiry: counter 190; narratives 4, 31, 141, 151, 176, 187, 202, 230, 240–2
navel gazing 21–2
Nelson, M. E. 32, 141, 146, 197
Nelson, M. E., Hull, G., & Young, R. 141–4, 147–8, 151, 154
neoliberal 175–6, 187
Norton Pierce, B. 14–16, 18

Observation 18–19, 67, 104–106, 124: neutral observer 18; participant 19, 82, 87, 144, 161, 163–64, 203, 240
Occupy movement 33, 172, 174, 177–80, 188
Ochs, E., & Capps, L. 47, 65, 67
other 9, 15, 16, 18, 25, 30, 100; otherness 25, 117, 199; processes of othering 9–10, 12, 24–5, 235; self and other 4, 9–12, 22–6, 32–4, 81–3, 103
Otsuji, E., & Pennycook, A. 29, 36

Pavlenko, A. 21, 23, 47
pedagogy 14, 34, 46, 139, 159, 213–16, 242
Pennycook, A. 11, 14–15, 21, 23, 27–9, 122, 155, 180, 194, 198
Pérez-Milans, M. 34, 65, 107, 214
performance 11, 16, 20, 27, 30, 32, 86; performativity/performativities 21, 34, 189–90; representation 3, 11, 23, 147, 180, 204
phenomenology 12–13, 17, 100, 102, 105, 236, 241
Pillow, W. 20
Pink, S. 207–8

Index 253

polyphony 169
polysemy 9, 27
polyvocality 23
positioning 3, 5, 7, 12, 20–1, 24–7;
    ideological 8, 15, 34, 153; social
    15, 220
power: relations 9, 16, 31–2, 88,
    119, 129, 132, 205, 241;
    representational systems 25, 35,
    238; semiotic 94, 96; symbolic
    37, 94, 173
privilege: approach 91, 107, 178;
    inequality 7, 8, 9, 11, 21;
    language 76, 174, 208

questioning 15, 18, 23, 44, 75, 169–70,
    174–6; self 102, 116, 123, 141,
    224

Rampton, B. 12, 24, 27–8, 222, 232
reflexivity 2–5, 23, 34–5, 234–8,
    240–1; awareness 20–3, 27,
    36, 45, 83, 138–41, 155, 189;
    construct 1–2, 15, 27; criticality
    12, 13–15, 25, 103, 213,
    234, 237; hyper-reflexivity 4,
    12, 23–6, 33, 165, 240, 241;
    journey 123; language, 31, 64;
    process 1, 15, 75–6, 83, 92,
    141, 147, 209; reflexivity of
    discomfort 20–2; self-reflexivity
    2, 20, 47–8, 60, 103, 176, 240,
    242; uncomfortable 20, 25, 51,
    113
relationality 100–1, 103, 108, 116
representations 3, 4, 12–13, 21–2,
    27, 112, 240, 243; cultural/
    social 176, 200; data 18;
    ideological 24, 76, 82, 174–6,
    213; linguistic 16, 139; power
    25, 26, 110; self 5, 8, 15, 23,
    91, 190, 241; symbolic 13, 20;
    writing/textual 64, 68, 77, 138,
    141, 197
role-taking 83, 86, 90–2

Said, E. 25
Scollon, R., & Scollon, S. W. 84, 101,
    146, 173, 176, 179–80, 189
semiotic, social 139, 140–3, 144,
    155; intersemiotic 176, 182,
    189; landscape 143, 146;
    (meaning)systems 28, 228;
    oscillation 138

Séror, J. 3, 64, 68, 77, 164
Shohamy, E. & Gorter, D. 176, 180
simplexity 238
Smith, T. 95, 134
social class 7, 9, 161, 165, 175, 194–5,
    236
social constructions 2, 20, 22–4
social processes 15, 34, 216, 225
socialization 15, 31, 73, 77, 93;
    language 64–5, 67–68, 74–5
sociology 13–14, 29; reflexive 19, 240
sojourns/sojourners 30–31, 43–4, 53,
    105, 111, 114–17
space 2–3, 25, 173, 180, 194–5, 207–8;
    dialogic 174, 176, 189–90;
    everyday 11; institutional 166,
    173, 216, 231; new 20, 34,
    173–4, 200, 203, 223, 230;
    public 172, 180, 188, 190
Spivak, G. 24–5, 27, 36
Statistics Canada 121
strategies 25, 31, 52, 85–6, 90, 105,
    139, 147; self-presentation 92,
    94, 96, 113
Stroud, C., & Mpendukana, S. 179,
    180, 183, 189
structured reflection 43, 46–7, 60
study abroad 43–4, 53, 58, 60, 66, 76;
    exchange 7, 31, 43, 49–54, 58,
    65–6, 81, 242
subjectivities 15–16, 20–1, 23–4, 81,
    90, 194, 222, 224, 228
symbolic violence 125, 127, 129, 131,
    164; Bourdieu 134, 163
synaesthesia 144, 148, 157

tensions 64, 129, 142, 153, 214–15,
    220, 222–5, 238; tensions
    between structure and agency
    34, 85, 164, 180, 225
Terrion, J. L., & Leonard, D. 127, 134
textualization/textualizing 21, 76, 116,
    138–41; textual 144, 150–2,
    158–60, 166, 226, 229
Thomas, D. R. 67
Thomas, W.I. & D. S. Thomas 2, 13
transformation 16–17, 35, 44, 76, 107,
    113, 144–7, 193, 224, 246
transgressive 147, 172, 180, 221
Turner, J. 81, 121, 123
Turner, K. (2012). 121, 123, 133

United States 5–6, 48, 50–1, 141, 172,
    224, 235

University of Ottawa 119, 120–2, 124, 128, 130, 133

Vertovec, S. 198
Visweswaran, K. 24
voice 102, 131, 158, 188; authorial 142–3, 144, 146, 151–2; giving voice 68; 106, 160; researcher's 48, 130, 196; voices 107, 110–12, 143, 149–51, 166–70, 215, 237–8
Volkart, E. H. & Thomas, W.I. 13
vulnerabilities 4, 21, 25–6, 30, 35, 238

Wacquant, L. 165
weaving 193–4, 196, 209
Weber, J.J. & Horner, K. 7, 11
Wikan, U. 13, 19, 29
wiki 33, 162

Yin, R. 66
Youtube video 177–8, 180, 183–4, 187, 189–90

Zittoun, T., & Perret-Clermont, A-N. 129
Zuengler, J., & Cole, K. 65